COLLOQUIA PONTICA

VOLUME 4

ANCIENT BEREZAN

COLLOQUIA PONTICA

Series on the Archaeology and Ancient History of the Black Sea Area

Editorial Address:

Department of Classics, Royal Holloway and Bedford New College,
University of London, Egham, Surrey TW20 0EX, UK
(Tel. (0)1784-443203; Fax: (0)1784-439855)

ANCIENT BEREZAN

*The Architecture, History and Culture of
the First Greek Colony in the Northern Black Sea*

BY

S.L. SOLOVYOV

EDITED BY

JOHN BOARDMAN
GOCHA R. TSETSKHLADZE

BRILL
LEIDEN · BOSTON · KÖLN
1999

This book is printed on acid-free paper.

939.5
SOL

143861X

Library of Congress Cataloging-in-Publication Data

The Library of Congress Cataloging-in-Publication Data is also available.

Die Deutsche Bibliothek - CIP-Einheitsaufnahme

S.L. Solovyov:
Ancient Berezan : the architecture, history and culture of the
first Greek colony in the Northern Black Sea / by S.L. Solovyov.
Ed. by John Boardman and Gochha R. Tsetskhladze. – Leiden ;
Boston ; Köln : Brill
(Colloquia Pontica ; 4)
ISBN 90–04–11569–2

ISSN   1389–8477
ISBN   90 04 11569 2

Contents

Introduction to the Series

This is the first issue to be published by Brill. It is a long time since issue No. 3 was published by Oxbow and the announcement by them of issue No. 4. I apologise to readers, the author and all those who put time and effort into this issue for the long delay. I apologise also to the authors of subsequent issues which have also been held up. These delays were not caused by the Series Editor or issue editors. Suffice it to say that the series has changed publisher.

Thanks to enormous efforts by Job Lisman, the Acquisitions Editor at Brill, *Colloquia Pontica* lives on with a bright future in the hands of an academic publisher of the highest repute. I wish him a bright future, well deserved, as he departs for pastures new and give him my sincere thanks for his initial offer which has brought *Colloquia Pontica* to its new home.

The new publisher has required some changes in organisation and structure; the aims of the series remain as they were stated in issue No. 1. The principal change is in the composition of the former Advisory Board, which has been split into an Editorial Board and a new Advisory Board. The Editorial Board will be closely involved in the preparation of the issues. Whereas the original target of two issues a year was not met, now it will be, with the likelihood that it will be exceeded.

Gocha R. Tsetskhladze
Series Editor
London, June 1999

Introduction to the Issue

Gocha R. Tsetskhladze

Greek colonization of the Black Sea is one of the most important and, at the same time, most heavily debated problems in Pontic archaeology. Study of the first settlements helps considerably our understanding of the initial stage of this crucial phenomenon. It is well known that Berezan was the first Greek colony in the northern Black Sea. Excavation of this site began in the last century but, unfortunately, little has been published about it. There are dozens of articles in Russian, but only a very small quantity of brief information has appeared from time to time in the West (most recently: Y.G. Vinogradov in *Expedition* Vol. 36, Nos. 2/3, 18–28; J.G. Vinogradov and S.D. Kryžickij, *Olbia* [Leiden 1995], 62–66; and J.G. Vinogradov and J.V. Domanskij in O.D. Lordkipanidzé and P. Lévêque [eds.], *Sur les traces des Argonautes* [Besançon 1996], 291–96. This last article was written in 1990). Hitherto we have lacked an overall picture of the settlement. This present issue of *Colloquia Pontica* aims to fill this gap, at least in part. Not all the author's interpretations and conclusions are beyond challenge (for example on the rôle of the local population, trade, etc. – see my chapter in *The Greek Colonisation of the Black Sea Area: Historical Interpretation of Archaeology* [*Historia* – Einzelschrift 121, Stuttgart 1998, 9-68]), but the book is the first to present a first hand, general survey of the development of the settlement, and I hope it will form the starting point for all future discussion and study. Whilst Oxbow was incubating this book, the Hermitage gave birth to a new international project: the full publication of the Berezan collection, which has been kept at the Hermitage for more than a century. Several volumes are planned to be written by Russian and Western classicists (with parallel Russian and English texts) and work is already underway on the study of objects.

Dr Sergei L. Solovyov works in the Department of History and Culture of the Ancient World, Hermitage, St Petersburg. He has participated in the excavation of Berezan for many years, and has been its Director or co-Director for part of that time. He is also Keeper of the Hermitage Berezan Collection. For several years Dr Solovyov excavated the *chora* of Nymphaeum (with the collaboration of a Polish team). Currently, he is Director of the archaeological project "Island of Sindice" and is studying the rural settlements in the south-west of the Taman Peninsula. He has been a Visiting Fellow at the University of Warsaw and has visited Great Britain under the auspices of the British Academy.

I am most grateful to the Society for the Promotion of Hellenic Studies for its financial help towards the costs of translating this book from Russian. I should like to thank Prof. Sir John Boardman, who kindly agreed to edit the issue with me and write a Preface. Thanks are also due to Dr J.F. Hargrave and to the author for his patience in waiting for his book to be edited and published.

This issue, ready for the printers since autumn 1998, was prepared by Oxbow and passed over to Brill for publication. Thus it resembles the first three issues in typeface, typesize and layout. All subsequent issues will be Brill products in their entirety.

Preface

John Boardman

The relaxing of political tensions in recent years has made it possible for far closer contacts between scholars of East and West on matters of common concern. A major area of common interest, at a time when Mediterranean studies are beginning to focus on the period of Greek colonization of Italy and Sicily, has been the comparable Greek experience in the Black Sea, and not least the local population's experience of the Greeks. A major problem has been accessibility of literature and language. This is being gradually answered from the eastern side, and with western encouragement, by books such as this which present a detailed survey and assessment of excavations and interpretations mainly available hitherto only from literature of limited circulation, and often only from brief abstracts of articles in western languages. Some western scholars have tried to keep up but have easily underestimated both the work that has been done on Black Sea sites and the considerable exercises in social and historical interpretation undertaken by Soviet, Russian and other eastern European academics.

The northern Black Sea sites are now divided between Russia and Ukraine and both countries are busy on them, often beside teams from western universities. Greek colonization in the area is revealed as a no less complex process than it was in the western Mediterranean, and decidedly not a matter to be regarded as peripheral to Greek archaeology and history. For western scholars, who may have had in the past better opportunities to become acquainted with the realia of the type exported to the Black Sea and often copied there, the need to understand both the sites and the finds has become acute. Publications such as this by eastern scholars can only help both to a better understanding of problems which were by no means confined to one area alone. Moreover, in the Black Sea the Greeks met and had to live beside, deal with and sometimes serve the interests of peoples whose culture was no less sophisticated than that of the Etruscans or Italic peoples, and in the Black Sea questions arise also of relations with the greater empires and nomad populations of the east.

Berezan was probably the first place to see a degree of settled occupation by Greeks on the northern shore of the Black Sea. Its relations with the local population, and its relations with its strong Greek neighbour at Olbia, present engrossing archaeological and historical problems. This book deals largely with the architectural development of the site and what it has to suggest on these matters. It is clear that the results presented here are the result of long series of excavations over many years and by different teams. We need now more such works which summarise for us in detail the architectural history of these sites, and at the same time we must hope that it will prove possible to rework for fuller publication the results and finds of earlier excavations which are often known only from brief reports or selective publication of interesting finds. The results of past exploration should engage the attention of scholars now no less than what they may hope for from new exploration.

Author's Foreword

The ancient Greek settlement on the island of Berezan, located in the estuary of two major southern Ukrainian rivers – the Dnieper and the Lower Bug (Fig. 1) – is known to be one of the oldest settlements in the northern Black Sea region dating to the period of Greek colonization. Berezan serves as the key to understanding a broad range of issues and problems connected with Greek colonization, a process which was immense in scale for the period and which in the course of two centuries grew to occupy nearly the entire Mediterranean and Black Sea coasts. This was a crucial period in the history of ancient civilization.

The Berezan settlement, known in the ancient world initially by the name Borysthenes, was the first link in a chain of Greek city-states (*poleis*) which appeared

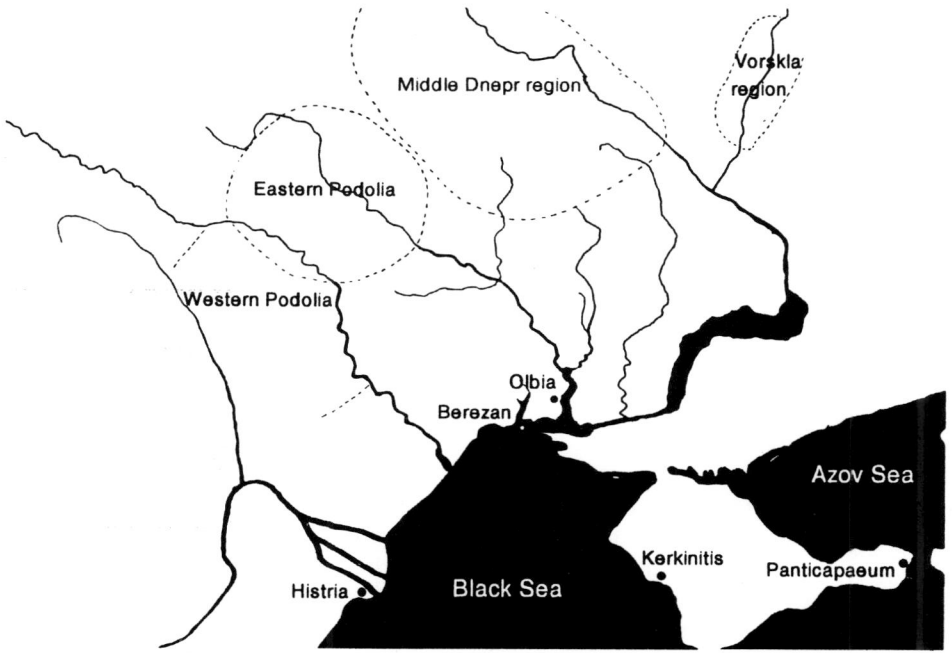

Fig. 1. Map of the North-Western Black Sea Littoral.

on the northern littoral of the Pontus. Together with these other city-states, Berezan became an active participant in the cultural and trading expansion of the ancient Greeks in the northern Black Sea, and in the transmission of Greek culture to the vast territory of forest-steppe and steppe Scythia. As a contact zone of interaction between the Greeks and indigenous peoples, located in the middle of Herodotean Scythia, Borysthenes became a powerful "magnet", drawing leading representatives of many tribes and peoples into its economic and political sphere. These people left numerous traces of their presence in the material and spiritual culture of Berezan.

Archaeological studies of the Berezan settlement have continued for more than 100 years. More than 30 years were given to the work of two expeditions, which were organized by the Institute of Archaeology of the Ukrainian Academy of Sciences and the State Hermitage Museum. Several generations of Russian and Ukrainian scholars devoted the best years of their lives to the study of Berezan. As a result of their work, more than 2ha of the territory of the ancient settlement and its necropolis, which were surrounded by numerous buildings for household use, have been uncovered. Also found were many works of both Greek and local arts, some of them unique and of high quality, which made up in both literal and figurative senses a treasure trove of ancient achievement.

Still, it is important to point out that, unfortunately, the archaeological materials of Berezan have not been well-known to a wide audience, even though until quite recently the island was visited by tourists nearly every day. These visits, however, were made for an entirely different reason – the island is also known as the place of execution of Lieutenant P.P. Smidt and his colleagues, who were the leaders of a revolutionary insurrection in the Black Sea fleet in 1905. The ancient Greek colony is usually mentioned only in passing. The former USSR's perpetual shortage of the resources and materials needed for the systematic restoration of the settlement, its undeveloped infrastructure for tourism, and the frequently uncoordinated actions of local authorities and academic organizations prevented ancient Berezan escaping from obscurity and taking its rightful place among such archaeological monuments as Olbia, Chersonesus, Panticapaeum, and Gorgippia.

The beginning of *Perestroika* in the USSR, which led to the overthrow of past ideological idols, ought to have awakened in people an interest in the eternal value and importance of ancient history. With this kind of understanding of cultural priorities, ancient Berezan and its remarkable collection of classical applied arts would not be forgotten, and its study would receive a new, powerful impulse. However, almost the exact opposite has taken place. In 1992 the Berezan archaeological expedition of the State Hermitage was denied permission from the Field Committee of the Institute of Archaeology of the Ukrainian Academy of Sciences to carry out archaeological excavations on the island. To this day permission still has not been granted, despite the active desire of the Hermitage to conduct studies on ancient Berezan.

The decentralization of sovereignty which has taken place in the past few years in the former USSR has evidently had a positive influence on the emergence of post-Soviet national cultures. Yet the same process has also generated some negative tendencies in the development of those cultures; in particular, it has distorted and even ruined what was at one time a unified cultural space. Nevertheless, both Russians and Ukrainians have been able to direct their efforts toward solving the immediate tasks of preserving and studying ancient sites. The future of the Berezan settlement too depends on the resolution of this issue. It is important not to forget that the island itself is slowly, inevitably being destroyed by the sea. Regarding Berezan, in my view the foremost tasks are the restoration and conservation of those archaeological objects already discovered and still preserved, especially architectural remains, and the creation on the mainland of a modern research facility and museum capable of providing regular and reliable means of preserving, treating, and restoring archaeological materials. I am convinced that those who are truly concerned about the fate of ancient Berezan and its collections would hardly wish to recommend any other course.

In preparing this book I have had to look many times to the help and advice of my colleagues and friends – Konstantin K. Marchenko, Eugenii Y. Rogov, Yurii P. Kalashnik, Sergei V. Pokrovskii, Julii A. Livshits and Natasha F. Solovyova, to whom I would like to express my deepest gratitude. I am also very grateful to John H. Pollock, who took on the far from simple task of translating this work. Thanks are also due to Prof. Sir John Boardman, Gocha R. Tsetskhladze and James Hargrave for their invaluable help, and the Hellenic Society (London) and the British Academy for their financial support.

Sergei L. Solovyov,
St Petersburg, Winter 1995

Introduction

Of the very few islands found in the Black Sea, only two – the islands of Zmeinyi and Berezan (Fig. 1), located just a few kilometres apart – were fortunate enough to become a part of history. The former island was known to the ancient Greeks as Leuke,[1] the final resting place and pan-Hellenic sanctuary of Achilles, legendary hero of the Trojan War. According to ancient written records which have come down to us from the Byzantine chronicler Eusebius (*Chron.can.* 95b Helm.), the latter island, called Borysthenes, was chosen by settlers from Miletus, who were the first Greek colonists in the northern Black Sea region. Many scholars follow Eusebius in placing this migration in the years 647–646 BC.[2]

The archaeological data from Berezan are richer and more varied than the testimony of ancient authors suggests. They contain information pertaining to many different periods and to many diverse aspects of life. The earliest traces of human activity on the island are connected to the Late Bronze Age. This most ancient period in the history of Berezan is represented by two burials and by separate finds in the levels of later settlements (Kopeikina 1981, 165). Most remarkable, both for its unusual length and for the sheer volume of archaeological materials, is the period of time encompassing the second half of the seventh through the first half of the 3rd centuries BC. Furthermore, both in the Middle Ages and in modern times, settlement on the island has been revived only periodically, and never for very long. Soon after 1825, the island became completely uninhabited.[3]

Owing to the key rôle which ancient Berezan evidently played in the destiny of the northern Black Sea region, generations of academics have focused their attention on the island's history and culture. Scholars and field researchers have returned again and again to one and the same questions about the appearance, functioning, and

---

[1] The first book on this island appeared recently: Okhotnikov and Ostroverkhov 1993.

[2] The fullest and most thorough survey of ancient literary evidence concerning the foundation of Berezan, and the historiography of this issue, is the monograph of Y.G. Vinogradov (1989). The studies of V.P. Yailenko (1982, 258–309) and B. Bravo (1974, 111*ff*; 1994) also deserve attention.

[3] The most recent period of Berezan history has also turned out to be the most destructive for the ancient site. Long-term use of the island as a military stronghold (as a fort defending the entrance to the Dnieper-Bug estuary), first by the Turks and then by the Russians, brought about intensive military-engineering construction from the end of the 18th through the first third of the 19th centuries. Later on, military interest in Berezan waned. However, in the 20th century, just prior to World War I, the island regained its importance, apparently being the only naval testing-range then available to Russian military engineers. The numerous remains of defensive installations from that period have created the contemporary landscape of Berezan island.

decline of settlements on this small piece of land, the area of which is hardly more than 20ha. Among the main questions, I will list here some of the most important:

- the time of the initial settlement of the island, according to written and archae-ological data;
- the social and economic characteristics of the Berezan settlement and its significance for the course of Greek colonization in the Lower Bug area and northern Black Sea region overall;
- the volume and character of trade relations between Berezan and the Greek world, as well as trade relations with the barbarian periphery;
- the characteristics of building practices and techniques on Berezan;
- the form and direction of interaction between the Greeks and native peoples;
- the political history of the Berezan settlement;
- the periodization of the cultural and historical development of Berezan in antiquity.

Initial investigations into these issues were undertaken in the 19th century by the first researchers on the settlement of Berezan: B. V. Farmakovskii (1898, 211–2), E. R. von Stern (1900; 1901, 88–91; 1904, 97–100; 1907, 41–9; 1908, 35–8; 1909, 50–8; 1909a, 139–52; 1910, 66–75; 1912, 84–93; 1913, 105–17; 1913a, 536–58; 1914, 76–108), and G. L. Skadovskii (1900) (although, to be more exact, the very first scholar to excavate on Berezan was R. A. Prendel 1886, 216–9). Since that time, a large body of scholarly literature has been devoted to issues and questions surrounding Berezan, although strangely among this work there has not been a single monograph (perhaps with the exception of a popular scientific pamphlet by K.S. Gorbunova (1969) and an unpublished manuscript by V. V. Lapin (1978)). Over the years definite successes have been achieved in developing an understanding of Berezan, including the study of imported and local (that is, Greek and native) pottery and epigraphic materials. By several means a whole complex of questions regarding the architectural appearance, daily life, and political organization of the Berezan community, and its place in the socio-economic and political structure of the Olbia *polis*, have been satisfactorily resolved (Enman 1911; Mantsevich 1927; Boltenko 1930; 1953; 1960; Artamonova 1940; Nudelman 1946; Kobylina 1948; Fabritsius 1951; Slavin 1956; Skudnova 1955; 1957; 1957a; 1960; Kaposhina 1956; Domanskii 1961; 1970; 1979; Lapin 1963; 1966; Gorbunova 1964; 1966; 1968; 1970; 1973; 1973a; 1976; 1982; Kopeikina 1968; 1970; 1970a; 1970b; 1970c; 1973; 1975; 1977; 1979; 1979a; 1981; 1981a; 1982; 1982a; 1986; Vinogradov Y. G. 1971; 1971a; 1976; 1979; 1983; 1989; 1994; 1994a; Vinogradov Y./ I. G. *et al.* 1988; 1990; Yailenko 1974; 1975; 1979; 1979a; 1980; 1982; Marchenko 1976; 1980; 1988; Marchenko and Solovyov 1988; Rusyaeva 1979; 1984; 1986; 1987; 1992; Kryzhitskii 1982; 1987; Kryzhitskii and Otreshko 1986; Mazarati and Otreshko 1987; Olgovskii 1980; Ruban 1982; 1990; 1991; Krapivina 1986; Ilina 1987; 1994; Bolshakov and Ilina 1988; Solovyov 1992; 1993; 1994; 1995; 1995a). Meanwhile a large number of other general and particular issues, bearing directly on the Berezan settlement and its rôle in the early period of Greek colonization in the northern Black Sea region, remain topical and unresolved today. Interest in these outstanding issues has grown even more as a result of the accumulation of relevant material and observations.

Today, as before, one of the most important remaining questions concerns the time when permanent settlement first took place. It is becoming clear that Eusebius's well-known report regarding the date of the founding of Berezan will be irreconcilably contradicted by archaeological data on the construction of the earliest dwellings, on the beginning of the formation of its cultural levels, and on the appearance of the first graves in the necropolis. Recent efforts to reconcile these two heterogeneous sources of information have not been successful (Vinogradov I. *et al.* 1990a, 121–39), since, even allowing for all possible assumptions and strained interpretations connecting Eusebius's date with the aforementioned events (which do not go beyond the last quarter of the 7th century BC), there remains a time break of at least two decades. The gap is explained by the following factors: first, the destruction of the most ancient part of the settlement by coastal erosion, and second, incomplete study of the site (Vinogradov I. *et al.* 1990a, 128). This assumes the possibility, through future field and underwater investigation, of revealing the original focus of settlement.

If the shakiness of the first argument is self-evident – it can be neither confirmed nor refuted by empirical data – then the second argument is also not sufficiently persuasive. It is hardly possible to reveal chronologically uniform or nearly undisturbed sections of a cultural level at the bottom of the sea in the well-known hydrological conditions of the Berezan region, as the results of underwater research recently conducted off the island's coastline confirm (Nazarov 1990, 82–3). The probability of finding the supposed earlier part of the settlement through excavation looks equally weak, insofar as beyond a doubt the lowest, northeastern part of the ancient peninsula, offering easily obtainable sources of drinking water, was settled first. This area has been sufficiently well studied.

A few dozen fragments of imported, decorated pottery serve as the single authentic material evidence of the presence of Greeks at such an early date. This evidence is usually treated as a decisive argument that the Berezan settlement existed and was functioning actively in the third quarter of the 7th century BC (Kopeikina 1982, 31). As corroboration, there is occasional reference to the data collected by M. F. Boltenko and K. S. Gorbunova, who proposed that certain of the pits and wells they exposed were of the second half of the 7th century BC (Boltenko 1949, 35; Gorbunova 1970, 247). A re-examination of these materials, however, has assigned them to the 6th century BC (Kopeikina 1981, 166–7; Solovyov 1989, 7).[4]

Moreover, it must be noted that very few fragments of decorated Greek pottery dating from the second half of the 7th century BC have actually been found in the cultural level of the settlement (Kopeikina 1982, 6*ff*; 1986, 2*ff*). Even allowing that the number of pieces corresponds to a quantity of whole vessels, it is a pity that the first inhabitants of Borysthenes had to be satisfied with such meagre utensils for an extended period of time. It is important to pay special attention to the composition of this pottery, which is almost exclusively represented by narrowly specialized vessels adapted not so much to the preparation of everyday food as for use in celebrations.

---

[4] Furthermore, there is little doubt that the presence of some sort of local well cannot indisputably demonstrate the existence of a settlement there, especially given the well-known absence of a fixed population in the Lower Bug region in the 7th century BC.

Fundamental changes in the typology and composition of imported pottery become noticeable only at the end of the 7th century BC.

Following from this, I have come to the conclusion that there is insufficient evidence to place the rise of Berezan in the third quarter of the 7th century BC. In my view, there is another more profitable approach: the large-scale settlement of Berezan was preceded by a more or less prolonged period during which a very small group of settlers (Rusyaeva 1986, 35), perhaps scouts and traders, familiarized themselves with the region, its population, and its natural resources. Of course, such a small group of pioneers would hardly have the ability to establish a permanent, flourishing settlement. Most likely in the first few seasons the Greeks would have visited the Lower Bug region only periodically, but the continuity and regularity of such visits would have depended to a large degree on navigational conditions in the area and on climatological and demographic factors.

Therefore, it makes more sense to look at the pottery fragments found on Berezan as the remains of special celebrations or gifts for a local tribal aristocracy, whose good graces first had to be secured in order to ensure successful trade, the safety of the early settlers, and the prosperity of the future colony (Marchenko 1991, 19). The small quantity of such items on Berezan and, importantly, in forest-steppe Scythia (Onaiko 1966; Domanskii 1979, 83–4; Kovpanenko *et al.*. 1989, 50*ff*; Vakhtina 1989, 74–88), provides evidence that such ware was not a major commodity of trade in the early phase of interaction between the Greeks and the indigenous people. Clearly, Greek pottery at first was not widely used in the lives of the majority of the local population. Moreover, the very presence of this pottery in an area so distant from the coast suggests that the indigenous society invested it with special, most likely socially significant (possibly prestigious) functions. One cannot eliminate the further possibility that such vessels were used for ritual, ceremonial purposes.[5]

The socio-economic organization of the Berezan settlement at different periods, especially the earliest, remains a subject of discussion. Formerly, this issue was studied through traditional conceptions of Greek colonization – that is, through trade or agriculture (Domanskii 1961; *cf.* Lapin 1966). However, a more balanced approach to resolving the problem has recently begun to prevail in Russian scholarship. Scholars usually prefer to talk about the domination of one or another type of economic activity at different points in the history of the colony (Brashinskii and Shcheglov 1979, 44; Marchenko 1980, 138; Rusyaeva 1986a, 294; Kryzhitskii *et al.* 1989, 15; Kryzhitskii 1989; Vinogradov Y. G. 1989, 49*ff*; Otreshko 1994). In this regard, academics have usually contrasted trade, agriculture, and local commerce. Even if one agrees in principle with this approach, it must not be forgotten that in the history of Berezan there were periods when either no permanent settlement existed (as, for example, in the second half of the 7th century BC), or when Berezan fulfilled a special function (for example, as a religious centre of Achilles Pontarches in the 1st century AD). In both these instances, Berezan strongly influenced historical development in the northern Black Sea region.

---

[5] The probability that the native people used decorated pottery in this way is indicated by the find of an East Greek cup of the 7th century BC on an altar in a dugout building at Trakhtemirovskii site in forest-steppe Scythia (Ilinskaya and Terenozhkin 1983, 267).

The importance of the Berezan settlement in the historical fate of the indigenous population of the Northern Pontus is an issue directly linked to the resolution of the aforementioned question concerning economic organization. If one gives preference to the opinions of those who believe that the Berezan economy was characterized primarily by trade and agriculture, then considering the very weak development of these sectors it is necessary to limit the influence of the Berezan economy exclusively to the Lower Bug region. Such a concept of the rôle of Berezan is certainly justified in respect of the later phases of its history, which fall in the Hellenistic and Roman periods. As for the early history of Borysthenes, all the archaeological and historical data suggest that the most persuasive point of view is one which emphasizes the centrality of trade and commercial interests in the region.[6]

In the literature there are frequent efforts to disregard the rôle of trade in the establishment and development of the settlement, mainly on the basis of the very small quantity of imported Greek pottery found in areas far from the coast in Scythia. It is difficult to call this evidence convincing. This sort of approach to the archaeological facts of ancient Scythia ignores a fundamental part of the Berezan archaeological material: the enormous amount of ceramic imports which eventually found their way to the island from cities in Ionia and mainland Greece during the 7th to the 5th centuries BC. In this period, Borysthenes was undoubtedly stronger and for a time even became the single transit point for trade for the northern Black Sea coast. Evidently, the island did not long remain so, and after the middle of the 5th century BC it became the *emporion* of the Olbia *polis* – the "Borysthenes *emporion*" of Herodotus (4.17; 24). Having lost its former power, the island gradually reverted to a provincial town, and later became a small, anonymous fishing settlement.

The issue of Berezan's political status has gained special importance as a result of a great deal of essentially new and significant information about the site, which has brought about a fundamental change in earlier conceptions of Berezan as a settlement deprived of political independence first by Miletus, and then by Olbia (von Stern 1900; Boltenko 1960; Domanskii 1961; Kopeikina 1979). Today's picture of Borysthenes' political life is much more complex and dynamic. In the opinion of many scholars, the Berezan settlement initially held the status of *polis*, and later was made into a part of the Olbian state, either as an *emporion* or simply as a small, rural population centre (Lapin 1966, 147; Bravo 1974; Wasowicz 1975, 62; Vinogradov Y. G. 1976; Yailenko 1982, 266; Kryzhitskii and Otreshko 1986). Even if one agrees with this outline of Berezan political development, it still must be allowed that certain specific issues related to these questions demand more detailed examination and elaboration (especially given the extent of new archaeological data).

Issues surrounding the political structure and status of Borysthenes are closely linked to a large group of questions regarding spatial organization and the evolution of construction techniques and practices on the island. This line of study still remains a point of disagreement among Russian scholars. Along with the accumulation of materials, the study of related issues has been consistently channeled into two extreme

---

[6] It is important to add that in this case reciprocal relations worked quite well, largely because a certain part of the local population in the hinterlands was interested in developing trade relations with the Greeks.

attitudes.   Although they agree on the cultural characteristics of aboveground dwellings, which both see as a consequence of the activities of Greek colonists, the two sides take diametrically opposed positions, however, in their views on earthen, dugout construction, which was the characteristic feature of building practices on Berezan for most of antiquity (Solovyov 1995b).

The first, earlier, point of view held that dugout buildings served as dwellings for the local, indigenous population of the Lower Bug region, which had found itself in or been drawn to the trading area of the Greek colony on Berezan (Kaposhina 1956; Stitelman 1956). Supporters of the second point of view looked at dugout construction as an activity of the Greek colonists, who found themselves in a new and unfamiliar cultural and natural environment (Lapin 1966, 156; 1978, 116–34; Kryzhitskii and Rusyaeva 1978; Rusyaeva 1979; Kryzhitskii 1982, 29). Without going too deeply here into polemics on the issue of Greek colonization in the northern Black Sea region, it is still important to note that both approaches remain more or less equally unconvincing in regard to the question of the form and particulars of dugout construction. To a significant extent this may be explained by the fact that the small amount of specific scholarship which has been done in this field is frequently offset by opinions and judgments of a rather general type. However, even following the logic of basic study, it should not be forgotten that a dwelling-place is always a reflection of the everyday culture of an *ethnos*. In this way, dwellings may be seen not only as a type of structure characterized by a certain set of formal indicators (principles of volume and layout, building methods, materials, construction, and so on), but also as a relatively stable model of human activity, or as an ethnocultural tradition. Of course, in both instances the basis of the difference between building types may be explained by the different methods used by people to create living space under varied environmental conditions. The difference may also lie in the phase of social development attained by the Greek world and by the indigenous peoples on its periphery; forms of dwellings and the overall specific character of construction are to a significant extent shaped not by the physical and geographical conditions of a colonized region, but by the social and economic, political and cultural features of a specific people.

Several generations of academics have been studying another important problem at the Berezan site: the interaction between Greek and local populations in the northern Black Sea region. Interest in this question has increased sharply in recent years, as relevant materials have continued to accumulate. There have been definite successes. The main achievement which should be mentioned is the emerging repudiation in Russian scholarship of general, purely speculative ideas, and of highly oversimplified and one-sided representations of the complex process of inter-ethnic relations. Today, these approaches have been replaced by systematic models of Greek-indigenous interaction (Marchenko and Vinogradov 1989; Vinogradov Y. A. and Marchenko 1989; Marchenko 1991) which have been created on the basis of a sophisticated analysis of diverse written and archaeological sources, each of which has previously been studied individually. Among the latter, preference is justifiably given to those things which have the greater capacity to differentiate among ethnic groups and provide differential indicators – above all this means pottery (particularly hand-made), adornments, cult objects, building techniques, and other cultural products of those peoples who in antiquity entered into various forms of contact in the northern Black Sea region, including on the island of Berezan. In recent years these factors have been the subject of a great deal of study.

Previous intensive investigation of the aforementioned issues allows us today to resolve one of the most important problems: the periodization of the historical and cultural development of ancient Berezan. It is certainly not the case that this subject did not attract serious attention in the past; on the contrary, it was resolved through a heated struggle among differing points of view on the history of Berezan. Underlying this conflict was the interpretation of E. R. von Stern (1900), which was supported by M. F. Boltenko (1960) and later corrected by Y.V. Domanskii (1961). In the 1960s this interpretation was subjected to serious criticism on the part of V. V. Lapin (1966; 1978) and his followers S. D. Kryzhitskii, V. M. Otreshko, S. B. Buiskikh, and V. V. Ruban (Kryzhitskii *et al.* 1989, 12*ff*). Their opponents, who continued to some extent to develop the earlier line of thinking, became L. V. Kopeikina (1981a) and K. K. Marchenko (1991). Only after the passage of several years did a substantial amount of research appear, which to one degree or another has resolved the problem (Yailenko 1982; Vinogradov Y. G. 1989; Solovyov 1989; 1994; 1995b).

The nearly one thousand year history of ancient Berezan is usually subdivided into periods which, as a rule, follow the generally accepted division of classical antiquity into Archaic, Classical, Hellenistic and Roman periods. Such a chronological articulation of the Berezan settlement, of course, seems highly artificial. The traditional chronology does not fully reflect the specific characteristics of Berezan's development. Therefore, in recent years investigation has tended to focus on the chronology of the site.

Thus, the history of the settlement in Archaic period, which encompassed more than a century and a half, is subdivided into two subperiods. The dividing line between these periods runs through the third quarter of the 6th century BC. In the opinion of some, the division lies closer to the beginning of this period; others believe that it lies closer to the end (Kopeikina 1981a, 197; Vinogradov Y. G. 1989, 64–8).[7] Very real changes in the cultural character of ancient Berezan took place in this quarter century (Kopeikina 1979, 110; Solovyov 1989, 9*ff*; 1994, 90–1). As a starting-point for Borysthenes, the date reported by Eusebius is usually accepted: 647–646 BC. The end of the Archaic period is, as a rule, fixed as the end of the first third of the 5th century BC, which corresponds to the time of fundamental changes not only in the Berezan settlement, but also in the whole Lower Bug area and in the northwestern Black Sea region (Marchenko and Vinogradov 1989, 803–13; Vinogradov Y. A. and Marchenko 1991, 149*ff*). Since the appearance on Berezan of the earliest living and working sites (Kopeikina 1979, 193; Solovyov 1989, 7; *cf.* Vinogradov I. *et al.* 1990) which can be reliably dated seems to fall into the last decade of the 7th century BC, the early period is sometimes divided into two stages: the first encompassing the second half of the 7th century BC, and the second occupying the first half of the 6th

---

[7] *Cf.*: Domanskii *et al.* 1989, 36*ff*. V.V. Lapin (1978, 73*ff*) adhered to this opinion, representing an early history of Berezan down to a beginning of the 5th century BC as undivided into periods. The view has partly declined nowadays (see Kryzhitskii 1982, 30, 45–6). See also J. Boardman in *Historia*–Einz. 121 (1998), 201–4 and Solovyov, *ibid.*, 205–26.

century BC (Domanskii 1979, 86; Vinogradov Y. G. 1989, 67–8). It is also possible to subdivide the second period into two further stages, the border of which stands at the end of the 6th century BC (Solovyov 1995, 90). At that time, the internal layout of urban blocks and the larger part of the buildings underwent essential changes, probably of a kind similar to those affecting other areas of the city. However, these changes did not entail creating a completely new layout of the settlement as a whole.

The third period of Berezan history occupied the remaining part of the 5th and the first quarter of the 4th centuries BC. In recent years excavation on the island have found new, important information about this period. The new data attest to fundamental changes in the culture, and to a general decline in construction: at this time there was a sharp reduction of surface building and a rise in dugout construction (Solovyov 1995a).

Up to now, very little information has been gathered on the fourth period in the history of Berezan. It is known only that it encompassed the larger part of the 4th century BC and at least the first third – perhaps the whole – of the 3rd century as well. The question of when this period came to a close remains under discussion. At that time, the inhabited area of the Berezan settlement was very small, and evidently did not stretch beyond the boundaries of the northeastern part of the peninsula. The surface building which was carried out here evidently approximated in its own way to the construction of the well-known rural settlements of the Olbian periphery of the second half of the 4th through the first third of the 3rd century BC.

Even less is known about the subsequent, fifth period. In many years of digging on the island, few remains of Late Hellenistic construction have been revealed, although a few material finds from this time have become known. This paucity suggests the absence of a permanent settlement on Berezan in the Late Hellenistic period, or is perhaps a consequence of the destructive powers of nature, which have destroyed even feeble traces. The future will tell. Even if such a settlement existed at that time, it most likely lived the life of an ordinary agricultural and fishing settlement, barely noticeable against the background of other populated areas in the Olbian rural region.

In the 1st century BC through the 1st century AD – the sixth period – the island for a short time became the state sanctuary of Achilles Pontarches (Shelov-Kovedyaev 1990). Although cult-related buildings of that time are still not known, the large number of dedicatory inscriptions found on Berezan confirms that the hero was honoured here.

The revival of settled life on the island took place only some time in the middle of the 2nd century AD. It is known that the island flourished through the whole second half of that century and into the first half of the next. A final period of ancient Berezan's history – the seventh – emerges at this time; and it is interesting to note that a combination of both surface and underground construction of dwelling-places became one of the fundamental peculiarities of this last period. The fact that the marble slabs with the remnants of dedications to Achilles were used in construction of these dwellings indicates that the spirit of Hellenic culture was alien to the builders. An end to life on Berezan probably coincided with the downfall of Olbian society and with the decline of Olbia itself as a result of the first Gothic invasion (Kryzhitskii et al. 1989, 155–6).

One book, of course, cannot hope to answer in full all the above questions concerning the historical development of ancient Berezan. The tasks here are more modest: to acquaint Western scholars with new archaeological material and with the current state of affairs in the field of ancient studies in Russia.

PART 1

The Historical Geography and
Topography of Berezan

No one will dispute the assertion that reconstructing the historical past of any ancient population centre would be incomplete if account were not taken the palaeogeographic features of the region in which the settlement is located. A special approach is needed when examining sites located on river estuaries or seacoast; that is, in zones of very specific hydrological conditions. It is well known that coastline configurations in such areas depend on a complex of natural actions, among which the most important rôles are played by cumulative processes of wind and erosion.

It goes without saying that the northwest coast of the Black Sea, across from which the modern island of Berezan is located, comprises one such complex hydrological area. The island is separated from sea by the estuary shared by two of the largest rivers in Eastern Europe – the Dnieper and the Lower Bug (Fig. 2). Evidently in ancient times two other quite considerable waterways spilled into the estuary directly across from the island (nowadays these are barely-noticeable streams by the names Berezanka and Sosik; possibly there was another stream which flowed through the modern Tuzla channel, but which no longer exists). The Berezanka and Sosik rivers, flowing together into one channel not far from Berezan, form the Berezano-Sositskii estuary which opens to the northeast of the island. The Tuzla riverbed is located to the west.

It is known that this region of the northwestern Black Sea coast is part of a gently sloping tectonic flexure called the Black Sea depression, which maintains a steady declivity from north to south (Zenkovitch 1960, 2–80; Kvasov 1975, 210ff). Now, as in ancient times, the landscape of this territory forms a steppe plain broken up by differing degrees of erosion. The river valleys are broad, as a rule, with banks higher on the right (western) side and lower on the left (east), and the slopes of the riverbanks are fissured with deep ravines and gullies. As indicated, in ancient times the river channels were deeper and narrower than they are today (Shilik 1975, 56). The broad, swampy floodplain, submerged during spring floods, possessed abundant meadow vegetation, and the valleys and ravines were covered with coniferous and broadleaf forests in which numerous animal species thrived (Zhuravlyov 1983; 1983a). For their part, the high plains were composed of typical grassland steppe with fertile, chestnut-colored soils. It is thought that in the middle of the 1st millennium BC the climate of this region was more humid than it is today, and proximity to the sea made the climate warmer and less continental than in the deeper regions of Scythia (Ievlev 1992).

The island of Berezan itself is a section of the seacoast, 470 × 860m, possessing a roughly triangular outline and extending from north to south. The island is ringed

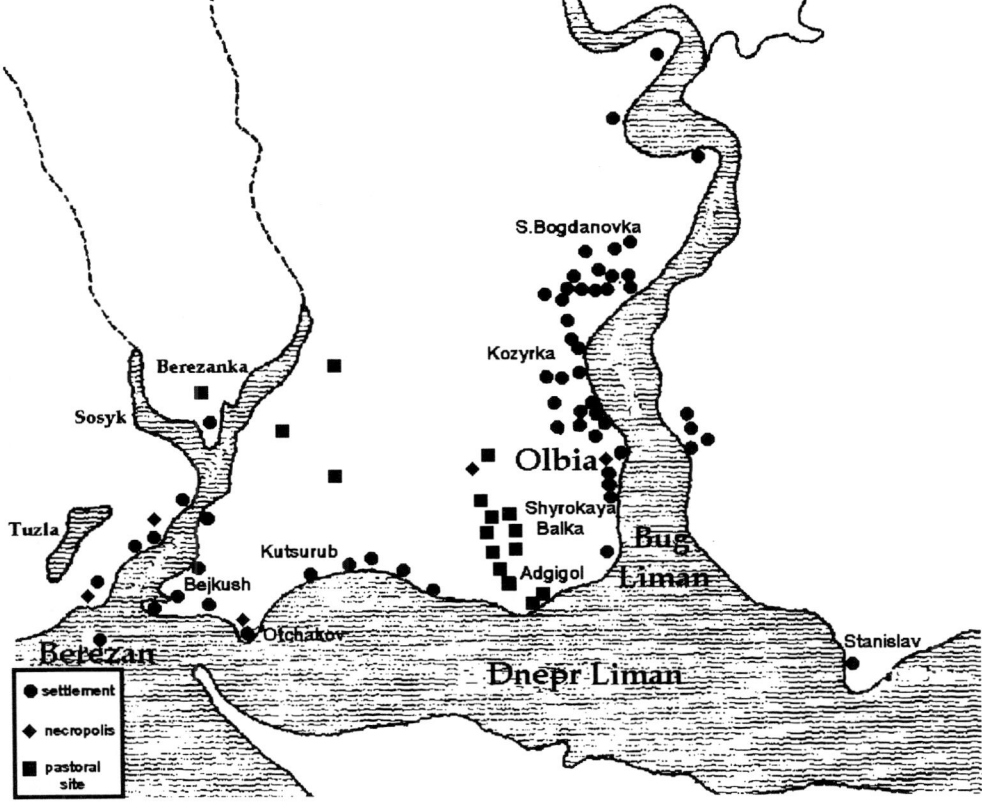

Fig. 2. Map of the Low Bug region.

by steep cliffs of porous limestone, with narrow sandy beaches which have reached almost to the base of the cliffs. In geomorphologic terms, the island shows the stratification of Quaternary loess and clay (Zenkovitch 1960, 2*ff*). The island's elevation rises toward the southern side, and reaches an altitude of 21m above sea level.

In accordance with contemporary reconstruction of physical and geographical conditions in the region of the Dnieper-Bug estuary, it is considered a fully proven fact that Berezan was a peninsula during the initial period of Greek colonization in the Lower Bug River region.[8] Investigation has shown that the formation of the near-modern coastline of the northwestern Black Sea took place during the maximum of the New Black Sea Transgression, which is believed to have occurred in the middle of the 2nd millennium BC and which raised the modern level of the Black Sea by

---

[8] Doubts about this issue were dispelled by V.V. Lapin (1963, 36–7; 1966, 129–37), and were later persuasively repudiated by A.N. Shcheglov (1965, 107–10). The question was finally resolved by the detailed study undertaken by P.V. Fyodorov (1978) and K.K. Shilik (1977; 1978).

2m. The initial formation of the island of Berezan, having been cut off from a section of the mainland coast to the west of the modern town of Ochakov, is believed to date from this time. The appearance of shallow estuaries contiguous to the shore, and especially the formation of an accumulative ledge (projecting sharply into the territory of the island) before the watershed between the Tuzla and the Berezano-Sositskii estuary, probably also took place at the same time (Zenkovitch 1960, 70; Shilik 1975, 11–2; 1977, 158–62).

It has been established that with the coming of a phase of Phanagorian Regression major changes took place in the coastline. Scholars suggest (Shilik 1978, 77; Shcheglov 1978, 17; Fedorov 1978, 157) that in its period of maximum, which occurred in the middle of the 1st millennium BC, the level of the Black Sea fell by 4–12 m,[9] which revealed large coastal terraces. As a result, a broad piece of land joining Berezan to the mainland was formed.[10] It is known that the beginning of Greek colonization in the northern Black Sea occurred at just the same time, as did the appearance of a

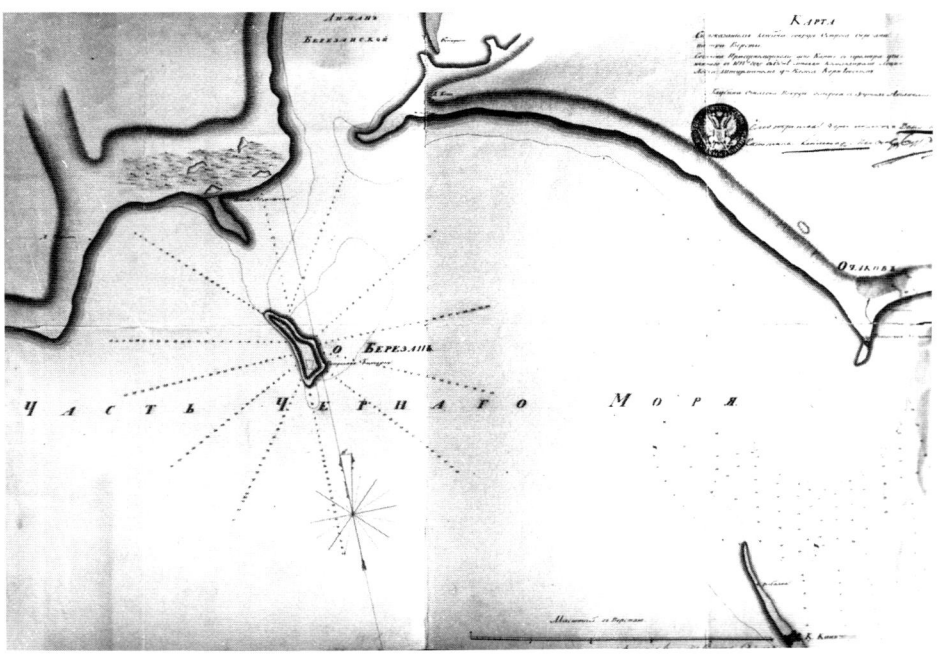

Fig. 3. Map of the surrounds of Berezan Island 1817 (CGA VMF F.3L, L.23, 1324).

[9] Such a broad range of sea level variations can be explained by local tectonic movements of both land and the sea floor. It is believed that the area in question experienced sea level 6–8m lower than the modern level, as defined by P.V. Fyodorov (1978, 157).

[10] The remains of such a connecting piece of land are still visible on maps of the region dating from the beginning of the 19th century (Fig. 3). Even up to the present day, at certain times of the year and in the presence of particular wind conditions the location of the ancient land-bridge can be seen by the unaided eye. It projects northward several hundred metres from the island toward the mainland coast in the form of shallow water or sand-bars.

permanent settlement on Berezan (which evidently remained a peninsula during almost the entire ancient era). Furthermore, it is thought that a new phase of the transgression began in the 3rd century BC and continued right down to the 5th century AD; in the opinion of K. K. Shilik (1978, 78), sometime in the 3rd or 4th centuries AD Berezan again became an island.

Along with changes in sea level and the displacement of seafloor sediments, one further natural factor significantly influenced the formation of the modern Berezan island – coastal erosion, which occurs very strongly in this part of the seaboard. Today the island experiences erosion, with varying degrees of intensity, on practically all sides – with the exception of its accumulative part, the sandbar to the northeast. According to geological research (Zenkovitch 1960, 71), the erosion rate averages 0.3–0.5m a year.

These details allow us to estimate, although roughly, the dimensions of the ancient peninsula at the beginning of colonization. From them it is reasonable to conclude that over the past 2500 years the territory of Berezan has decreased to at least half. Since in modern times the area of the cultural level, excluding the necropolis, occupies about 8–10ha, in my opinion it would not be mistaken to propose that the ancient settlement at the height of its development reached an area of 16–20ha, perhaps slightly less. Up to the present time, no more than 1.5–2ha of that area has been studied.

One major stumbling block for archaeological study of the Berezan settlement has been the lack of a revised archaeological map of the island. Even with sufficiently exact topographical information – which does not exist[11] – it is almost impossible today to locate reliably many of archaeological sites, especially those excavated long ago. There are many reasons for such a distressing conclusion, but key among them are the full or partial absence of documentation of successive fieldwork seasons, sketchy and fragmented excavation plans; and, at times, insufficiently precise descriptions of sites, objects, and their locations. Unfortunately, all the research and excavation plans published by A.S. Uvarov (1851, Pl. 25), R.A. Prendel (1886), G.L. Skadovskii,[12] and E.R. von Stern (1909, 51 Fig. 64, 57 Fig. 65; 1910, 67 Fig. 58, 71 Fig. 60; 1912, 85 Fig. 76, 91 Fig. 79; 1913, 107 Fig. 154) suffer from these shortcomings.

In contrast, the research plan put together by M.F. Boltenko in 1947 was more detailed in an archaeological respect (Fig. 4). The importance of Boltenko's work consists in the fact that it precisely indicated certain sites researched by E.R. von Stern, his excavations, and much of the modern surface damage which occurred during the Second World War. Still, in many cases the fixing of the exact locations of sites worked earlier demands serious correction.

---

[11] In recent years, major work on this problem has been performed by the Moscow geomorphologist and surveyor D.B. Belenkii. His topographical survey of the entire island is the most detailed cartographic source available today. Unfortunately, its richness of detail, which is vital for archaeological work, makes it technically very difficult to publish it in its entirety. The next step is to plot topographically all the archaeological sites excavated over the years, must be done by trained archaeologists. Of course, this can only be done through a meticulous comparison of the local terrain with the results from an analysis of the field-notes from past excavations.

[12] I have in mind the plan of Skadovskii's excavations on the necropolis of Borysthenes kept in the Archive of the State Hermitage and published by V.V. Lapin (1966, 112).

Fig. 4. Plan of Berezan Island (after Boltenko 1947).

Two new archaeological research plans for Berezan were created in the 1970s. The great merit of both was that they were set up on a reliable topographical foundation – specifically, on a map of the island created by professional surveyors in the late 1960s. To be sure, one of the plans (by L.V. Kopeikina: 1981a, 193 Fig. 1) was actually a rather conventional diagram of the location of only the main excavations. In comparison, V.V. Lapin's plan (1978) was much more detailed; it showed most of the sites excavated and their states of preservation in 1976 (Fig. 5). However, even here the localization and configuration of parts of the excavations of R.A. Prendel and E.R. von Stern are debatable, furthermore a series of sites under index K is missing. Evidently Lapin's plan was based on an archaeological map which was later republished by J.G.F. Hind (1984, 79 Fig. 9). In my opinion, the new chart was not very successful and suffers from many inaccuracies.

Therefore, having taken Lapin's plan as a starting point for an archaeological map of Berezan, I have attempted to create a new, more complete map reflecting the state of contemporary archaeological investigation on the island, adding its essential

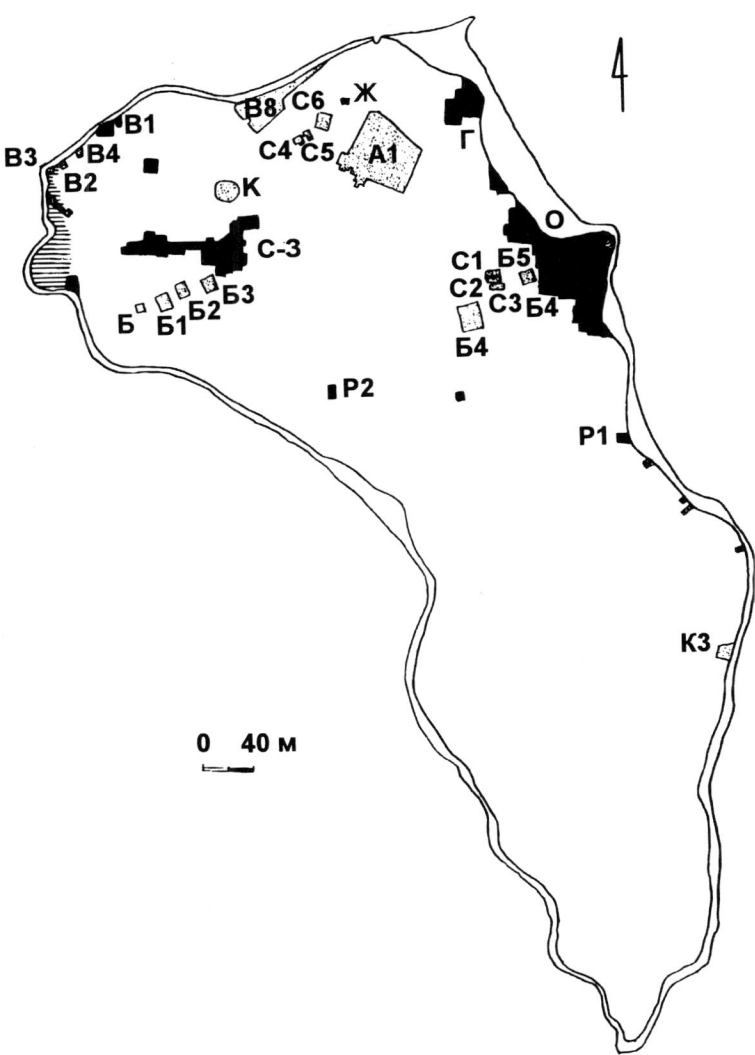

Fig. 5. Plan of Berezan Island (after Lapin 1978).

topographical characteristics (Fig. 6). This cannot, of course, claim to be a full and complete depiction of archaeological studies on the island of Berezan. In general, a more accurate localization of early excavation sites is hardly possible due to the absence of reliable documentation and because there have been significant changes in the topography of the island. There is also a lack of information on the past five years of excavation, since in 1992 the work of the Russian expedition to the island was prohibited by the Institute of Archaeology of the Ukrainian Academy of Sciences.

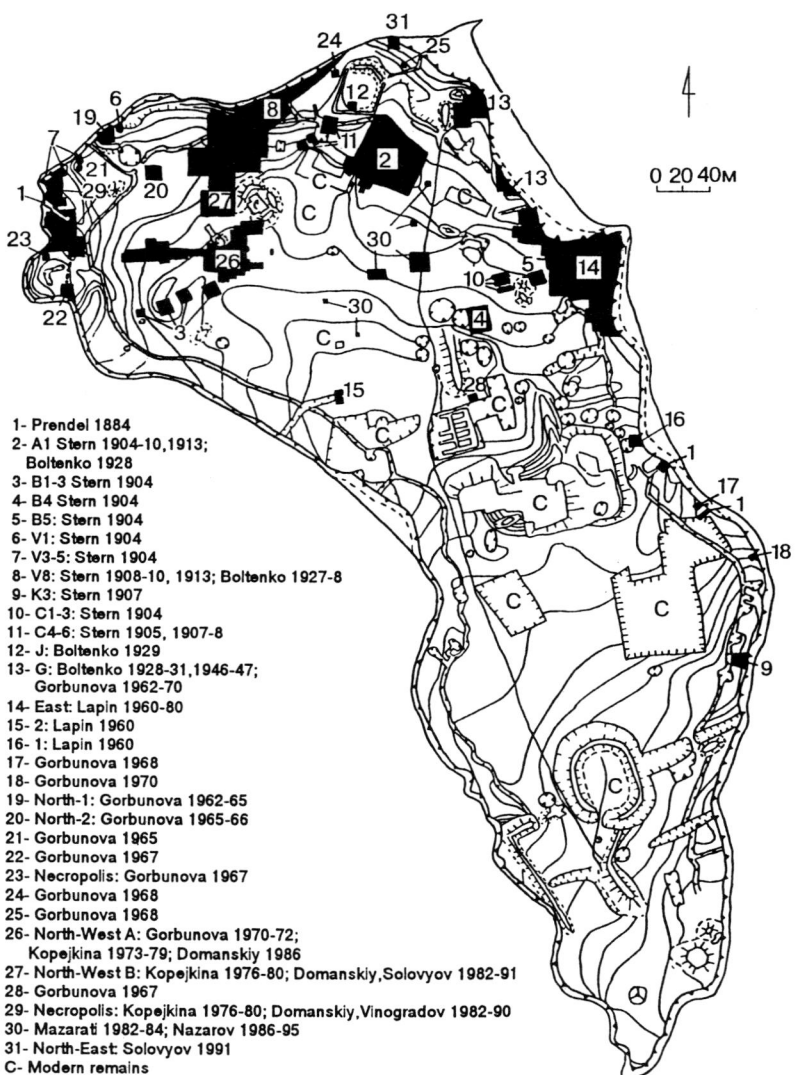

1- Prendel 1884
2- A1 Stern 1904-10,1913;
   Boltenko 1928
3- B1-3 Stern 1904
4- B4 Stern 1904
5- B5: Stern 1904
6- V1: Stern 1904
7- V3-5: Stern 1904
8- V8: Stern 1908-10, 1913; Boltenko 1927-8
9- K3: Stern 1907
10- C1-3: Stern 1904
11- C4-6: Stern 1905, 1907-8
12- J: Boltenko 1929
13- G: Boltenko 1928-31,1946-47;
    Gorbunova 1962-70
14- East: Lapin 1960-80
15- 2: Lapin 1960
16- 1: Lapin 1960
17- Gorbunova 1968
18- Gorbunova 1970
19- North-1: Gorbunova 1962-65
20- North-2: Gorbunova 1965-66
21- Gorbunova 1965
22- Gorbunova 1967
23- Necropolis: Gorbunova 1967
24- Gorbunova 1968
25- Gorbunova 1968
26- North-West A: Gorbunova 1970-72;
    Kopejkina 1973-79; Domanskiy 1986
27- North-West B: Kopejkina 1976-80; Domanskiy,Solovyov 1982-91
28- Gorbunova 1967
29- Necropolis: Kopejkina 1976-80; Domanskiy,Vinogradov 1982-90
30- Mazarati 1982-84; Nazarov 1986-95
31- North-East: Solovyov 1991
C- Modern remains

Fig. 6 . Plan of Berezan Island.

Nevertheless, the new map was the first to include sufficient information on archaeological excavation on Berezan and the main characteristics of its historical topography, in particular disturbances of the cultural levels of the settlement which occurred at various times during the construction of military facilities.

The earliest of these military sites, as established in the records of the State Archives of the Russian Navy, date from the second half of the 18th century – the remains of a Turkish fort which was located on the southern extremity of Berezan. Other, less

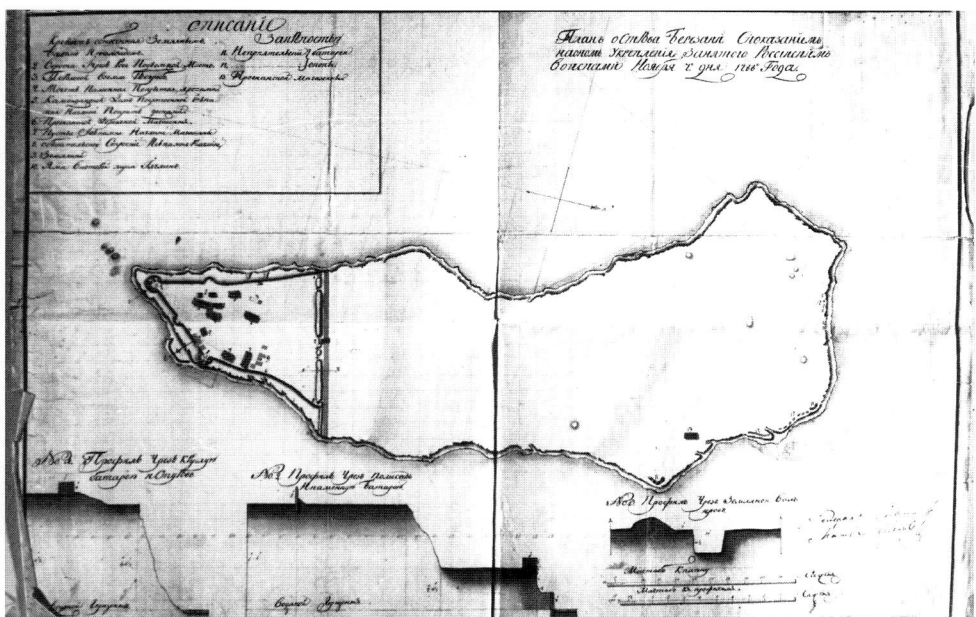

Fig. 7. Plan of Berezan Island -1788 (CGA VMF F.3L, L.23, 1330).

significant fortifications were scattered in other parts of the island (Fig. 7). Practically no traces of this system of fortifications have survived to this day. After the fort was taken by Russian forces in 1788 (Kovalevskii 1906), a Russian fortress was erected in its place, and improvements to the fortress continued to be made until 1825 (Fig. 8). During this time, a strong central fortification was built in the southern highlands, and on the opposite, lower (northeast) part of the island a redoubt with two bastions was erected. However, soon after 1825 military authorities came to realize that it was pointless to keep a garrison on the island.

Military construction on Berezan resumed in 1910. Unfortunately, in contrast to the preceding century, this time the work took place mainly on the northern half of the island; that is, where the ancient settlement was located. Archaeological studies suffered irreplaceable losses as a result of large-scale soil excavation in various parts of the territory: in places the entire surface layer of soil was removed over a large area (Fig. 6). For this reason, the pages of newspapers of the time resounded with the protests of scholars and educated society, and the Imperial Archaeological Commission sent inquiries to the Ministry of War regarding the Commission's need to oversee any construction on the island. These actions, however, had no effect on the military authorities. Only the beginning of the First World War was able to bring a halt to the destruction.

Returning to the question of the map, it is important to note that the larger part of the ancient settlement remained available for archaeological study. During the last 100 years, excavators have been drawn mainly to the northern and eastern coasts of the island, and on the western shore the necropolis has been studied. If we leave

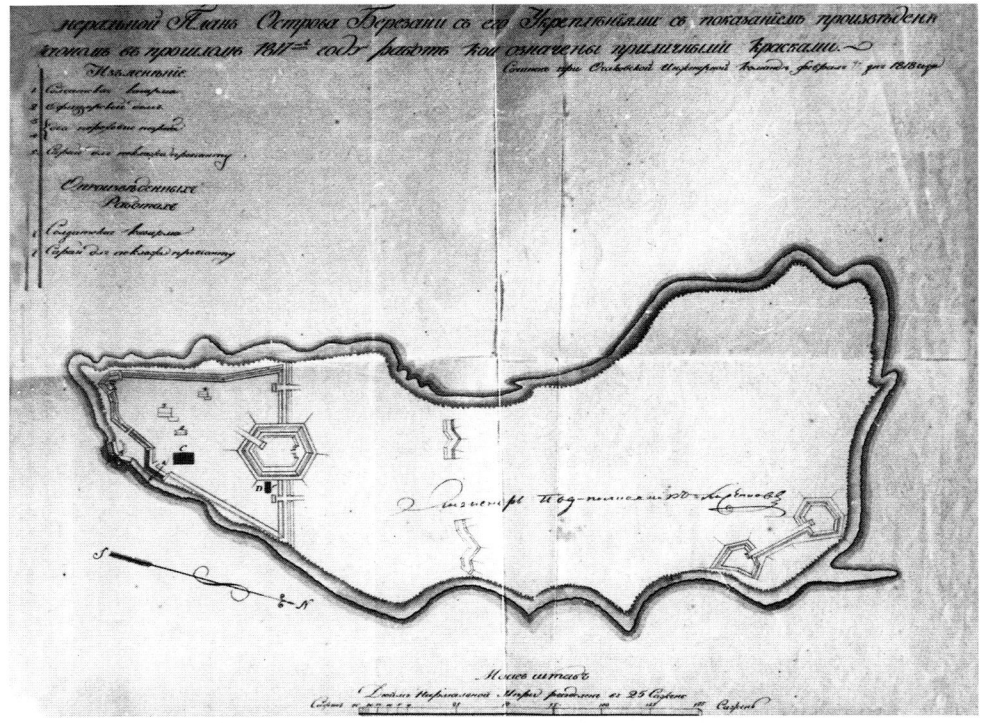

Fig. 8. Plan of Berezan Island -1817 (CGA VMF F.3L, L.23, 1325).

aside the smaller, exploratory shafts and excavations which are scattered all over this part of Berezan, then the main sites of archaeological investigation include areas 2 and 8 (excavations of E.R. von Stern), 13 (M.F. Boltenko and K.S. Gorbunova), 14 (V.V. Lapin), 26 (K.S. Gorbunova and L.V. Kopeikina), 27 (L.V. Kopeikina, Y.V. Domanskii, and S.L. Solovyov), 29 (L.V. Kopeikina, Y.V. Domanskii, and Y.G. Vinogradov), and more recently 30 (S.N. Mazarati, and V.V. Nazarov).[13] This will be discussed in further detail in the next section.

---

[13] This numeration is given in accordance with the map I have compiled, which of course is not intended to supersede the traditional system for excavations on Berezan, by which studied sites are designated by letters. The numeration used here is intended only to simplify current investigation for the reader. The standard lettering system is given in the map legend.

PART 2

The History of
Archaeological Investigation on Berezan

Berezan first became known to Russian scholarship as an ancient archaeological site in the first half of the 19th century, as a result of visits to the island by the St Petersburg scholar K. Kohler (1826, 627–8) and the head of the Moscow Archaeological Society, Count A.S. Uvarov (1851). Kohler published inscriptions found on the island, and Uvarov composed a description of Berezan itself. In particular, Uvarov's work reported that "the soil is all strewn with pottery fragments, white marble, and green stone." In the northern part of the island, Uvarov located six ancient burial mounds, and to the northeast of these (nearer the shore) he noted ditches and moats remaining, so he supposed, from a temple of Achilles (Uvarov 1851, 141–2). In Uvarov's opinion, the remains of buildings of ancient cult had been scattered by Turks during the construction of fortifications on the island. It is, of course, difficult to say if that is indeed the case. It is more likely that Uvarov mistakenly took abandoned Turkish military fortifications (built in 1781: Boltenko 1960, 45) for the remains of a temple. On one map of Berezan composed by Russian military cartographers soon after the island was taken by Cossacks in 1788, one of the Turkish artillery batteries is shown on the supposed site of the ancient temple (Fig. 7).

Archaeological research on Berezan was initially proposed by R.A. Prendel (1886, 216–9), a member of the Odessa Society of History and Antiquity. In 1884, he visited the island with the aim of uncovering traces of prehistoric peoples. Excavations were conducted in four places: three were located on the eastern shore of the island, and one – a form of trench – was situated on the western shore. Although he never decided on the main goal of his investigation, and finally admitted to its lack of success, Prendel nevertheless uncovered on Berezan numerous pottery pragments, an ancient interment site, and a grave dating from a later time. Prendel composed a highly detailed description of the island's physical appearance, in which he noted in particular that "a concentration of kitchenware remains" was found only in the northern area, the broadest part of the island.

Prendel reported the results of his excavation to the VI Archaeological Congress, which took place that same year in Odessa. His report did not go unnoticed. The remains of ancient gravesites on the island aroused the greatest interest among archaeologists. At the time, reconnaissance in southern Russia comprised the main, if not only, tendency in archaeological investigation into ancient cultures. In academic circles and in society rumours circulated about the remarkable finds from ancient Bosporus.

Still, resuming archaeological study on Berezan became possible only in 1896, when the island was briefly visited by B.V. Farmakovskii. One of the top specialists of the time in classical archaeology, one may rightly call Farmakovskii the father of classical archaeology in Russia. The small-scale excavation he undertook in the northern part of Berezan discovered in all only three burials of the 1st century AD (Farmakovskii 1898, 211–2). More successful was G.L. Skadovskii – Marshal of the Nobility (*predvoditel' dvoryanstva*) of Kherson province – but, unfortunately, not an archaeologist. To Skadovskii went the honour of discovering the huge, ancient Berezan necropolis (von Stern 1901, 88–91). In two field seasons – 1900 and 1901 – Skadovskii managed to unearth more than 500 graves, most of which dated from the beginning of settlement on the island. Unfortunately, for scholarship much information on these burial complexes was irretrievably lost, owing to a lack of professional skills on the part of the excavators and because of losses of documentation on the digging and parts of the collection itself during the Second World War. Consequently, one cannot consider the well-known, contemporary publication (Radlov 1910; Enman 1911; Turaev 1911; Fabritsius 1951, 57*ff*; Kaposhina 1956, 214*ff*; Skudnova 1957; 1960; Dzis-Raiko 1959; Lapin 1966, 102*ff*; Bolshakov and Ilina 1988; Ostroverkhov 1989; Okhotnikov and Ostroverkhov 1993), of the results of Skadovskii's work, and the remains of his collection (which have been preserved by the State Hermitage, Kherson, and Odessa museums), as fully exhaustive; nor is the interpretation of these finds fully convincing.[14]

Many honorable pages in the history of excavations on Berezan are linked to another scholar, E.R. von Stern, a senior contemporary of Farmokovskii and Professor of Novorossiisk University (Odessa) and a member of the Imperial Archaeological Commission. Studying the ancient world of southern Russia, von Stern enthusiastically accepted the opportunity which was offered him to conduct archaeological research on the island. The main task which he pursued during the first years of his stay on Berezan – in 1903 and 1904 – was the traditional one for archaeologists of the time: to study the embankments and hollows of supposed ancient burial sites not far from the area which was excavated earlier by Skadovskii (von Stern 1904, 97–100; 1907, 41–9). Encountering traces of building activity and numerous pottery finds everywhere he dug, von Stern evidently came to the conclusion that on Berezan there had to have been not only a necropolis, but also an established settlement. Therefore, as early as 1904 one of the goals of his research became, in the words of von Stern himself, "finding the ancient settlement" (von Stern 1907, 42). Later on this task would become his primary aim.

Von Stern devoted seven field seasons to archaeological research on Berezan. During the period 1904–1909 and 1913, a significant portion of the ancient settlement was unearthed, mainly in the northern part of the island (von Stern 1910, 71 Fig. 60). As a result of this work, the basic stratigraphy of the site was marked, and the characteristics of the cultural levels were determined. These observations taken together served above all as a basis for determining a relative chronology for the Berezan settlement, a project to which von Stern devoted particular attention.

All the building remains found at the site were divided into two groups, according to two criteria: the position of walls relative to the level of continental soil, and the

---

[14] Indeed, the richest materials from Skadovskii's excavations are still unpublished. Until that happens, any speculation about the data from the Berezan necropolis will remain incomplete and unconvincing.

type of leveling. Walls were found which dated from an early time, built of well-worked stone and standing either on the subsoil or on a thin cultural level. Those walls of soft quarry-stone which were erected on the cultural level, and which in some instances attained a width of 1.4m, were connected to a later period.

Relying on the dating of ancient pottery, von Stern discerned a definite chronology of the site. In his opinion, the settlement arose in the 7th century BC, the early period consisted mainly of the first half of the 6th century BC, and the upper chronological limit of the later period fell at the end of the 6th/beginning of the 5th centuries BC. As a result of this kind of approach, in von Stern's view the cultural and historical development of ancient Berezan had two phases: Ionian and Attic. The former was characterized by the predominance of East Greek ("Milesian", according to von Stern) pottery; the latter saw a growth of imported Athenian pottery. Finally, the presence of a small quantity of Roman pottery and the remains of dedicatory inscriptions to Achilles were explained by von Stern as traces of seasonal visits to the island in the 1st century AD by fishermen and by devotees of the cult of Achilles.

Von Stern carried out important work determining the boundaries of ancient Berezan. His excavations in the northwest, southwest, and southern parts of the island showed that the ancient settlement occupied almost the entire broad, northern half of the island. Most of the raised areas examined by him turned out to be later burial complexes, in the foundation of which were found household pits and the remains of surface constructions dating from the time of the ancient settlement.

It is important to give proper due to the consistency and firmness with which von Stern expounded his views on the history and archaeology of Berezan. These qualities were reflected in his reports published by the Imperial Archaeological Commission, and also in a series of articles on the ancient history of the northern Black Sea region, all of which in one way or another touched on the development of the Berezan settlement (von Stern 1900; 1901; 1904; 1907; 1908; 1909; 1909a; 1910; 1912; 1913; 1913a; 1914). Of course, it is impossible now to agree with all of the views articulated by von Stern. Furthermore, certain archaeological facts were left unexplained, or were given explanations that now seem unclear.

The nearly total absence of information relating to dugout residential buildings found on the island seems very strange. During all the years of excavations only two such dugouts are mentioned (von Stern 1912, 87), while all subsequent researchers on Berezan noted numerous dwellings of this type in virtually all areas of the Berezan settlement. Also unclear is the question of the so-called "burial pits" which von Stern singled out as a special group and which contained a large quantity of pottery fragments, scorched human bones and terracotta figurines of Cabiri – "cloud demons," as von Stern called them (1912, 92–3). Not one pit of this type was subsequently found on Berezan.

In addition, von Stern's research was generally not very clear on the characteristics of buildings found in the excavated parts of the settlement and on the layout of individual residential houses. To von Stern (1913, 108), residential construction on Berezan seemed to consist of a set of buildings of rather small size, which, judging by the published map of the excavations, looks an improbable conclusion. However, he committed more serious errors in the dating of these building remains and in determining their chronological sequence. These errors resulted from his carelessly chosen criteria for the chronology of the buildings and by the almost total absence in those years of information on the specifics of local residential construction.

Of course, such a critical evaluation of the results of von Stern's work in no way diminishes his contributions to the study of Berezan and to the preservation of the ancient settlement for scholarship. He was among those who spoke out sharply against the engineering work on the island carried out by the Ministry of War in 1910–14 (von Stern 1914, 78–80), which sought to build an artillery testing ground for the Black Sea fleet – work which significantly damaged the ancient settlement (as mentioned in the introduction to this book). Even after his departure from Russia not long before the beginning of the First World War (Farewell 1911), von Stern never lost his vital interest in ancient Berezan; in Germany he actively continued his studies on the history of the ancient Greek settlement (von Stern 1912a).

The war years, and social revolution in Russia, pushed archaeological investigations aside for a long time. Such was the case for Berezan as well. Interrupted excavations on the island were able to resume only when social and economic conditions in the new Soviet state began to stabilize. The leader of this new work was M.F. Boltenko of the Odessa Archaeological Museum, a student of von Stern and in many ways his successor. Excavations were conducted (albeit with a few interruptions) over the course of several field seasons: 1924, 1927–31, 1946 and 1947; this work made important further contributions to understanding Berezan's past (Boltenko 1930; 1949; 1960). Unlike his predecessor, Boltenko made his primary task the study of the latest, already Slavonic, period, which had earlier been almost completely unknown (Boltenko 1947). His work was, without a doubt, remarkably successful. The absence of remains of a later settlement in the excavations of von Stern were justifiably explained by Boltenko as a consequence of the serious disturbance of the upper soil level during construction operations carried out by the Turks, as he surmised (Boltenko 1949, 32; 1960, 44),[15] as well as by Russian military fortifications on that part of the island. Furthermore, during Boltenko's excavations on Berezan a well-substantiated chronological and stratigraphic timeline was developed, which described the development of the settlement from ancient times to the Middle Ages. This scale remains relevant today.

Boltenko's view of the historical development of Berezan took the following form: from the moment of its founding in the second half of the 7th century BC, the settlement on Berezan was a major fishing and trading centre for the Ionians; its heyday was in the 6th century BC. At the same time, an indigenous population (which had appeared well before Greek colonization) continued to live on the northern coast of the island. It was supposed that dugouts served as residential quarters for both the Greeks and indigenous people. Further, in the course of excavations Boltenko discerned a distinctive type of dwelling used by the local population – "living pits", which the scholar (Boltenko 1949) and O.A. Artamonova (1940), who was working with him in 1931, believed dated to an early period of indigenous settlement on Berezan. According to Boltenko's conception, in the 5th century BC there occurred

---

[15] After Boltenko, other archaeologists also began to subscribe to this idea, having looked uncritically at the latest materials from Berezan. In addition, Russian naval cartographic data preserved in the Central State Archive of the Russian Navy in St Petersburg has removed all doubt on the subject.

a period during which the island was abandoned, an event connected to the political and economic growth of Olbia.

The unremarkable building remains and levels dating to the 5th through 3rd centuries BC were excavated only on the northeastern part of that area which had earlier been occupied by the settlement. Boltenko attributed the cessation of life on Berezan at the beginning of the 3rd century BC to a Galatian invasion in 280 BC. He explained the remains of dugout residential buildings dating from the 1st through 4th centuries AD as a minor revival of domestic activity at that time.

Owing to a growing interest in the history of the Slavonic settlement on Berezan, questions concerning the development of the ancient Greek colony were gradually and undeservedly moved to the back burner. Archaeological interest in the Greek colony also remained secondary for a long time because of the very small scale of the excavations carried out by Boltenko, who was probably not provided sufficient means for conducting significant study, in comparison with those which took place before the Russian Revolution. This situation could not but be reflected in the reports on investigation, which appeared from time to time in the press. This basically repeated and to a certain extent refined the ideas of von Stern, taking into account corrections made by Boltenko (Nudelman 1946; Fabritsius 1951; Slavin 1956; Kaposhina 1956; Domanskii 1961).

A new approach resulted from the work of V.V. Lapin, who devoted a significant portion of his life – from 1960 to 1980 – to excavations on Berezan. He looked very critically at the results of previous expeditions to the island. As early as the first field season, the main task of Lapin's research was to develop a more precise topographic and stratigraphic analysis of the site. That work enabled him to come to the following conclusions (Lapin 1961, 43):

– the boundaries of the settlement were not fixed; their maximum extent appeared to date to the 5th century BC;

– the largest quantity of building remains, including the very earliest, was concentrated in the northeastern part of the island, and the strength of the cultural level decreased in a southerly direction;

– the attraction of the initial centre of the settlement to the northeast can be explained not by the presence of a convenient harbour, but by the peculiarities of the local terrain; the best conditions for obtaining fresh water were in the very lowest, northeastern part of the island;

– the existing periodization of the cultural levels and building remains, which was developed by von Stern based on the predominance of one or another type of pottery, was not supported;

– the existing chronology of building remains, which relies on the level of foundation levels, is imprecise, inasmuch as it does not take into account the existence of basement and semi-basement rooms;

– the absence of a cultural level from Hellenistic times may be explained by the peculiarities of level formation.

It is worth noting that we have before us a comprehensive programme of study for the Berezan settlement. In subsequent years, the main features of it – the formation of levels and stratigraphy of the site, the typology and reconstruction of building remains, the historical periodization of the settlement – remained the focus of Lapin's attention. Despite the fact that he carried out excavations primarily on the eastern half of the island (Lapin 1967, 145–9; 1968, 150–5; 1972, 157–60), observations made on that basis appear to apply generally to the entire settlement. Lapin's ideas were grounded in a well-developed and original conception of cultural and historical development on Berezan (Lapin 1966, 86ff; 1975; 1978). The following are just a few aspects of this conception which demonstrate its distinctiveness.

As Lapin noted (1978, 73–4), the level corresponding to the founding of the Berezan settlement according to ancient sources was not uncovered in the course of excavations.[16] Incidental finds of ancient pottery on Berezan were only solitary. Lapin's studies characterized the material culture of Berezan in an entirely new way. He paid special attention to the development of residential construction in ancient Berezan, which he saw as an important ethnographic indicator (Lapin 1975, 101). He noted that dugouts,[17] and not "living pits," were the very earliest and only type of dwelling during the initial phase of Greek colonization in the Lower Bug region. Indeed, he fully and persuasively denied the existence of "living pits" at all. The development of dugout residential buildings seemed to him to take the following course: from an oval form (as he supposed, the most ancient), through structures with "apse ledges", ultimately to a rectangular form (Lapin 1978, 114–23). The further evolution of dwellings seemed to Lapin a process by which single-chambered dugout buildings were replaced by many chambered ones, followed by the construction of small and simple aboveground houses with semi-basement spaces, which led to the creation of many-chambered houses with basements of the classical type (Lapin 1966, 102; 1975, 101; 1978, 134).

In accordance with his concept of the development of residential construction, Lapin came to the conclusion that the ancient Greeks of the northern Black Sea were themselves a "culture of dugout dwellings," the genetic roots of which he traced to Bronze-Age cultures of Balkan Greece and the islands of the Aegean Sea (Lapin 1975, 101; 1978, 224). He also saw such ancient sources in certain features of funeral rites, inscriptions, and the hand-made pottery of ancient settlements of the northern Black Sea (Lapin 1975, 102). Furthermore, Lapin argued firmly against the dominance of trade during the early phase of Greek colonization on the northern shores of the

---

[16] In 1977 a section of the cultural level was fixed at a depth of 1.50–1.95m below the level of the modern surface. Lapin tentatively dated this section to the middle of the 7th – beginning of the 6th centuries BC. However, having examined the illustrations from his 1977 field reports, it seems that somewhat later date is preferred.

[17] "Dugout" (*zemlyanka*) is the term usually applied in the archaeological literature of the Soviet period and today to residential or household buildings dug into the ground, the lower part of which consists of a foundation-trench dug out to a depth greater than 1m (half the average height of a human being is sometimes accepted as the defining figure), and covered with a roof. A buildings whose depth measures less than 1m is usually called a partial or semi-dugout (*poluzemlyanka*). Both full and partial dugouts may have had aboveground construction as well, which as a rule consisted of walls of wood, mud-bricks, or stone.

Pontus, including Berezan, and also denied that local societies had any influence on the course and character of the colonization process (Lapin 1966).[18]

Today it is possible to disagree with one or another of the opinions developed by Lapin; some have undergone substantive reconsideration, and others have received little further encouragement. Among the latter may be included his views on the evolution of residential building construction, the interaction between Greek and indigenous populations in the region, the periodization of historical development, and certain other beliefs. All of this does not, however, diminish Lapin's contribution as a major study on ancient Berezan. Without a doubt, it is important to give just due to the meticulous planning, systematic character and high degree of professionalism demonstrated in his research.

In 1962 an archaeological expedition led by K.S. Gorbunova and organized by the State Hermitage Museum came to conduct research. Excavations were carried out in various parts of the island, mainly on the eastern and northern coasts, until 1970. In the west investigation was conducted to find the boundaries of the necropolis: in 1967–68, sixteen ancient burial sites were found here. The results of all this research were never published in full; they were recorded mainly in annual field reports and in minor, merely informational, communications (Gorbunova 1967; 1968a; 1969a; 1970a; 1971; 1972; 1974). Meanwhile the excavations of 1962–70 completely replenished the Berezan collection of ancient pottery. Gorbunova's research represented an important contribution to the study of ancient sites in the northern Black Sea region.

After 1970, the Hermitage expedition moved its excavations mainly to the northwestern part of the island (Kopeikina 1974; 1975a; 1976; 1977a; 1978; 1981b). Because well-preserved building remains from various different times (mainly the Archaic period) were found there, this section of the Berezan settlement gained special meaning for investigation on ancient Borysthenes. Recognition for the largest contribution to the study of Archaic levels on Berezan rightly belongs to L.V. Kopeikina, who replaced Gorbunova in 1973. In addition to studying various types and groups of ancient pottery, Kopeikina also paid close attention to questions concerning the development of the settlement, including its layout, the design of residential buildings, and construction traditions (Kopeikina 1975; 1979; 1981; 1981a).

---

[18] Among Soviet archaeologists, it was V.V. Lapin who most consistently developed ideas connected to the agrarian theory of Greek colonization, as applied to the conditions of the northern Black Sea region. Overall, Lapin (1966, 33*ff*) saw the colonization process as a primarily spontaneous, mass migration of the most impoverished parts of the population of the Greek cities of eastern Ionia. Lapin's views on the character of Hellenic colonization in the northern Black Sea found widespread support among specialists – archaeologists and ancient historians – in the former Soviet Union. The most active and consistent of his supporters were Ukrainian archaeologists under S.D. Kryzhitskii. On the basis of Lapin's ideas, these scholars have recently formulated and widely disseminated a new conception of colonization in the northern Black Sea (Kryzhitskii and Buiskikh 1988; Kryzhitskii *et al.* 1989, 26–31). Its main argument rests on the contrast between regulated and spontaneous means of settlement employed by the ancient Greeks on the northern coast of the Pontus; the latter interpretation is clearly preferred. These opinions have already been given mainly negative evaluation by specialists (Marchenko 1994) (in my opinion, a correct judgment). Without touching here on all the other debatable points of this conception, it is important at least to note that its main shortcoming is an almost complete lack of regard by the authors for any archaeological material which do not fit into a rigid framework describing the historical development of the northern Black Sea region in the Archaic period.

Within the boundaries of the Archaic period, Kopeikina (as did von Stern in his own time) discerned two primary types of construction. The first of these dated to the end of the 7th through the first half of the 6th centuries BC, and was characterized exclusively by dugout and partially dugout buildings, along with household pits. Kopeikina noted the absence at that time of any kind of regulation concerning construction in the settlement. In the fill found in the residential buildings a large amount of imported Greek pottery was discovered, a significant amount of which consisted of decorated East Greek wares.

Kopeikina believed that the second period of construction, which dated to the second half of the 6th through the beginning of the 5th centuries BC, was related to the appearance of brick and stone houses on Berezan. In her opinion, this type of structure was built according to a single plan based on a principle of orthogonal organization of the living areas with a developed network of streets. She saw in this construction plan evidence of a *polis* structure. She also believed the sources of these building traditions to lie in the ancient culture of eastern Ionia. It was further noted that the tradition of dugout construction also continued in the settlement at this time, but only as an exception. In contradiction to Lapin, Kopeikina demonstrated that the peak of social, economic, political and territorial development of Berezan occurred in the 6th century BC, and its decline should be dated not later than the first quarter of the 5th century BC.

Kopeikina's name must always be associated with renewed excavation of the Berezan necropolis, located in the western part of the island. From 1976 to 1980, 56 ancient burial sites were discovered here, complete with inhumation and cremation, and which were accompanied by distinctive sets of burial accessories. This material has included works by ancient masters, of rare artistic merit.

In 1982, Y.V. Domanskii became the Director of excavation on Berezan for the Hermitage. At the same time (1982–84), S.N. Mazarati headed excavation for the Institute of Archaeology of the Ukrainian Academy of Sciences; she was succeeded by V.V. Nazarov. The new investigation proceeded along the general lines set down by previous work. The efforts of both expeditions – that of the Hermitage and that of the Ukrainian Institute of Archaeology – were directed at studying all periods of archaeology and history of Berezan as thoroughly as possible. However, because of a number of distinctive features in the historical development of the settlement in the Archaic and subsequent periods, the two expeditions were presented with different concrete tasks. In particular, in the northwestern part of the settlement the main objects of study for the Hermitage expedition were the block of 6th-century BC residential buildings, the earlier construction remains dating from the Archaic period, and the necropolis dating from the same time (Domanskii 1985; Domanskii *et al.* 1986; 1989; 1991; Solovyov 1992a). In the eastern part of the settlement, the Ukrainian Institute of Archaeology expedition sought to uncover the construction techniques of Hellenistic and Roman times (Nazarov 1990; 1994). Of course, when urgently necessary both groups, in parallel, examined issues concerning life on Berezan at other times.

The excavations in the northwestern part of the settlement discovered fundamentally new information about the Classical period (Solovyov 1994; 1995a). These excavations also significantly expanded our knowledge of Roman Berezan.

Apart from anything else, this knowledge was supplemented by new written sources on a very poorly studied part of Berezan history – the 1st century BC, during which time the island replaced itself for Leuke as a pan-Hellenic sanctuary of Achilles (Shelov-Kovedyaev 1990; Vinogradov Y. G. 1994). And, finally, a completely unexpected event – the discovery of a necropolis on Berezan dating from the early Middle Ages, which was found in this part of the island above ancient building remains (Solovyov 1992a).

For its part, work in the eastern part of the island also extended beyond the framework of basic research tasks. Investigation here shed light on separate and distinct moments in the history of the Berezan settlement in Archaic, Classical and Roman periods (Nazarov 1990; 1994). Moreover, the expedition of the Ukrainian Institute of Archaeology initiated the first undersea archaeological research in the waters off Berezan. In the event of their successful conclusion, it is reasonable to expect important new data on the history of ancient Berezan, above all on the initial stage of Greek colonization in this area of the northwestern Black Sea.[19]

---

[19] In recent years, the Ukrainian expedition has also carried out reconnaissance and study of the latest building remains, especially Turkish fortifications. Today, given the overall limitation of financial and technical means to conduct archaeological excavations, these other interests have unfortunately weakened the investigation front on ancient Berezan.

PART 3

Archaic Berezan

A. The Berezan settlement down to the end of the third quarter of the 6th century BC

As already noted, the natural environment of the Lower Bug region in the 7th-5th centuries BC included flat, open country and fertile lands covered with the vegetation of the steppe and indented with a network of ravines and river valleys, with mixed floodland forests and rich animal life. Here, as in the entire northern Black Sea region, a humid, relatively warm climate prevailed by the middle of the 1st millennium BC, although it was cool in comparison with the modern climate (Ievlev 1987, 64–5; 1992, 134*ff*, *cf*: Shcheglov 1978, 27*ff*). It is thought that the region possessed significant natural resources, above all raw materials for construction and craftsmanship. It is believed that all this comprised a decisive factor in the choice of Greek colonists to found a new *polis* in this place. It is also believed that the absence of a permanent and numerically significant local population in the Lower Bug region also favored the decision to colonize (Kryzhitskii *et al.* 1989, 20; Vinogradov Y. G. 1989, 39*ff*).

Still, it would not be completely correct to characterize the Lower Bug area as a region totally devoid of people at the time of the appearance of the Greeks. Today there is good reason to assume quite the opposite, namely, that the entire area in the lower course of Borysthenes and Hypanis was, in early Scythian times, under the more or less permanent control of tribes from the forest-steppe region between the rivers Dnieper and Dniester (Marchenko and Vinogradov 1989, 806–7; Marchenko 1991, 18–9). Archaeological study on Scythian sites in right bank Ukraine have, especially in recent years, provided much evidence that the style of life and domestic activities of local tribes (especially the inhabitants of the steppe and forest-steppe border zone) combined both settled-agricultural and nomadic elements (Ilinskaya and Terenozhkin 1983, 227*ff*; Shramko 1987; Kovpanenko *et al.* 1989; Alekseev 1992, 56*ff*. The gradual change of climate in the arid zone of the northern Black Sea region in the middle of the 1st millennium BC, which brought greater warmth, was able to further the great economic and demographic potential of the Dnieper-Dniester region – not only in the sense of cultural growth, but also in terms of broad territorial expansion. The migrations of inhabitants of this region led to the creation of the Vorskla and western Podolia local groups of forest-steppe Scythian culture and eventually to their resettlement in the direction of the Lower Bug. This is a highly regarded fact of contemporary Scythian studies (Ilinskaya and Terenozhkin 1983, 304; Smirnova 1978; 1990, 28*ff*).

Few now doubt the presence of emigrants from the middle Dnieper and eastern Podolia regions in the Dnieper-Bug area, inasmuch as the assertion is strongly supported by the composition of hand-made pottery found by excavations on Berezan (Marchenko 1988, 107*ff*). However, it is thought that the numbers of these people in the 7th century BC were very modest. There may have been seasonal migrations for part of the forest-steppe population to the coastal regions, where both Borysthenes and Hypanis possessed swampy estuaries rich with vegetation, excellent conditions for wintering livestock. The absence of any traces of winter quarters in the Lower Bug region can be explained, first of all, by their total loss as a result of the inundation of ancient floodlands and the destruction of the shores of the Lower Bug and Dnieper rivers from a sea level higher than that of today; and second, by the insignificant occurrence of nomadic livestock-raising among the forest-steppe tribes, which primarily raised cattle of the pasturable kind (Tsalkin 1960; 1971, 14*ff*). A fully nomadic life was, evidently, the permanent occupation of a very small social group, which apparently consisted of the highest level of local society. This conclusion is supported strongly by a certain number of military (apparently local horse-warriors) burial mounds in forest-steppe Scythia, which are typologically very close to the nomadic style. There is also a small number of Scythian burial sites of a "royal" appearance in the steppe zone to the west of the Dnieper (Alekseev 1992, 56*ff*, 104*ff*, Smirnova 1990, 28).

In light of the archaeological evidence discussed above, the behaviour of the indigenous population toward the Greeks in the northwestern Black Sea region in the 7th century BC becomes more understandable. These actions were grounded in social and economic factors prevailing in forest-steppe Scythia at the time, and also in the interest that more well-to-do local inhabitants had in contact with the Greek colonists. The actions of the Greeks, unfortunately, cannot be understood and described in straightforward terms. The fault for this lies primarily in the disparity of data between the ancient written tradition and archaeological evidence on the question of early Berezan history (mentioned in the Introduction).

In this way it must be said that the sum total of archaeological evidence on the initial phase of Greek colonization in the Lower Bug region does not support the well-known source, Eusebius, and instead only indicates that in the third quarter of the 7th century BC Berezan became a place regularly visited by representatives from Miletus and, possibly, other Ionian city-states. The factors which pushed these people to undertake such a distant and risky enterprise lie most likely in the relations between Ionia and other states during the whole of the 7th century BC.[20] The international situation of the time was shaped largely by the expansionist policies of the Lydian empire and by continual raids carried out by Cimmerian nomads, and after that by Scythians who, according to some scholars, may have been the source of information by which the Ionian Greeks learned of the Dnieper-Bug region and of the people of forest-steppe Scythia (*cf*: Alekseev 1992, 95).

---

[20] On some aspects of the influence of the military-political situation in the eastern Ionia on a course of the colonization process, see: Vinogradov Y. G. 1989, 38*ff*, Koshelenko and Kuznetsov 1990, 38*ff*, Alekseev 1992, 9*ff*, Tsetskhladze 1994, 123–26.

As a result of the military and political instability on the eastern shores of Asia Minor in the 7th century BC, there was apparently a concomitant decline in social and economic conditions. In this situation, the Ionian *poleis* most likely needed new markets for raw materials and production in order to maintain themselves. With these goals in mind, reconnaissance became the main objective of Greek seafaring in the early stage of opening up the northwest Black Sea. The constant threat posed by Lydia and by nomadic raiders probably compelled the Greeks to mobilize all available resources for defence of the city-states and was not conducive to colonization. It is believed that setting up colonies occurred most frequently in relatively stable periods, after the danger of war had passed (Vinogradov Y. G. 1989, 57*ff*; Koshelenko and Kuznetsov 1990, 38*ff*, *cf*.: Tsetskhladze 1994, 123–6).

All of the factors noted above applied as well to Miletus, which took a leading rôle among the Ionian city-states and in the colonization movement. The dramatic upheavals and reversals of fortune in Miletus' conflict with the Lydian empire are well known (Hdt. 1. 15, 17–19). Emigrants from Miletus surely made up the most active and enterprising part of Ionian sailors and traders. Their commercial interests in the Lower Bug region most likely included the search for and acquisition of such goods as fish, timber, metals, and grain (Vinogradov Y. G. 1989, 53*ff*, *cf*.: Shcheglov 1990, 99*ff*).

The need of Milesian merchants for the first two categories of commodities could have been fully satisfied in the Dnieper-Bug region, but the rest only partially. Therefore one must acknowledge that the first settlers had very limited means, if any, to create a base of marketable agricultural production on Berezan or in its surrounding areas. Considering that for any metropolis the provision of food, especially bread, is of paramount importance, it is reasonable to suppose that setting up a stable and permanent relationship with the agricultural regions of forest-steppe Scythia became one of the key tasks of the Greek colonists. It is thought that in exchange for grain the Greeks were able to export wine (which was probably transported mainly in wineskins or in other some other kind of unbreakable containers), fine woollen fabrics, and other products of Greek manufacture and craftsmanship (initially, it seems, these were few in number and consisted of materials which have not survived to the present day) (Vinogradov Y. G. 1989, 54–5).

At first all the imported goods would have gone to the local aristocracy, and only later spread among the rest of the indigenous people, which gradually drew them to the area of direct contact with the Greeks. One result of the Greeks' successful economic policies was the decision by various groups within the indigenous population, including farmers and nomads, to settle on Berezan. This process probably began at the end of the 7th century BC, when the first fixed dwellings appeared on the peninsula. One cannot exclude the possibility that there had been even earlier dwellings much like yurts or tents, which are archaeologically unrecorded.

As a result of this influx, there began a new (second) period which lasted roughly seven or eight decades. As I already mentioned, within this time-frame it is possible to discern two distinct phases, one of the first quarter and the other of the second quarter of the 6th century BC. The end of the third quarter of the 6th century BC, which was a time of major change, stands as the lower limit of this period (Domanskii *et al.* 1989, 35–7; 1991, 11–5; Solovyov 1994, 90–1).

Evidently, at the beginning of the period in question there was no clearly planned and organized structure in the layout of the settlement. Construction of residential buildings proceeded haphazardly, mainly in the coastal areas of the peninsula (Figs. 9–11). Even in the settlement's early phase of development, inland areas were probably given over to economic and household use. As a rule, dwellings were primitive dugout

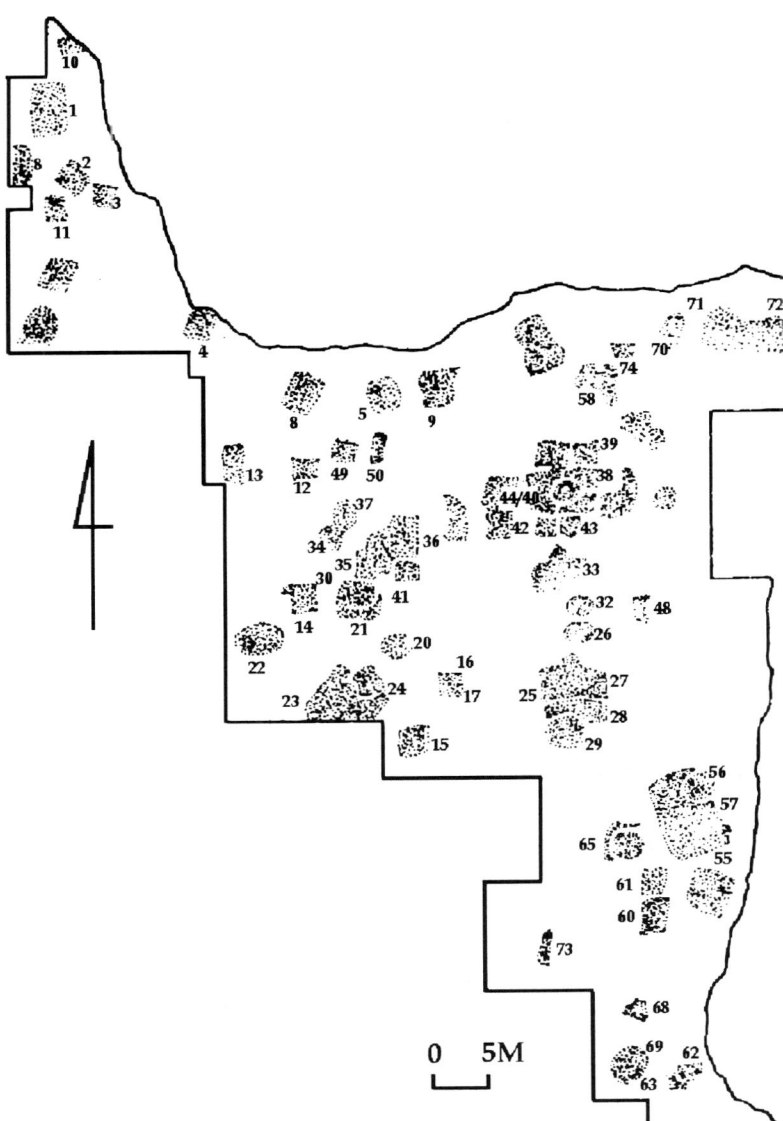

Fig. 9. Plan of Archaic dugout dwellings in the East Sector (after Mazarati and Otreshko 1987).

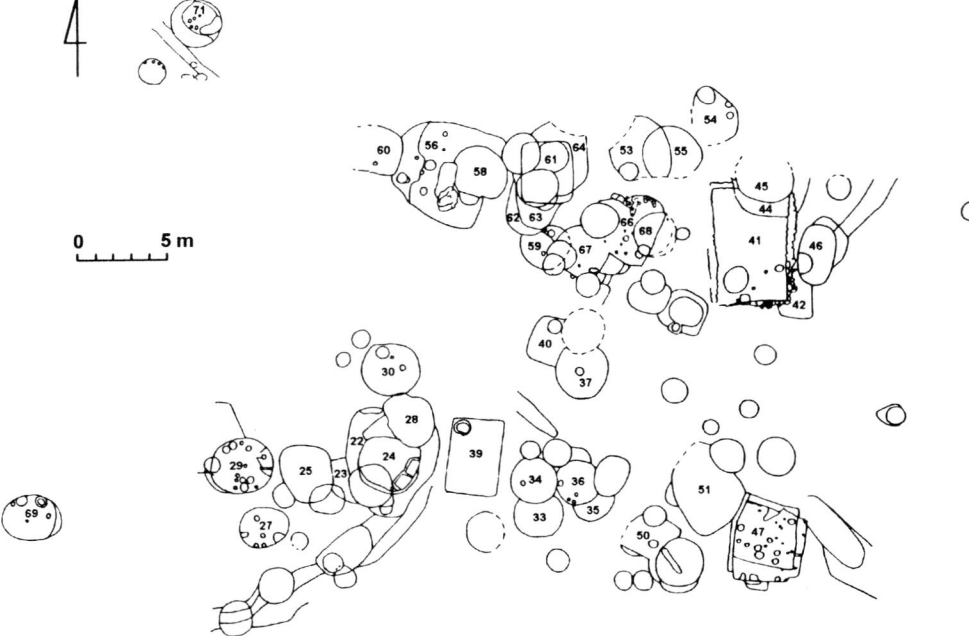

Fig. 10. Plan of Late Archaic dugout dwellings in the Northwest Sector.

Fig. 11. Late Archaic dugout dwellings in the Northwest Sector.

or semi-dugout buildings, of various forms; the space they occupied ranged from 3 to 14m² (Figs. 12–13). I would like to draw particular attention to the distinctive characteristics of these buildings, since to a significant extent they reflect the

Fig. 12. Late Archaic dugout dwelling 69 (Berezan, Northwest Sector).

Fig. 13. Late Archaic dugout dwelling 71 (Northwest Sector).

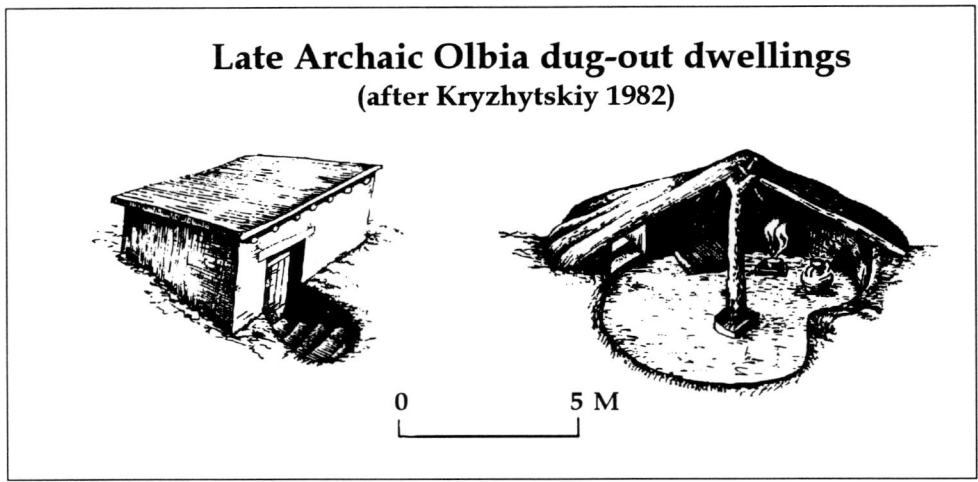

Fig. 14 . Late Archaic Olbia dugout dwellings (after Kryzhitskii 1982, Fig. 2).

characteristics of dwelling building not only in the Berezan settlement, but also in the Lower Bug region as a whole.[21]

More than 200 dugout structures have been excavated on Berezan up to the present time; of these buildings, about three-quarters have been more or less satisfactorily documented. However, certain vexing problems have arisen because, in their descriptions, scholars have tended to disregard certain details of construction. With the broad distribution of dugout buildings at sites across the Lower Bug region, questions regarding their construction have come up repeatedly (Lapin 1966, 153–9; 1978, 114–34; Kryzhitskii and Rusyaeva 1978; Kozub 1979; Rusyaeva 1979, 3–17; Kopeikina 1981a; Kryzhitskii 1982, 11–4; 1993, 40–2; Marchenko and Domanskii 1981; 1986; Mazarati and Otreshko 1987; Solovyov 1992). According to general opinion, a typology of this kind of construction may be generated by taking the following into account: dimension, layout, volume, and function.

Today there is little serious disagreement among academics regarding analyses of dugout structures according to the latter two factors. Depending on the depth of the foundation-trench, the structures can usually be subdivided into dugout and semi-dugout categories. In the former case, this means that the building is embedded in the ground to the full height of the walls; in the latter case, it is assumed that there were aboveground walls of stone, brick, or wood, and the depth of the foundation-trench is not less than 0.20–0.30m (Kryzhitskii and Rusyaeva 1978, 3). The construction of the roof of fully dugout buildings depended on the particular layout plan and the

---

[21] As I have already written in the Introduction to this volume, these buildings are believed to be the work exclusively of the Greek colonists, who built them as temporary dwellings on Berezan and on other ancient sites in the northern Black Sea region (see, for instance, in Olbia [Fig. 14]: Kryzhitskii 1982, 13 Fig. 2). Therefore, for the present study I have considered it essential to provide a more detailed description of the main features of this aspect of culture of ancient Berezan than is ordinarily found in this type of studies.

placement of pits in the floor for holding support posts. It is believed that dugouts of a circular form utilized a conical roof with a central support column, while those of a rectangular-trapezoid design used either a simple sloping or gabled roof; the unbraced type design was supported by aboveground brick walls, while the braced type relied on wooden support columns. Both types of roof can be seen among dugouts of oval design. The roofs themselves were made light, probably of thatch held together with clay. The inclination of the roofs could reach 40–50° (Kryzhitskii 1982, 13–4).

The placement of the entrance into most dugout dwellings is unknown because most frequently it was set inside the chamber. Only in very rare instances is there evidence of steps cut into the sides of the foundation-trench. One can only assume that the entrance may have been set either on the face or the side of the buildings. Considering that in an unusually large number of ancient Berezan dugouts particular interior elements were typically placed on the southern side of the building, it appears that construction had a northerly orientation.

It is also important to note that the abovementioned principle of subdividing these buildings into fully and partially dugout categories can only be applied in exceptionally rare cases and only when the construction complexes themselves are well-preserved. In reality there is a broad range of dugout depths seen among the structures, and as a rule the sites are poorly preserved. But if one takes the average human height (1.6–1.8m) as a norm, then half of that (or a figure close to it) can serve as a more acceptable and precise criterion for separating fully from partially dugout structures. Using this technique, all buildings deeper than 0.8–1.0m would be considered fully dugout (*zemlyanka*), while those of shallower depth would be considered partial dugouts (*poluzemlyanka*). Previous criteria should also be maintained, however, since they define the very concept of a "dugout dwelling".

Analyzing the Berezan dugouts using the proposed criteria, it appears that, with few exceptions, they fall into the category of semi-dugout. The depth of these buildings hovers around 0.3–1.0m. However, the remains of aboveground walls have not been found anywhere. Mounds of bricks traced inside separate dwellings may serve as indirect evidence of the existence of surface walls. Levels of stone were found in six partial dugouts; as a rule, these levels were arranged alongside one of the sides of the trench, evidently as reinforcement. Such rare use of stone walls and their obviously careful facing indicates that this kind of technology was used in dugout construction only in exceptional cases.

Fully dugout dwellings, for their part, showed a depth ranging from 1.1–1.95m. Despite the fact that for the most part these buildings functioned in the first half of the 6th century BC, against the backdrop of such a large number of semi-dugouts it seems difficult to support the widespread opinion that possibly there had been an evolutionary progression from full to partial dugout construction (Kryzhitskii and Rusyaeva 1978, 3). Finds suggest that at times both types of buildings had existed on the island. Furthermore, it is reasonable to propose that the optimal combination of dugout and aboveground parts of the buildings was achieved near a depth of 0.8–1.0m. Those buildings which were dug out to about half the height of a man made up about 45% of all semi-dugouts on Berezan.

As a rule, full and partial dugouts are also categorized according to their function, for living or production purposes. Working out objective criteria for this kind of division is made more complicated by the relatively low level of social and economic development of the Berezan inhabitants in the early years of the settlement, and by the absence of diagnostic materials (that is, finds *in situ*). As a result, dugout constructions can barely be differentiated by functional indicators, since various types of domestic and handicraft activity could have arisen spontaneously in any of the dwellings. However, jumping a little ahead, it is important to note that certain features of some buildings allow us to interpret them as workshops with ironworking functions.

The absence of heating equipment, any interior detailing or amenities, and an overall small size serve as indirect evidence of a non-residential, more domestic-economic and production-oriented function of some dugouts. Altogether only 12 building complexes display these characteristics to some extent. This group consists of both full and partial dugouts of various forms, with an area ranging from 2 to 10m², and a depth from 0.3 to 1.5m. The number of these buildings is so small that it is hardly necessary to describe them in detail. Greater interest has rather been aroused by those building complexes which appear to have been utilized for production. Judging from the levels of iron rust and remains of metallic slag found in them, these seem to have been connected in some way with ironworking and production.

Four such complexes have been discovered in the eastern part of the settlement, and were described by V.V. Lapin (1961, 47; 1978, 223). Three of them had the shape of rounded basins, with a diameter of 3.5–4.0m and a depth of 1.1–1.3m; the fourth possessed a rectangular plan 3.2 × 3.8m in size and with a depth of 1.2m (Mazarati and Otreshko 1987, 118). Three additional buildings which appear to have had a similar purpose, but which differ in form from those previously described, were discovered in the northwest part of the settlement. Of these, only one (unearthed in 1983: Domanskii 1985, 272; Domanskii *et al.* 1989) requires a detailed description. This building is oval with dimensions of 6.4 × 4.8m and a depth of 0.75m. Given the presence of cuts in the side of the trench, the entrance to this construction appears to have been located in its northern side. An open hearth constructed of a clay-and-straw (pisé) material was placed by the southern wall. The central part of the building (with a diameter of 2.8m) was dug out to a depth of 0.20m relative to the rest of the interior space, and was filled with rust and pieces of iron slag. Pits used to hold support columns for the roof were discovered in the floor, in the centre and along the edges of the depression. A small fire-pit, which possibly used to forge iron, was also found here. These complexes may also have served as workshops for the initial processing, purifying, and enrichment of iron ore (Lapin 1961, 47).

For determining residential buildings, without a doubt the most significant factors are elements of interior amenities for living. In these types of full and partial dugouts as a rule one finds a clay coating on the floor and, occasionally, on the walls. In order to heat the building, and also for preparing food, open hearths were usual, seen more rarely were portable braziers (Fig. 15) and (only very rarely) fixed and permanent ovens (Fig. 16). As a rule, such ovens were constructed of clay-and-straw pisé, and had a round shape and footings of stone or pottery fragments set into a level of sea-sand or shells. The interior of this type of dwelling is distinguished by its simplicity. Depressions in the floor were used to hold cooking vessels or amphorae; sometimes

Fig. 15. Late Archaic brazier in dugout (B.87.290).

Fig. 16. Late Archaic oven in dugout.

in the same place small pits were dug and used for storing foodstuffs. Occasionally a few recesses were set into the sides of the foundation-trench, possibly for storing kitchenware. In all likelihood the so-called "apse ledges" – a particular type of large recess found in two dugouts in the eastern part of the settlement – served the same kind of household purpose. Found in three dwellings were so-called stove-benches, which were placed alongside the walls in the form of a kind of earthen shelf with a width of 1.0m and a height of 0.20–0.30m.

One interesting detail of the interior of dugout residential buildings was the "tables" seen at many sites in the Lower Bug region (Kryzhitskii and Rusyaeva 1978, 8 Fig. 8; Kozub 1979, 15–6 Fig. 12; Marchenko and Domanskii 1981, 64). On Berezan, these "tables" (found in more than 20 semi-dugouts), showed the following construction: the "table" was usually a pisé platform 0.7–1.0m in length, 0.5–0.9m in width and 0.2–0.5m in height, frequently faced with smooth stones. The edges of the platform were slightly raised, with a width and height of about 0.1 m. On rare occasions the surface seems to have been scorched and covered with a level of coals and cinders. As a rule, these "tables" were situated on the southern side of the dwelling alongside the trench; next to them one or two pits for holding large vessels similar to amphorae or hand-made clay pots have often been found.

Scholars' opinions about the purpose of the "tables" vary widely. Some propose seeing them as cult related constructions (Kozub 1979, 16); others view them as having an ordinary household use (Kryzhitskii and Rusyaeva 1978, 9), for instance as a place to set up portable braziers (Lapin 1972, 158). In my opinion, in the absence of other diagnostic materials it makes more sense to assign the "tables" to a category of multifunctional structures. It is also evident that as an element of interior design in this type of dwelling, these "tables" have turned out to be characteristic of dugout buildings across the Lower Bug region, and are unknown in other areas of the northern Black Sea. Material from the Berezan settlement have shown that this type of interior detail first appeared not earlier than the middle of the 6th century BC, and its use became more widespread by the second half of that century. The most recent structures of this type have been found in dugouts dating from the first half of the 4th century BC, both on Berezan (Solovyov 1995a) and in Olbia (Kozub 1979, 15). In dugouts on Berezan, brick enclosures built alongside the walls have also been found; these enclosures are similar in size, and possibly in purpose, to the "tables" described above. Examples of enclosures of this type are well-known as well at other sites in the Lower Bug region (Marchenko and Domanskii 1981, 65 Fig. 5, 7).

To complete a description of the interior of dugout dwellings on Berezan, it is also important to point out the gradually increasing complexity of the interior design of these buildings; this stands as an important feature of dugout development. Simplicity may indeed have been the key characteristic of the interior arrangement of both full and partial dugouts in the first half of the 6th century BC, but by the third quarter of the same century their interior space was distinguished by significantly greater variety. In virtually every second building of that time one or several of the enumerated amenities was found: a "table" or a brick enclosure, pits for holding vessels or household niches, storage pits, or "benches".

One of the key characteristics of dugout construction, which on Berezan is represented by buildings of various forms, is the layout and design of the structures themselves. As opposed to other typological indicators, the question of layout and design has not been clearly resolved. Analyzing this aspect of dugouts on Berezan, Lapin in his time discerned two groups of dugout buildings: an oval, nearly circular, type; and rectangular (Lapin 1978, 114). In his opinion, dugouts of curvilinear form predominated in early times on Berezan. From this, Lapin developed the idea of an evolution in the design of the dwellings toward a rectangular form (Lapin 1978, 118, 123). These ideas were criticized convincingly by S.D. Kryzhitskii and A.S. Rusyaeva (1978), who relied mainly on the results of research on ancient Olbia. It was they who determined that dugouts of all forms existed simultaneously; this was later corroborated by other research from sites in the Lower Bug region dating from the second half of the 6th century BC.

Although he rejected the idea of evolutionary development, in other respects Kryzhitskii accepted and further refined the typology created by Lapin. According to Kryzhitskii (1982, 12), the fundamental layout types were rectangular and circular. Among the former there were two subtypes: dwellings with clearly cut corners, and those with more rounded corners. The latter group also possessed two subtypes, dwellings in the form a true circle, and those of more oval shape. In my opinion, this is an incorrect and very misleading division, entirely too dependent on the state of preservation of the actual building, on the length of time which passed from the time the building ceased functioning as a dwelling to the time it was finally filled in with soil or household rubbish, and on how accurately the structure was laid out in place by ancient builders.

A different typology of dugout structures was proposed by Rusyaeva (1979), who discerned three layout types: rectangular (with variants having either rounded corners or the so-called "apse ledges"; circular; and oval. If (for the reasons given above) the variability of rectangular dwellings is excluded, then in my opinion Rusyaeva's classification appears more precise, since it corresponds to current data on ancient Berezan.

Figuring out the layout of both full and partial dugouts is directly related to the number of rooms found in a single dwelling. Special study has shown that single-chambered dugouts were widely distributed in the Lower Bug region of the Late Archaic period (Kryzhitskii 1982, 20). However, in Lapin's opinion (1972, 158; 1978, 134), the Berezan settlement was an exception: he presumed that many-chambered building complexes had existed there. In Lapin's view, these complexes served as an important link in the evolution from single-chambered dugouts to aboveground houses. This thesis, however, was not subjected to sufficiently well-grounded criticism, even though it was not documented convincingly enough to demonstrate the objects in question. Therefore, today it makes more sense to propose simply that a single-chambered design scheme generally dominated dugout construction.

Relying on archaeological data from ancient Berezan, I attempted to portray through drawings the dynamics of change in dugout construction on the island, taking into account different dugout forms and their temporary characteristics (Fig. 17). These latter, despite a certain vagueness, were by and large deduced empirically on the basis of stratigraphic observations and further critical sources. For example, in the course of excavation in the northwestern part of the settlement in 1984, four semi-dugouts were discovered; these dwellings seemed to have succeeded each other consecutively during the third quarter of the 6th century BC. Therefore, the length of time any one of them functioned averaged about 5 to 7 years. Located to the west of these buildings was one more concentration of buildings, five of them built during

S. L. Solovyov

General

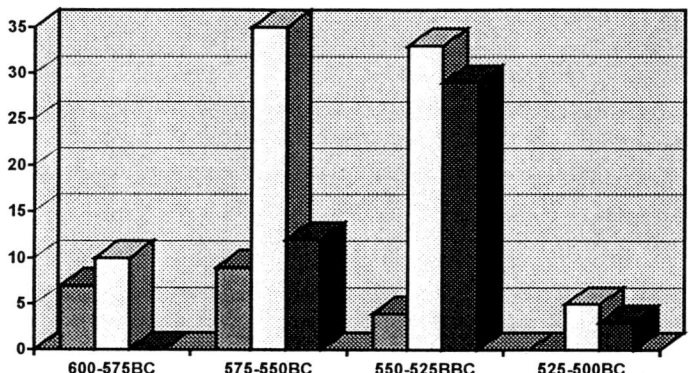

East Sector

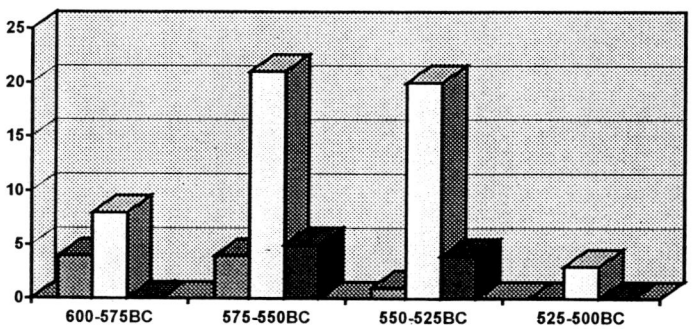

North-West Sector

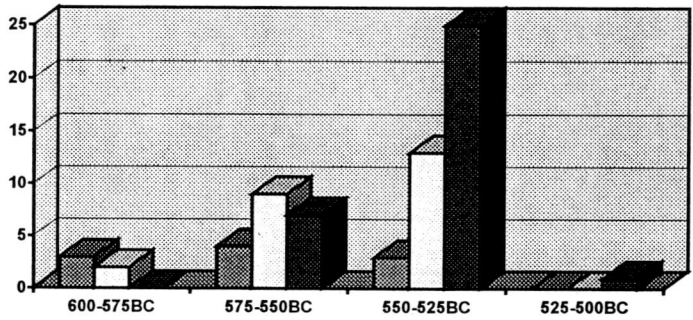

Fig. 17. Dynamics of dugout home-buildings.

the second and third quarters of the same century. It follows that in this case each complex functioned for a comparatively longer time – 10 to 12 years.[22]

That may be, but the period I have proposed describing the development of dugout construction on Berezan (which lasted for approximately 25 years) should be considered reliable also because it closely corresponds to the duration current theories have established for the functioning of dugout dwellings. It is thought that these dwellings could not have functioned for longer than a single generation (Vinogradov I. *et al.* 1990).

As the diagrams in Figure 17 show, many years of excavation on Berezan have revealed not more than two dozen building complexes which can be dated reliably to the first stage of the period in question; even taking into account the fine preservation and relative ease of conducting study at the site, the small numbers of buildings attest that there had been an extremely small number of inhabitants. Dugout dwellings of a circular plan appeared at the beginning of the second phase (that is, in the second half of the 6th century BC). It is important to add that after that time the concentration of dugout constructions began to increase, especially in a northerly direction. This occurred mainly as a consequence of an increasing number of building complexes of both circular and rectangular form. As material from the eastern and northwestern areas of the settlement indicate, in the second phase the number of dugout structures doubled every 25 years; by the end of the third quarter of 6th century BC the number had reached somewhere between 70 and 80. It is reasonable to assume that a similar pace of construction prevailed in other areas of the settlement – except in the central region, which at the time was not included in the household zone.[23]

Despite the fact that dugout dwellings of all three design types – circular, oval, and rectangular – were utilized throughout the Berezan settlement, the particular frequency of dugouts of one kind or another varied by area, and so ultimately it is possible to discern the characteristics of the buildings. For example, in the southern part of the northwestern area in the third quarter of the 6th century BC the dispersed character of the buildings corresponded to a polymorphous structure seen in both full and partial dugouts. A different picture is observed only 80m to the north of this site, where semi-dugouts of a circular plan predominated. The particular placing of these buildings in this part of the settlement was probably planned to some extent, since they apparently formed a separate and distinct concentration; perhaps distinguished by a specific kind of domestic activity including at least a quarter-century of replacing and rebuilding one or two dugout dwellings.

It is not yet clear whether there was any kind of conscious regulation in the residential zone, or if that regulation was more spontaneous. The area of the settlement was certainly insufficient for comprehensive metrological observations. Today it is

---

[22] The continuing existence of dugout dwellings in less densely-built areas of the settlement evidently reflected that which has been discerned in areas of more intensive construction. In addition, the reasons for the peculiarities of the settlement's spatial organization will be found in one particular aspect of the traditional culture of ancient Berezan – its ethnic heterogeneity (Solovyov 1992).

[23] This interpretation is corroborated by the results of von Stern's investigation at "Excavation A". At that site, over the course of many years, von Stern (1912, 87) found several dozens of household pits (which preceded aboveground building), and in all only two building complexes of the dugout type. In my opinion, the material from von Stern's excavation in this case deserve full confidence. Certain doubts which have been raised (Lapin 1978, 65*ff*) seem to me completely groundless.

only possible to affirm that the distance between the centres of economic activity ranged from 15–25m. Furthermore, even a simple comparison of this phase of dugout construction with the previous phase indicates that the boundaries of separate and distinct domestic activities probably began to take shape in the second quarter of the 6th century BC.

Dug-out dwellings of the second phase did not differ very much in external appearance from earlier buildings. As before, the materials used in the construction process consisted mainly of brick and wood; stone was still used very rarely. Moreover, during the second and third quarters of the 6th century BC the number of earthen buildings with stoves and hearths increased noticeably. In addition, nearer the end of the period in question new, previously unknown interior features began to appear, including the "tables" already mentioned.

Following this analysis of home-building on Berezan during the first three quarters of the 6th century BC, it seems to me entirely clear that the sources must lie in local traditions of dugout construction (Solovyov 1989, 12ff; 1992, 47–51). It is not only particular morphological features which indicate local sources; it is also the spatial structure of the settlement itself. The latest was set up haphazardly and without any regulation on construction: most likely the building was subject to only the most elementary rules of communal living and to the requirements of domestic-economic activity. This lack of regulation (along with a whole set of other factors) resulted in the technological backwardness of dugout construction, narrow building techniques, conservatism and other issues. The true urbanization of Berezan simply could not have been carried out in this stage of its development (cf.: Kryzhitskii and Otreshko 1986, 10–11; Vinogradov Y. G. 1989, 66–8). In all of these ways Berezan resembled other population centers which arose in the Lower Bug region around the middle of the 6th century BC, especially Olbia.[24] The attempt recently made to contrast Berezan and Olbia as two fundamentally different types of settlement (Kryzhitskii et al. 1989, 40–1) does not seem convincing in the light of the factors discussed above.

Unlike the majority of scholars (who explain the specific features of dugout buildings using only a variety of purely technical methods), I have proposed differentiating dwellings based on layout design as a manifestation of various architectural and construction traditions brought to Berezan by indigenous peoples as part of a complex of other cultural elements (Solovyov 1989, 15; 1992). I do not intend to repeat here the development of this argument, but to limit myself to a short exposition of its basic points.

Thus, it has been established that certain particular features of the construction of dugouts on Berezan, which at first glance appear accidental (specifically, the three volumetrically-planned types of buildings, changes in the frequency of their occurrence

---

[24] Despite (in comparison with Berezan) scholars having devoted more attention to Olbia, many aspects of its early history still remain unclear, beginning with the date of its founding and ending with its particular characteristics at that time. The most detailed examination of these issues can be found in: Kryzhitskii 1982, 14ff; 1985, 57ff; Vinogradov Y. G. 1989, 42ff and Vinogradov I. et al. 1990, 83ff. However, their judgments about the sequence of events in the early history of the Olbia city-state do not fully accord, and are at times even diametrically opposed. A desire to eliminate these contradictions can probably explain the recent publication of the joint study of both authors on the history of the Olbian state (Vinogradov J. G. and KryzictskiJ 1995).

Fig. 18. Late Archaic hand-made pottery from dugouts (B.85.149, B.89.160, B.82.214).

in separate areas of the settlement, and the apparent absence of construction regulations in general), in fact directly reflected the diversity of the local culture. The fact of this heterogeneity became clear primarily as a result of the observed combination of specific characteristics of Berezan dugout construction with other features of daily life for the inhabitants. Most important in this regard was the combination of dugout features with the types of hand-made pottery widely used in everyday life and discovered in fill inside both full and partial dugouts (Fig. 18). From statistical analysis of the ceramic assemblage from Berezan dwellings of that time, the proportion of hand-made pottery ranged from 10–36%, sometimes more. The remainder consisted of imported Greek vessels. Analysis of the composition of the latter revealed amphorae almost exclusively, which cannot be seen as a distinct functional category of the social culture of Berezan.[25]

It has also been noted (Fig. 19) that in places where circular dugouts were concentrated, pottery related to that of eastern Podolia and the central Dniester region (areas very much under a tangible Thracian cultural influence) tended to predominate (Fig. 20). In areas of Berezan occupied by rectangular (and to some extent oval) structures, a different type of hand-made pottery predominated (Figs. 21–22), one which can be linked only to the pottery of the central Dnieper and Vorskla regions, which was brought at that time into the areas resettled by forest-steppe Scythian tribes.

---

[25] In other words, unlike other types of pottery, the wine-jugs of the Greeks did not have a functional analogy in the ceramic complex of the local population, and so in view of their broad distribution in the economic and household activities of both peoples wine-jugs apparently cannot be ethnically differentiated in the way that, for instance, Scythian weaponry can. One additional matter involves the particular use of this category, which in certain circumstances tends to take on an ethnic colouration.

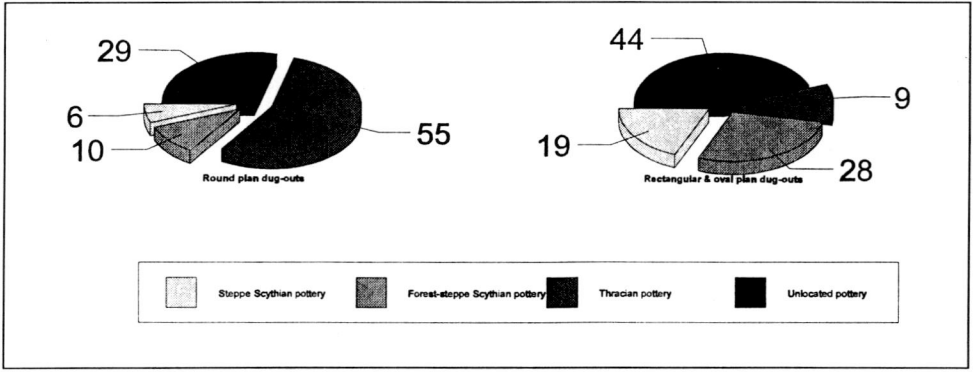

Fig. 19. Correlation between dugout plan and hand-made pottery (according to Northwest Sector finds).

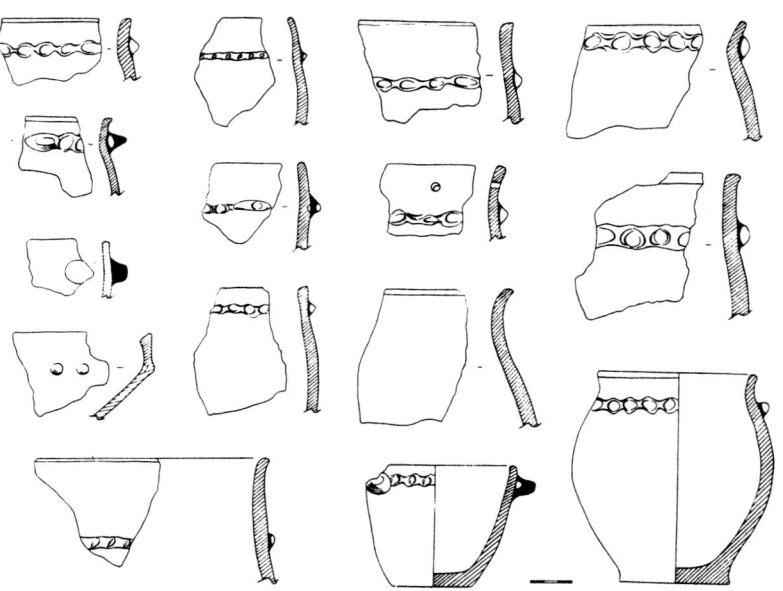

Fig. 20. Late Archaic hand-made pottery from round plan dugouts.

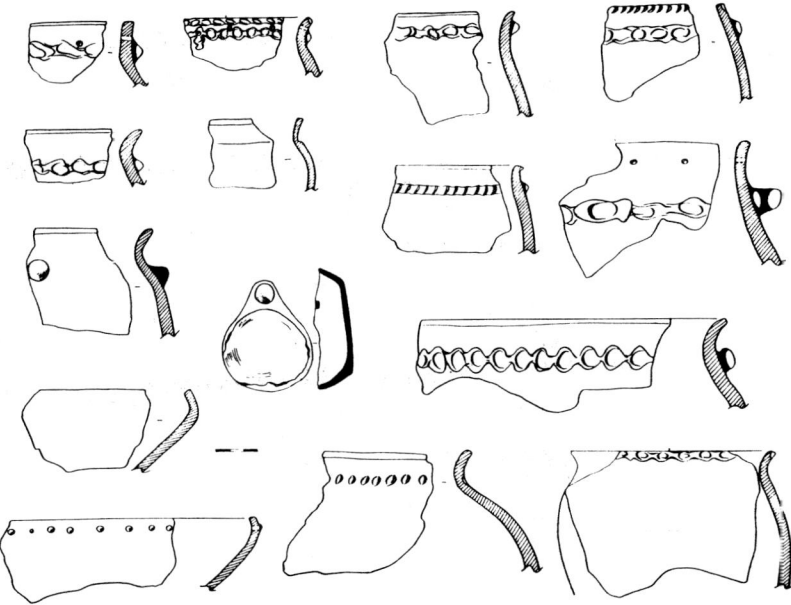

Fig. 21. Late Archaic hand-made pottery from rectangular plan dugouts.

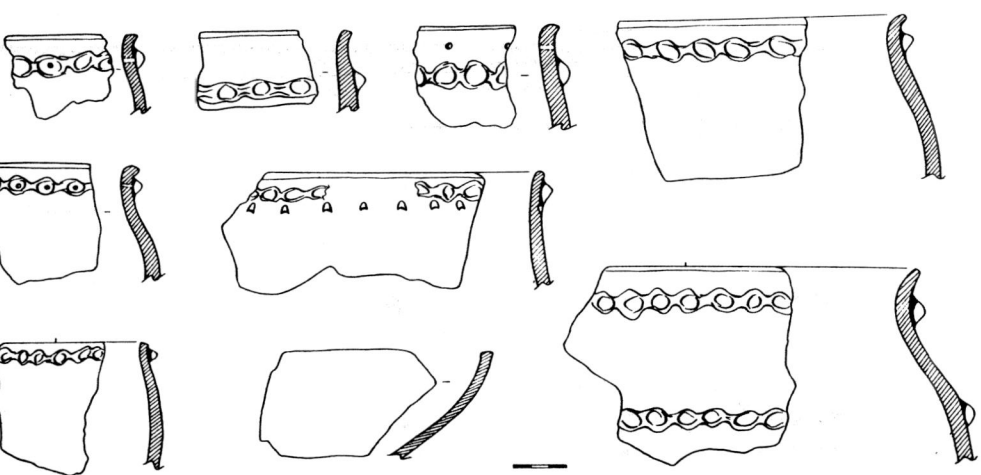

Fig. 22. Late Archaic hand-made pottery from oval plan dugouts.

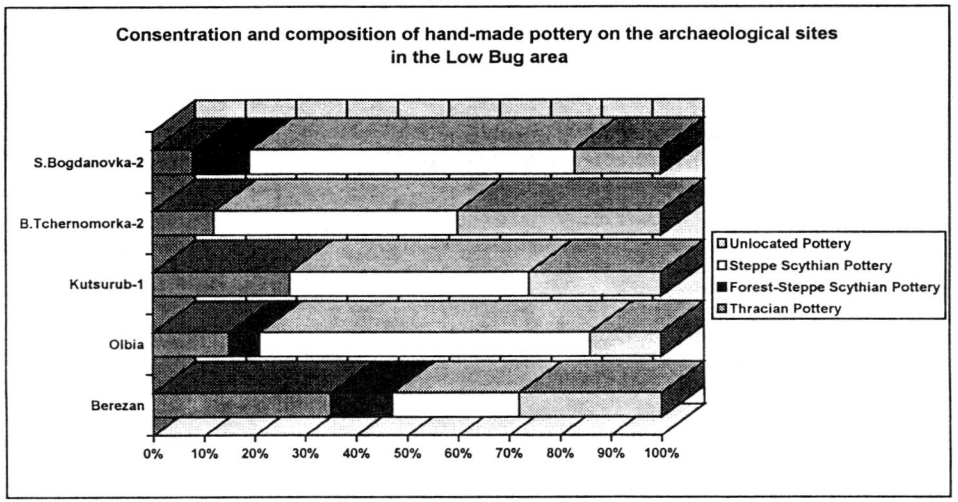

Fig. 23. Concentration of hand-made pottery on the archaeological sites in the Lower Bug area.

Statistical analysis of this type of material from Berezan (Fig. 23), supplemented by analogous data from a series of other sites in the Lower Bug region (albeit, of a somewhat later time period), demonstrates the significance of the correlation discussed above (Solovyov 1992, 50; 1994, 87–90). Up to the present, however, there has been an absence in the literature of judgments and opinions which convincingly clarify the facts just noted, which compels me to repeat conclusions already given. According to the data we have today, in the course of Greek colonization in the northern Black Sea, the active and successful economic activities of emigrants from Miletus and other eastern Greek *poleis* drew also some very significant groups from forest-steppe Scythia into the process of occupying the Lower Bug region. Owing to certain particularities of their culture (particularly in the areas of building and in the technologies of making and decorating hand-made pottery), the forest-steppe Scythian groups were drawn mainly to two areas of the Lower Bug zone: specifically, the middle Dniester and Dnieper regions. The culture of the nomadic Scythian population, which is also reflected in archaeological materials at the site, probably comprised a third component of indigenous cultural influence on ancient Berezan.[26]

---

[26] Owing to specific characteristics of its nomadic way of life, steppe-Scythian culture was very heterogeneous and included components of those cultures with which the nomads in one way or another came into contact. Thus, the derivation of one of the groups of hand-made pottery used in the nomads' everyday lives (and found almost exclusively on Berezan: Fig. 24) can be linked confidently to regions settled by tribes of the Kyzyl-Koba (or earlier Taurian) culture of the Crimean peninsula (Solovyov 1995). This fact provides evidence that the inhabitants of the Berezan settlement were familiar with these areas at a very early time. It is possible that this knowledge promoted the trading expansion of the Ionians in the northwestern Crimea, persuasive evidence for which is provided by clear traces of their presence in the area of modern Evpatoria (Kutaisov 1990, 35–9) and on the Heraklean peninsula (Zolotarev 1986; Vinogradov I. and Zolotarev 1990) in the second half of the 6th century BC (not to mention the Greek colonies in the European part of the Bosporus: Smidt 1953; Sidorova 1962; 1992).

Fig. 24. Late Archaic Kyzyl-Koba (Taurian) hand-made pottery.

Cultural differences between the groups of local inhabitants who (willingly or unwillingly) ended up residing in the Lower Bug region can be seen not only in the type of building or in pottery complexes, but also in other details of everyday life on Berezan. Particularly important in this regard are types of work-tools, weapons, and adornments, all of which have been found in great quantities on Berezan and the great majority of which are linked to local cultures (Olgovskii 1980). To mention just a few of these: bronze nail-shaped pins (Fig. 25) and mushroom-shaped pendants (Fig. 26), glazed paste

Fig. 25. Late Archaic bronze pins
(B.86.303,305; B.90.290).

Fig. 26. Late Archaic bronze pendant
(B.86.307).

Fig. 27. Late Archaic stone dish (B.89.374).

*Fig. 28. East Greek oinochoe of the early 6th
century BC (B.83.19).*

*Fig. 29.1. East Greek dinos of the early 6th century BC
(B.82.8).*

*Fig. 29.2. East Greek dinos of the early 6th cent:
(B.91.233).*

beads, bone tools for working hides, arrowheads, stone dishes (Fig. 27) and many other objects. Of course, all of these require further study in terms of their relationship to indigenous cultures.

Therefore, there is no doubt that many of the more visible features of ancient Berezan culture were rooted in the local cultures of the northern Black Sea. However, it is also clear that part of it must have belonged to the Greek colonists.

The large number of imported ceramics which appeared here at the end of the 7th and first quarter of the 6th

Fig. 30. East Greek chalice of the early 6th century BC (B.82.40)

centuries BC (primarily from Ionia and Corinth) serve as evidence of the physical presence of Greek colonists on Berezan (Kopeikina 1986, 32, 42). Judging from the small number of finds on Berezan, Corinthian ceramics must have ended up in the Lower Bug region thanks to Ionian merchant-middlemen, who consisted mainly of emigrants from Miletus, Samos, Chios, and northern Ionian cities. The overall production of Ionian ceramics, which dominate the general mass of pottery found on Berezan, is typologically varied (Figs. 28–35). It is worth noting, however, that (with only rare exceptions) this pottery did not show great artistic merit and can

Fig. 31. East Greek plate of the first half of 6th century BC (B.89.37).

Fig. 32. East Greek pottery of the first half of 6th century BC (B.88.2,8,9,14,20).

*Fig. 33.1. Chiot chalice of the early
6th century BC (B.85.42).*

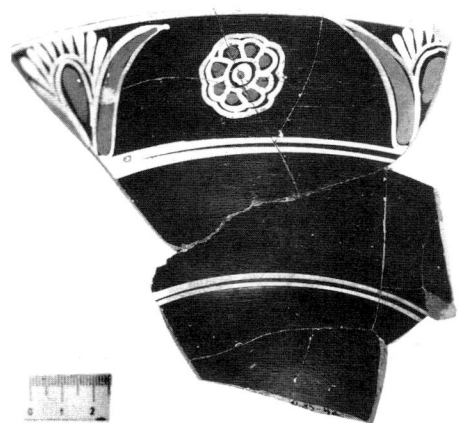

*Fig. 33.2 . Chiot chalice of the early
6th century BC (B.85.42).*

Fig. 34.1. Chiot lekane lid of the first half of 6th century BC (B.90.25).

Fig. 34.2. Chiot bowl of the first half of 6th century BC (B.90.25).

Fig. 35. Ionian dinos of the first half of 6th century BC (B.83.72).

justifiably be assigned to the category of goods produced to meet mass demand, which distinguishes this material substantively from the imported pottery of the previous period *i.e.*, of the second half of the 7th century BC).

The nearly complete absence of imported ceramic kitchenware on Berezan suggests that locally produced pottery fully satisfied the inhabitants' cooking and food-preparation needs, regardless of their ethnic roots. In the first quarter of the 6th century BC and after, this local ware consisted mainly of functionally specialized vessels (Marchenko 1988, 107–9 Fig. 36).[27]

Today it is rather difficult to make judgments regarding other categories of ancient imports which ended up in the northwestern Black Sea in the first quarter of the 6th century BC. It is only possible to suppose that there was a gradual increase in the importation of wine and other such goods. Judging from the numerous fragments of amphorae on Berezan, the main import suppliers at that time were the Greek islands of Chios, Samos, and Lesbos. In comparison with these places, other cities, particularly Miletus and Clazomenae, at the time had a much more modest share in the wine trade. Other types of products – works of metal, bone and glass, for instance – were also imported to the Lower Bug region, but these were significantly fewer in number. The reasons for relatively smaller trade in these types of items probably hinge on

---

[27] Bearing in mind that in ancient societies the making of vessels for household needs was primarily a woman's task, then the hand-made pottery found in the dwellings of Greek colonists in the Lower Bug region may indicate that local women also resided there. It is important, however, not to interpret this circumstance too broadly and absolutely, as some scholars insist (who are trying to explain the presence of hand-made pottery at ancient sites exclusively in terms of the presence of women: Kryzhitskii *et al.* 1989, 91*ff*). This kind of explanation is unjustified, since it disregards other non-Greek elements of the culture present at the sites, not to mention the well-known heterogeneity of the hand-made pottery complex itself.

specific characteristics, and a certain conservatism, of tastes and customs among the indigenous population (Vinogradov Y. G. 1989, 54), as well as on the rapid development of local handicraft industries (Ostroverkhov 1979, 115*ff*). Local production met not only the everyday needs of Berezan inhabitants for to work tools, weapons and ornaments, but also made it possible as well to export certain goods. This conclusion is supported by frequent finds on the site of iron, bronze, and bone work tools, weapons, simple decorations and ornaments and other personal items (Son 1987, 118–25; Otreshko 1987, 125–7). The majority of these reflected local cultural traditions, and should be seen as the result of the development of local industry on Berezan (Olgovskii 1992).

Furthermore, in my view, the initial processing of ferrous metals had by this time already taken on a market-oriented character. This supposition is supported by the discovery on Berezan of the four semi-dugouts mentioned earlier, which were evidently used precisely for the initial processing and dressing of raw materials. According to one opinion (Ostroverkhov 1979, 118–20), local haematite-rich sand and haematite-magnetite ore from the Krivorozhskii basin and northern Taurica (Crimea) could have served as raw material for ironworking production on Berezan. Still, the main center of ferrous and non-ferrous metalworking in the Dnieper-Bug region at such an early time was the Hylaea region. Hylaea's primary natural resource was forestland (Hdt. 4. 18–19), which was needed in large quantity for charcoal and without which local industry would have been simply impossible. According to material from the so-called Yagorlitskii industrial region (which was closely linked to Berezan economically and politically), bronze-smelting and iron- and glassworking were concentrated in the Hylaea region (Ostroverkhov 1978, 41–9; 1978a, 26–36; 1979, 120*ff*). It is thought that these industries functioned seasonally (Marchenko 1980, 135; Olgovskii 1987, 52), mainly in the spring and summer when navigation was easier. However, this interpretation overlooks the fact that these industries seemed to have been oriented not only towards internal market demand for everyday objects, but also towards the needs of the Greek homeland, which was experiencing shortages of raw material for industry.

Among the important occupations of Berezan inhabitants was raising cattle; but judging from the small quantity of bone remains from that time found on the island, it is entirely possible that livestock production was organized principally for trade. According to study on the osteological materials of the Berezan settlement (Zhuravlyov *et al.* 1990),[28] during the entire Archaic period herds on Berezan were composed mainly of small cattle, sheep and goats, numbers of which were sufficient to provide fully for the dietary needs of the local population. Evidence for this is provided by the large quantity of bones of (mostly) young domesticated animals (sheep and goats) found on the island (Zhuravlyov 1990, 98, 100, 110).[29]

---

[28] I would like to express enormous gratitude to Dr O.P. Zhuravlyov of the Institute of Archaeology of the Ukrainian Academy of Sciences, Kiev. During the Hermitage expedition's many years of research on the island, Dr. Zhuravlyov wholeheartedly and selflessly performed osteological analyses of Berezan materials with great thoroughness and a high degree of professionalism.

[29] It is also important to note the observed numerical similarities in herd composition between the Berezan settlement and sites in forest-steppe Scythia (Tsalkin 1966; Zhuravlyov 1983a, 81). These similarities provide evidence of the preservation of livestock-raising traditions in areas inhabited by Scythian population. In the given case, of course, the different species of domestic animals are very significant;

Aside from this, the main export from the Lower Bug region was probably grain. In all likelihood the grain was received here from forest-steppe Scythia, which comprised the principal agricultural region of the time. Here it is worthwhile to mention the message of Herodotus about the Scythian ploughmen who sow wheat for sale (Hdt. 4.17). There is little serious dissension among scholars on the fact that the Scythian ploughmen were located on the lands lying between the Dnieper and Dniester rivers (Dovatur *et al.* 1982, 288–90), that is, in exactly the place which had been drawn earlier and more actively than other regions into cultural and economic exchange with Greeks. Judging from the economic and demographic conditions and potential of the Berezan settlement in the first quarter of the 6th century BC, there can be little doubt that its grain trade did not have a sufficient basis for development by itself.[30]

In my opinion, it was the shared economic interests of the Greeks and the indigenous population (especially the tribal aristocracy) in the further expansion of trade that became the primary, if not exclusive, reason for the spread of the contact zone between the groups and for their increasing interaction in the second and, especially, third quarters of the 6th century BC (*i.e.*, the next stage of the second historical period of ancient Berezan). An analysis of Greek pottery brought to Berezan at the time reveals the following specific, trade-related features.

The Greek islands of Chios, Samos and Lesbos remained the principal suppliers of wine-related products. There was also an increase in the volume of imports from Clazomenae, and a to smaller extent from Miletus. Finally, wine and possibly olive oil from the cities of mainland Greece also appeared, sporadically. Exports of decorated table-pottery from these cities, especially from the Athens (Fig. 36), gradually increased in volume; by the end of the third quarter of the 6th century BC the Berezan marketplace was full of these kinds of products from East Greek workshops (Fig. 37) (Kopeikina 1986, 42–3).

It is also evident that in terms of quantity imported tableware of all kinds took second place only to amphorae. As I have noted, the proportion of amphorae in the composition of the Berezan ceramic complex ranges from 70–90%. From this observation two conclusions naturally follow: during its entire early period, the Berezan settlement was above all a major transshipment point for the wine trade on the northern coast of the Black Sea; the primary, if not exclusive, activity of the Greek residents

---

there are some very diverse (at times completely contradictory) opinions, depending on the theoretical outlook of a scholar. Thus, the well-known fact that polled (hornless) cattle were widely distributed in the Lower Bug region is sometimes explained (most often by advocates of an agrarian conception of Greek colonization: Zhuravlyov 1987, 35–7; Kryzhitskii *et al.* 1989, 74*ff*) as a consequence of the Greeks acquiring this type of cattle from the Scythians. These authors also allude to the difficulties of transporting large domestic animals across the sea. For its part, the fact that in the Lower Bug region the sheep raised were of a larger size than those in forest-steppe Scythia is usually interpreted by these same scholars as evidence that the animals were brought in from the Greek homeland.

[30] Recently, the possibility that grain was exported from forest-steppe Scythia has been placed in question (Shcheglov 1990; *cf.*: Pashkevich 1990; Vinogradov Y. G. 1989, 50 *ff*). This doubt is based on the absence of reliable archaeological data on the cultivation of the determined sort of wheat (*golozernaya*), which was the primary grain of Greek agriculture. In addition, it is important to note that up to the present time little is known about the structure of agriculture in ancient Berezan itself, just as little is known of agricultural activities at other Greek colonies on the northern coast of the Pontus. Therefore, a sufficiently accurate comparison of the particular features of agriculture in the two regions is practically impossible.

Fig. 36. Attic black-figure krater of the third quarter of 6th century BC (B.85.89).

Fig. 37. Ionian lekythos of the third quarter of the 6th century BC (B.87.31).

of Berezan may have been trading as middlemen. The widespread use of imported pottery in the daily lives of the local population is evidence of the settlement's successful development; however, the locals did not entirely give up using vessels made without a potter's wheel. Unlike the latter, the composition of imported Greek pottery found on Berezan indicates little about the ethnocultural identity of its owners and instead reflects the state of affairs of trade and politics at one or another moment in the Black Sea and Aegean.

Returning to the issue of the composition and proportion of the complex of Hellenic cultural materials at Borysthenes in the first three quarters of the 6th century BC, it is also important to point out that the components of the complex (with the exception of wheel-made-pottery) are rather weakly represented in material found at the site. For instance, there is the already-mentioned scarcity of imported handicrafts of metal, glass and bone. It is also worth noting that, for the time in question, terracotta finds and other traces of the Greeks' religious activities on Berezan and in surrounding areas are very rare; the same cannot be said about these sites in later times (Figs. 38–41). Moreover, up to the present day no remains of early cult-related buildings have been found at the settlement.[31]

Material from the necropolis could be a great help in determining the ethnic origins of the first inhabitants of Berezan. Despite their large number, the earliest burials found on the island remain poorly studied and published.[32] It is not yet quite clear what changes were taking place as to the boundary between the settlement and the necropolis. Scholars are in general agreement that the earliest part of the necropolis has been lost as a result of coastal abrasion. More attention should be paid to Lapin's view (1966, 120–1) of the character of the territorial development of the necropolis. As he believed, a significant part of the cremations of the 7th-first half of the 6th century BC opened by Skadovskii were, in fact, storage pits of the earliest part of the settlement in an area subsequently (from the second half of the 6th century BC) covered by the necropolis.

The material known from the Berezan necropolis does not contradict this conclusion. Of the numerous and diverse Archaic burials only a few can, with complete relaince, be ascribed to the first half of the 6th century BC (Fabritsius 1951, 59; Kaposhina 1956, 225; Vinogradov I. *et al.* 1990, 127; Vinogradov J. and Domanskii 1996, 294–5). A large proportion were cremations and child burials in vases, on the

Fig. 38. Late Archaic terracottas (B.89.239, B.85.241, B.85.238, B.83.266).

---

[31] All this, of course, does not contradict the fact that there were temples and shrines in the Lower Bug region dedicated to various Greek deities, mainly Apollo the Healer and Achilles. Natural forms, such as a small grove, a spring, or something similar may have been objects of native devotion.

[32] During excavation by G.L. Skadovskii between 500 and 800 burials were opened (Fig. 60) (Kaposhina 1956, 217, note 1; Lapin 1966, 120). The excavations of E.R. von Stern discovered how wide was the chronological spread of burials on Berezan. Sixteen burials were discovered in 1967–68 (Gorbunova 1969, 20–5). A further 213 graves were studied in 1976–90 (Vinogradov J. and Domanskij 1996, 294).

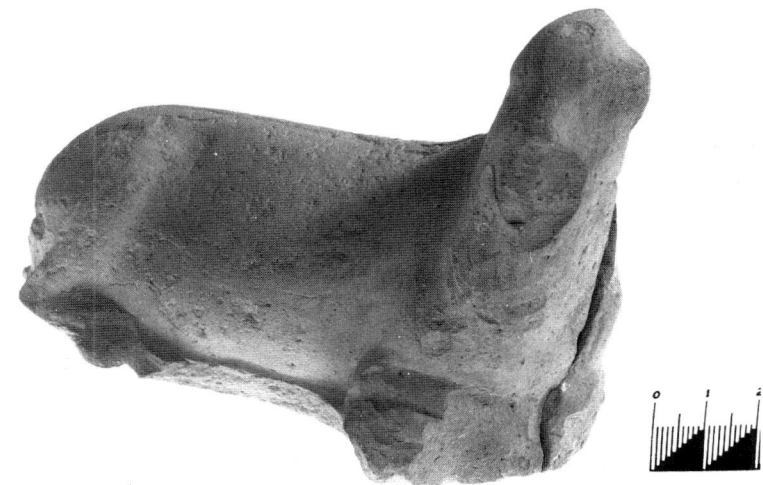

Fig. 39. Late Archaic terracotta of a bull (B.90.205).

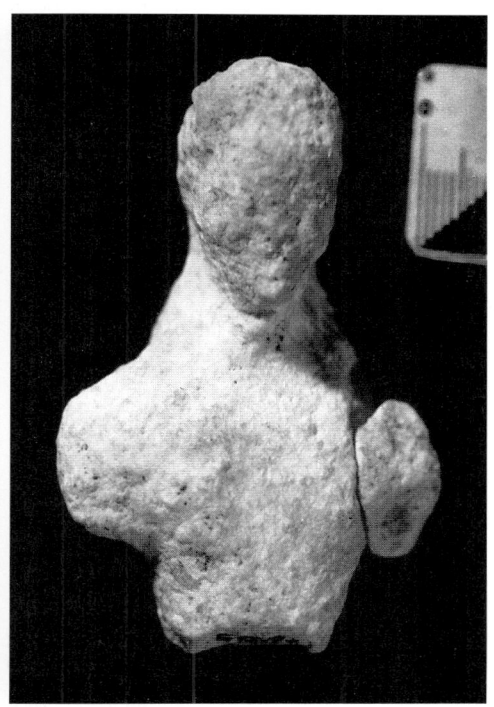

Fig. 40. Stone kouros (B.86.222).   *Fig. 41. Late Archaic paste pendant of*
                                             Horus (B.87.313).

periphery of the earliest part of the necropolis. The lack of any large number of early Greek graves is an indication of the small proportion of Greeks amongst the first inhabitants of Berezan. Material from the necropolis testifies to the sharp growth in the number of Greek colonists in the second half of the 6th century BC.[33] It is possible that the location of the cemetery of the indigenous population is unknown as yet.

The small amount of evidence relating to non-material Hellenic culture of the first three quarters of the 6th century BC which has been found in ancient settlements of the Lower Bug region consists exclusively of inscriptions mainly scratched onto vessels or fragments (Vinogradov Y. G. 1979; 1994a, 63–6; Yailenko 1980, 89*ff*; 1980a; 1982, 258*ff*; Rusyaeva 1987, 146*ff*). Most of these consist of separate letters and compositions of letters, the meaning of which is frequently unclear. To be sure, among these epigraphic finds are distinct inscriptions of sacred, political, and even economic meaning; still, in my opinion, they are not indisputable indicators of the existence of Borysthenes or Olbia *polis* at the time, but of some kind of Greek settlements.

The information contained in these inscriptions indicates more reliably that, in the Lower Bug region, emigrants from various Greek cities were engaged primarily in trade and were well-informed about the areas in which they were living. However, some of the Greek immigrants were also involved in importing religious cults and in serving sanctuaries consecrated to such Greek gods as Apollo (in his many forms: the Healer, Delphinius), Achilles, etc. These sanctuaries were traditionally linked to the area and were its patrons. That the colonists worshipped other deities as well – Herakles, Cabiri and others is observed in their striving to secure the support of these gods in their lives and in their daily activities (Rusyaeva 1992, 219*ff*).

During the first three quarters of the 6th century BC, the Greek settlers who arrived at different times in the Lower Bug area were probably incorporated into the structure of the larger local settlements,[34] one of which was located on Berezan and the other a little upstream on right bank of the Hypanis, in the area of the future Olbia.[35] According to current opinion, some of the dugouts at these sites must have belonged to Greek colonists (Domanskii and Marchenko 1975; Kopeikina 1981a, 202). Their use of dwellings of the local type was dictated not so much by specific climatic factors in the northwest Black Sea region or by the absence of a construction industry, as some scholars believe (Kryzhitskii 1982, 28*ff*, 45*ff*; Kryzhitskii *et al.* 1989, 41*ff*), but, in my opinion, was determined more by particular characteristics of the way of life and psychology of traders, which is what the first Greek settlers were. Without a doubt, the success of the traders' activities depended mainly on how much drive and

---

[33] More than half the burials excavated in 1982–90 were dated to the second half of the 6th century BC (Vinogradov J. and Domanskij 1996, 294–5). The ration was similar for Archaic graves found on Berezan in other years (Lapin 1966, 111).

[34] Apart from Berezan, at the present time only three settlements established in the first half of the 6th century BC are known in the Lower Bug region. These are Malaya Chernomorka-2 (Beikush), Shirokaya Balka-1, and Olbia (see: Kryzhitskii *et al.* 1990, 10*ff*, map). The first two are designated by Nos. 17 and 40.

[35] Unlike sholars who place the founding of the Olbia at the end of the 7th or beginning of the 6th centuries BC (Vinogradov Y. A. *et al.* 1989, 83–4), I hold a different opinion regarding the date of this event. I believe that it makes more sense to place the date in the second half of the 6th century BC; S.D. Kryzhitskii and V.M. Otreshko (Kryzhitskii 1985, 57–68; Kryzhitskii and Otreshko 1986, 5–8) have brought out some very convincing arguments in favour of this view.

Fig. 42. Late Archaic dugout 47.

ambition they had, on their abilities to communicate and to adapt to different and frequently changing living conditions, and last but not least on the burdens of domestic goods. Unlike other people of the Greek *polis*, especially the farmers and artisans, the traders, as a result of the particularities of their profession, were a more adaptable social group in terms of cultural interaction with other ethnic groups.

In this connection it is worthwhile mentioning four building complexes of the first half of the 6th century BC which can be distinguished from other full and partial Berezan dugouts by their relatively large dimensions, by the detailed, painstaking finish of the bottom and sides of the trench, and by the presence of stoves and hearths (which made use of the upper parts of amphorae, inverted and coated with clay). As I have mentioned, hearths of this type were not ordinarily found in typical dugouts on Berezan. Only in the second half of the 6th century BC did they become more widely used in the interior of the stone aboveground houses of Borysthenes. Furthermore, in one of these buildings it was observed that one of the walls was built of a layered system of mud-bricks similar in size to those used later in aboveground building (Fig. 42).

Owing to its clearly unusual qualities, one of these building complexes deserves closer attention. A rectangular construction, about 38m^2, cut 1m into the ground (Figs. 43–44), this building appears to have been functioning in the second quarter of the 6th century BC (Fig. 45) (Domanskii *et al.* 1989, 36; Solovyov 1994, 90). One of the most notable features is the placing of stone plinth walls, 0.5m wide, around the perimeter of the trench and to the full height of its sides. The aboveground portions of these walls were constructed of mud-bricks. The lower row of the plinth consisted of large polygonal slabs to a height of 0.55m. The slabs were set on their sides and

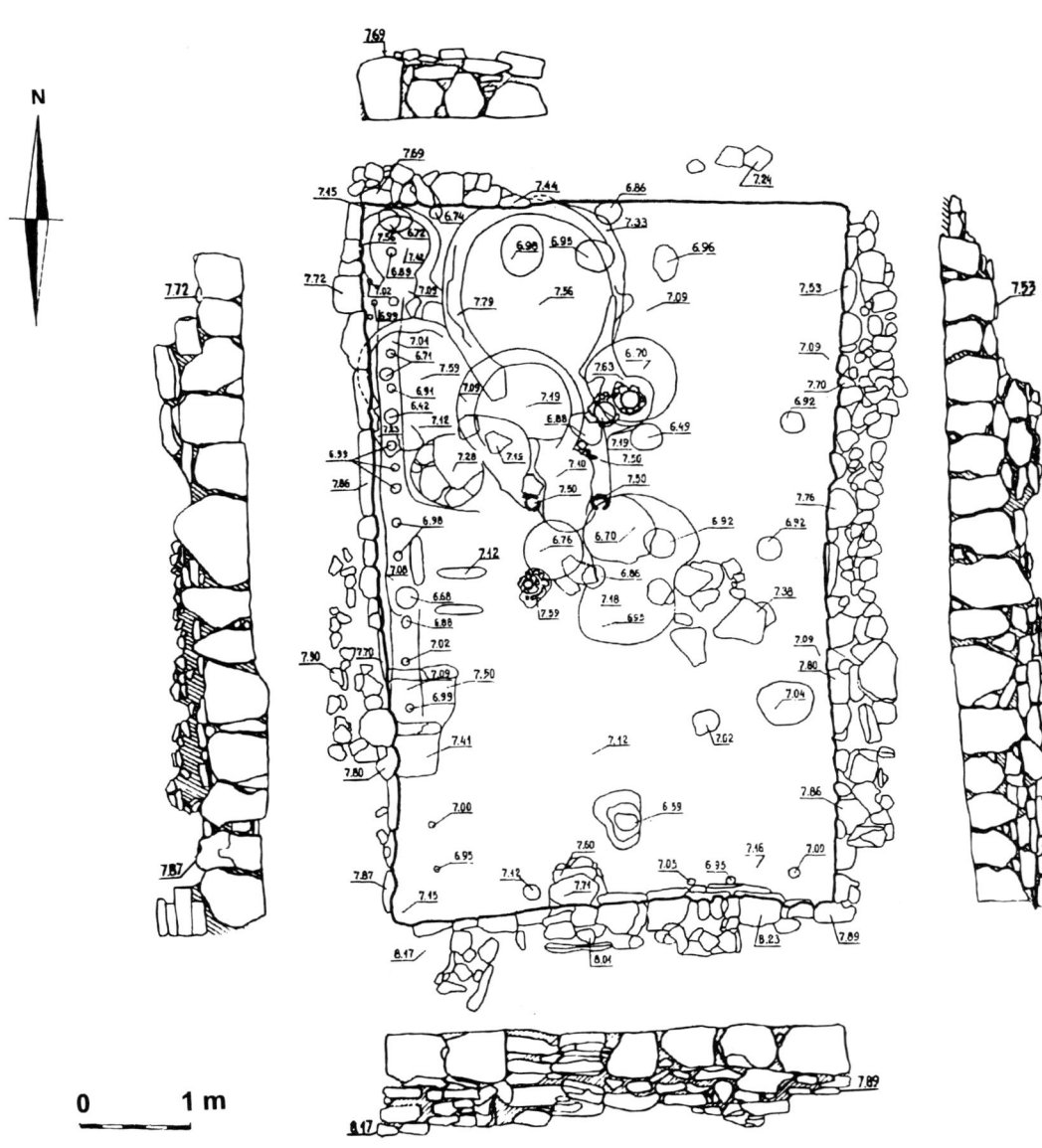

Fig. 43. Plan of the Late Archaic dugout 41.

Fig. 44. Late Archaic dugout 41.

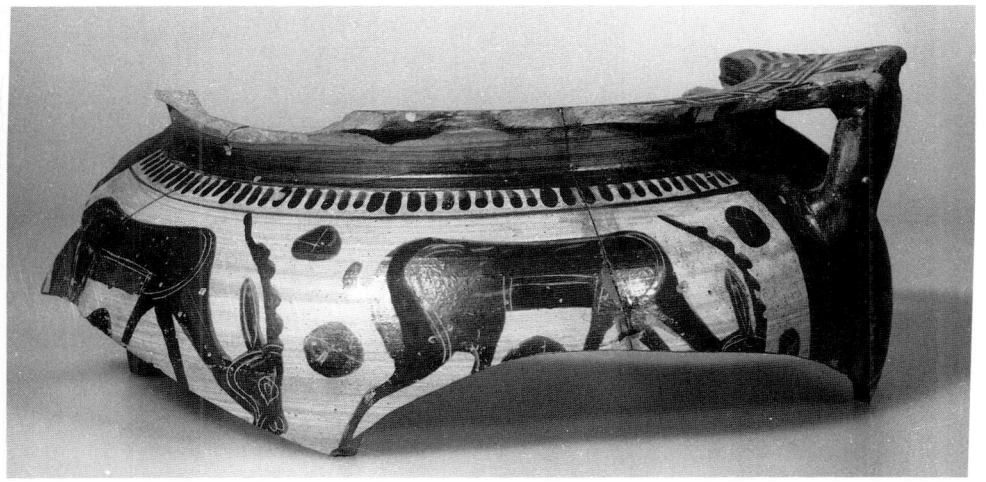

Fig. 45. East Greek krater of the second quarter of 6th century BC (B.85.1).

above them four rows of smooth stones were leveled. The entrance to this building
was set into the southern wall, and a four-step stairway constructed of stone slabs led
into the dwelling from the entry. The building consisted of a single chamber; however,
the inhabitants probably divided its interior space (with an area of about 28m²) into
two functionally distinct halves – for living space and for cooking. Kitchen space
occupied mainly the northwestern part of the dwelling, where the stoves and hearths
described above were also located. Portable braziers were also used. Alongside all of
these heating and cooking systems, pits were dug into the floor for holding vessels.
As stoves and hearths wore out, new ones were built, and the level of the floor rose
correspondingly due to alternating levels of clay coating. It is thought that a minimum
of four decades could have continued in this way.

Some of the depressions found in the floor of the building were associated with
constructing its roof; this allows a volumetric reconstruction of the building itself
(Fig. 46). To judge from the placement of pits (for supporting a gable) which were
dug in along the longitudinal axis of the dwelling, it appears that the building used
an unbraced type of gable (two-sloped) roof, which was supported by the purlins and
by the walls. Additional supports were apparently dug in along the walls on the sides
of the building. One side wall – on the western side (and possibly the southern one
as well) – was reinforced with wattle fencing, traces of which remain in the floor of
the dwelling. Taking into account the depth of the trench (1.0m), the height of the
doorway (not less than 1.7m), the pitch of the two sides of the roof (at least 180–200),
it is reasonable to propose that the maximum height of the building from the level

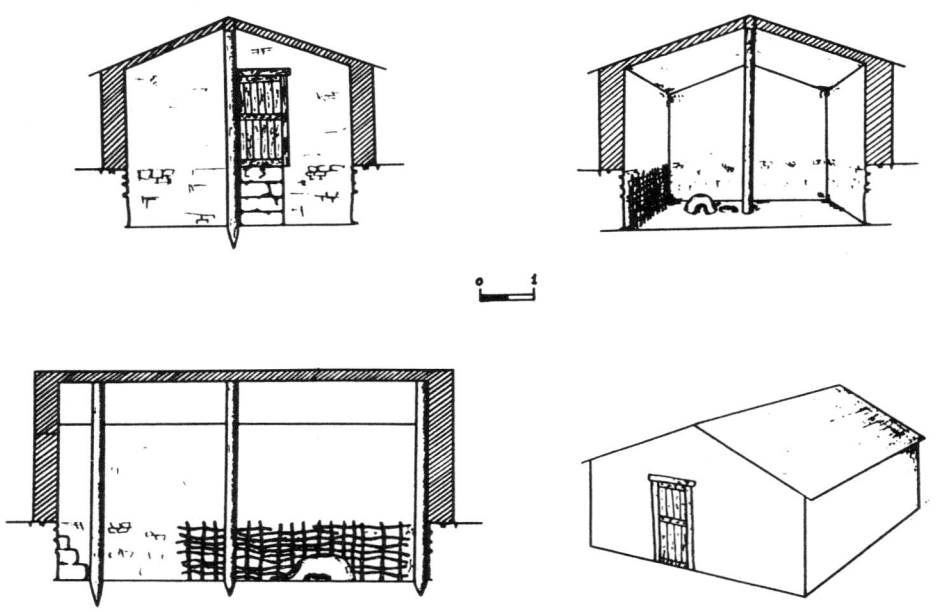

Fig. 46. Graphic reconstruction of the Late Archaic dugout 41.

of the floor was 3.8m and, correspondingly, its height above the ground level of the time reached 2.7m.

Up to the present day, buildings which appear much like those on Berezan, and which date from the same period of time, have been found at only one site in the Lower Bug region – Shirokaya Balka (Rabichkin 1951, 114*ff*),[36] which is located not far from where the Greek city of Olbia was situated in the second half of the 6th century BC. In my opinion, there is good reason to consider the dugout buildings of the first three quarters of the 6th century BC as dwellings used by early Greek colonists. These and certain other similarities between the Berezan and Shirokaya Balka sites also suggest the presence of Greek trading stations in the two areas.

The mutual interest of both the Greeks and local inhabitants in increasing the volume of trade probably stimulated the appearance of new population centres in the Lower Bug region whose number began to increase sharply in the second half of the 6th century BC (Kryzhitskii *et al.* 1980, 4–7). Today, hundreds of settlement sites dating from the Late Archaic period can be counted in the Lower Bug region (Kryzhitskii *et al.* 1990, 11 Fig. 4). From the construction of primitive dugout buildings similar in some ways to those on Berezan, and showing an analogous composition of hand-made pottery, it seems that most of the inhabitants of these buildings were indigenous people. Greek immigrants evidently comprised a numerically smaller number of inhabitants. The impression given by this data is that economic and (possibly) cultural integration between these two ethnocultural groups was not only an indispensable condition for, but also a consequence of peaceful, long-term, large-scale and mainly successful contacts between the Ionians and Scythians in the Lower Bug region and in the northwestern Black Sea in general.

This process did not take long to yield; by the second half of the 6th century BC such positive change was manifested in the large-scale settlement of the Dnieper-Bug region. It is also evident that interaction between the Greeks and indigenous peoples prepared the way for the establishment here of Greek colonies of the classical type, *i.e.*, which already possessed political organization and a diversified economy. My view is that this colonization process took place quickly at the end of the third quarter of the 6th century BC, first on Berezan, and then at Olbia.[37] From that time on, the cultural and historical development of the Berezan settlement took a course fundamentally different from that which had taken place before.

---

[36] It is interesting to note that another site has recently become known in the northern Black Sea, a place where similar buildings were erected: Myrmekion in the European Bosporus (Kerch Peninsula). Around the middle of the 6th century BC, dugout dwellings were constructed here (Vinogradov Y. A. 1991, 73; 1991a; 1994). Many of the features of these buildings, above all the layering methods of the stone walls, look much like those which have been described above.

[37] The establishment of Olbia as a major economic and political centre in the region, much like Berezan, can be dated to the second half (more exactly, to the last quarter) of the 6th century BC. Until that time, Olbia was probably politically dependent on Berezan or, at most, occupied an equivalent position (Kryzhitskii and Otreshko 1986, 12; Solovyov 1993, 41*ff*, *cf*.: Vinogradov Y. G. 1989, 43*ff*).

B. The urban culture of Borysthenes

The majority of scholars agree that substantial changes in the cultural development of the Berezan settlement occurred in the third quarter of the 6th century BC. Based on the results of recent archaeological investigation, some academics place the time of this historical event more precisely at the end of that 25–year period (Domanskii *et al.* 1989, 36*ff*, Solovyov 1994, 90) rather than at its beginning, as L.V. Kopeikina (1981a, 197*ff*) did in her time.

The most noticeable of these changes were in the construction techniques employed by the inhabitants of the settlement, which shifted toward building aboveground with undressed stone (Kopeikina 1975, 189*ff*, 1981a, 198*ff*. *Cf.*: Lapin 1966, 94–7; Kryzhitskii 1982, 30). According to the archaeological data, the turn toward this type of construction took place on most of the territory which had formerly been occupied by dugout buildings. However, it was primarily the north and northeast areas which were initially taken up by aboveground building. Over a very short period of time additional construction projects were carried out in this area, in the course of which the trenches of dugout buildings were filled in with earth and covered with a level of clay, and the ground was leveled and smoothed over. Meanwhile, outlying areas of the settlement (especially the eastern region), were built up as before with full and partial dugouts right up to the very beginning of the 5th century BC, when they too were finally replaced by aboveground buildings (Lapin 1966, 100; 1968, 152).

From the archaeological material available today, it is believed that aboveground (surface) construction on Berezan in the late Archaic period was mainly private. Furthermore, attempts have been made in the literature to interpret particular buildings as having either a public or religious purpose (Kopeikina 1975, 190*ff*, 1981, 197*ff*). In my opinion, it is impossible to agree with these interpretations owing to the lack of well-grounded arguments concerning similar propositions. It is known that in terms of size and layout these buildings differed little from other well-studied dwellings on Berezan. It is also likely that unusual material finds in these cases (Kopeikina 1977, 92–104) may attest, at the very least, to the functions of one or another area inside a typical dwelling.

One exception to this may be a surface building of the first half of the 5th century BC discovered by V.V. Lapin (1966, 118–21; 1967; 1972) on the eastern coast of the island in 1963–64. Although it would certainly be more appropriate to talk about this construction in the section devoted to Berezan in the Classical period, considering its uniqueness it is still relevant to discuss the building now. Oriented along a north-south longitudinal axis, the building had a rectangular form measuring 21.0×5.4m, and was finished on the north side with apse with a radius of 2.7m. The interior was partitioned into three spaces of almost equal dimensions. The territory on which the building was located was enclosed by a fence, the stone plinth from two sides of which have been preserved. In Lapin's opinion, such a building could have been only a temple (Lapin 1978, 194–201; Kryzhitskii 1993, 66*ff* Fig. 37, 2).

It must be noted that despite the undisputed value of Lapin's proposed reconstruction of the layout of the building in question, it is difficult to accept his interpretation of the site as an exclusively religious complex, above all because of an absence of contemporaneous material of a religious or cult character. Meanwhile, it is also clear that the construction could not have been a residential building. As is known, in the second half of the 6th–5th centuries BC such a highly archaic type of construction was occasionally used in Greek architecture for religious and cult purposes (the temple of Apollo on the Athenian Agora: Thompson and Wycherly 1972, 137 Pl. 4) and for public buildings (part of the bouleuterion at Olympia: Parnicki-Pudelko 1985, 174 Fig. 242). However, at the present time it is impossible to present a more detailed analysis of this particularly unique and important site in the northern Black Sea, owing to an absence of detailed publications.

The remaining newly-erected buildings possessed an area of 100–260m² (possibly even a little more than that), and were comprised of several living and household areas grouped in various ways around an inner courtyard (Figs. 47–48). Depending on their intended purpose, the rooms housed stoves, hearths, portable braziers, fireplace-type heating systems, paving-stones and drains. In the courtyards, which were partially paved with ceramic sherds and small stones, there were wells (Fig. 49), pits used as cellars, altars, and drains (Solovyov 1993; 1994).

The buildings were most likely single-floor, although it is impossible to exclude the possibility that a second level may have been set up in some places. This is not contradicted by the well-known characteristics of wall construction in Berezan buildings: the thickness of the stone plinth walls ranged from 0.4 to 0.6m. and they were arranged using systems of both irregular and regular leveling (Fig. 50). The latter usually consisted of 2 to 3 embedded levels, or were more rarely orthostatic. The leveling was done primarily in single rows. Around the middle of the first stage,

Fig. 47. Late Archaic block of houses (Northwest Sector).

[38] During excavation of this block, this house was designated No. 2.

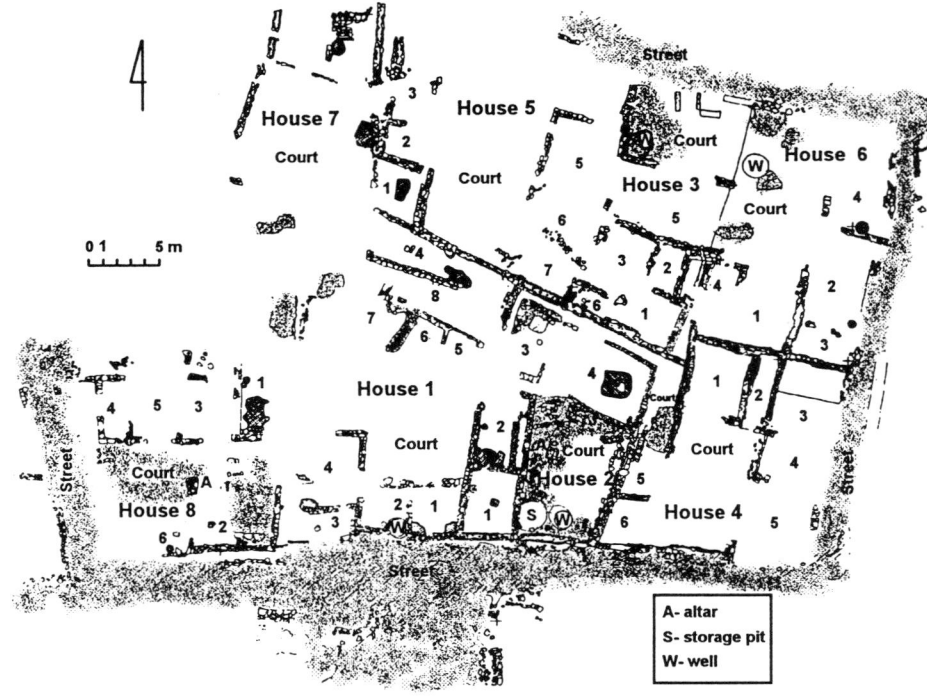

Fig. 48. Plan of the Late Archaic block of houses (Northwest Sector).

Fig. 49. Well in the court of House 3.

Fig. 50. House 5 remains of the last quarter of 6th century BC.

the builders began to apply a separate row at the base. The quality of construction work varied, and apparently depended on the economic well-being of the owner. Overall, there was a rather high level of technology applied in construction.

Two houses stand as examples of typical dwellings on Berezan at the this time (Fig. 51); they were part of a recently discovered residential block in the northwest part of the settlement (Domanskii *et al.* 1989, 36–8; Solovyov 1994, 90–1 Fig. 4). One of these houses[38] was built in the final years of the third quarter of the 6th century BC and by the end of the same century had already undergone reconstruction. This building stopped functioning completely some time during the first third of the 5th century BC. Stone plinths from the mud-brick walls of this complex have partially survived; their thickness measured 0.45–0.60m, with a height of 0.20–0.60m, and the partitions between interior spaces were 0.10–0.15m narrower than the exterior walls. As a rule, the walls were built of local limestone in a one- or two-layer single-row embedded arrangement (with some irregularities); boulders brought in from elsewhere were also added. The faces of some of the stones were poorly cut. In some circumstances a three-layer, single-row embedded layering system, in which the middle layer was filled in with small stones and clay, was utilized. The mud-brick parts of the walls were probably built using a single-layer embedded system.

In its first period, the building occupied an area of 123m²; it was composed of two interior spaces and an adjoining courtyard to the east (Fig. 52). Approximately 46% of the total area of the building was taken up by the courtyard. The entry to the building, with a width of 1–1.2m, was built into the blank southern wall of the courtyard. In this area, the ceramic paving of the street was reinforced with stone slabs leading up to the threshold of the entrance; the threshold itself was constructed a single row of flat stones.

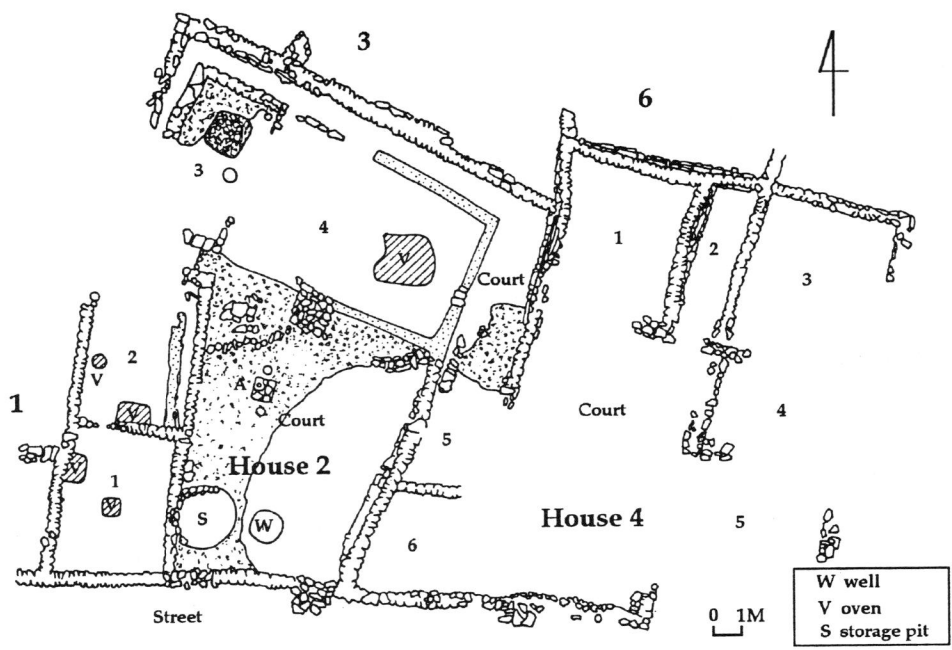

Fig. 51. Plan of Late Archaic Houses 2 and 4.

In the courtyard, to the left of the entrance, was a well 1m in diameter, the mouth of which was once reinforced with stones. To the west of the well was a meticulously constructed bell-shaped cellar-pit, the opening to which had a diameter of 0.90m. The western half of this cellar (which filled in earlier earthen constructions), was reinforced with stone layering connected to the plinth of the courtyard's western wall.

In the central part of the courtyard, near the residential complex, there was a rectangular altar measuring 0.85 × 0.90m, with a height of 0.20m. The altar was constructed of separate stones held together with a clay mixture. A small cup-shaped depression, 0.25m. in diameter, was located in the altar's northwest corner. There were small raised sides along the edge of the altar, with a width and height of 0.1m; these raised edges were built of small stones cemented together with clay. Two small pits were located to the north and south of the altar. The first of these was filled in with 114 pottery sherds; the remains of 38 first phalanxes of small hoofed mammals were found in the second pit.

As I have already indicated, the western part of the building comprised two unlike spaces. The southern room had an area of 18m², and its clay-and-straw (pisé) floor lay 0.65m lower than the level of the courtyard. Near the center of the space, a small area of the floor was scorched, apparently as a result of a portable brazier being placed there. The location of the entry to this space is unknown. Two large flat stones found lying on the courtyard side of the space, by its eastern wall, may be the remains of a threshold.

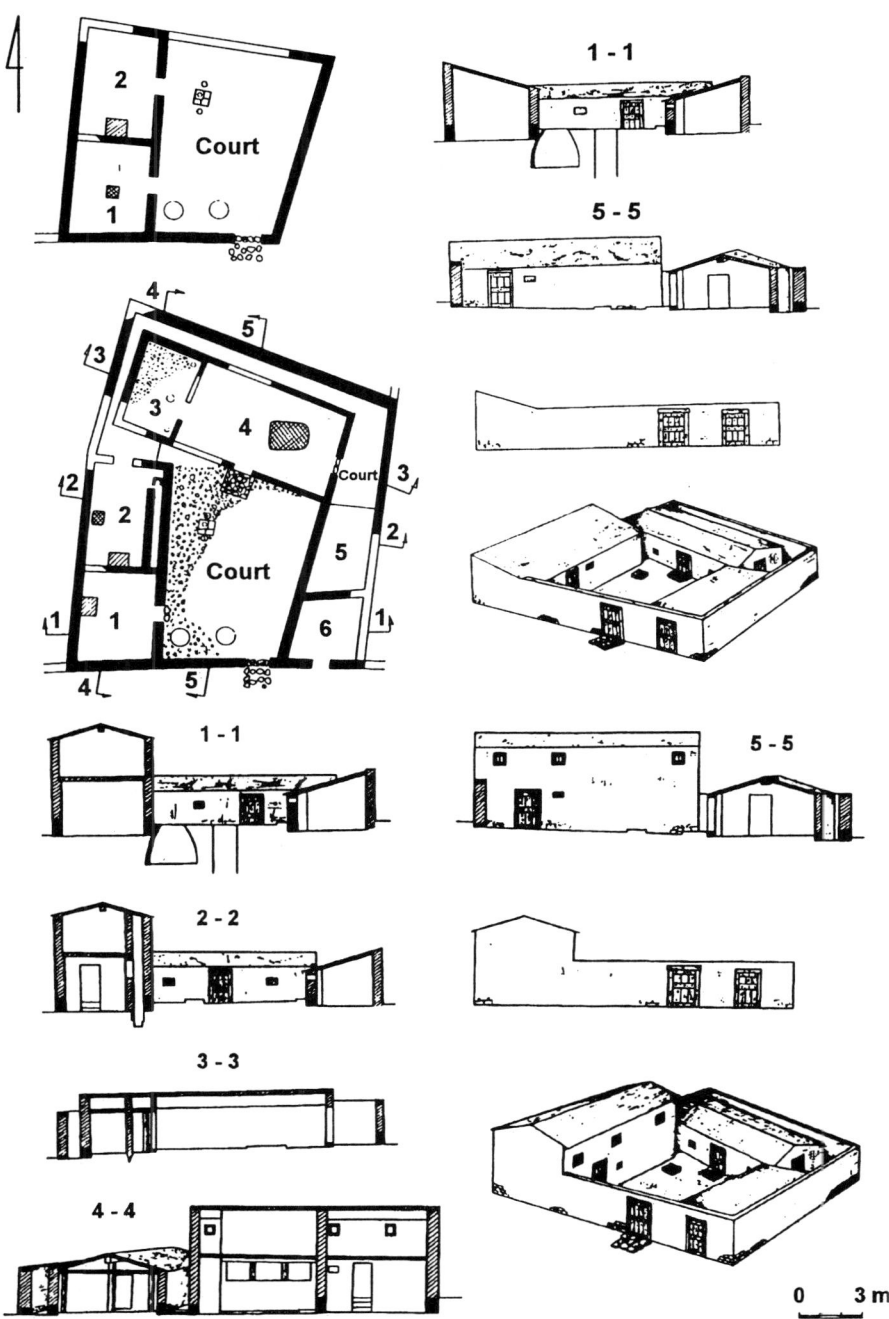

Fig. 52. House 2.

The northern room, with an area of 19m², was dug out to the same depth as the southern. Here too it is unclear where the entry may have been located, but considering the layout of the space, it was probably built into the room's eastern wall. By the southern wall, a stove built of stone and pisé was found in the floor.

Thus, this building represents a typical Greek dwelling in the first construction period, small in area and with the courtyard as its only functionally undifferentiated space. The volumetric reconstruction of the building will be substantiated below; however, it is already reasonable to assume that the house consisted of a single floor and that the interior space were covered by a one-sided adobe roof inclined toward the courtyard.

Residential houses of the type and layout described above began to appear in the northern Black Sea region at the end of the 6th century BC, as a consequence of the colonists' bringing in ancient building traditions (Kryzhitskii 1982, 74). The distinctive design of the building discussed above is visible in the lowering of level of the floor of the interior space relative to the surface of the courtyard, which can be explained by the particular climate of the region.

The appearance of House 2 changed substantially during the second construction period. At the end of the 6th century BC, the northern wall of the courtyard was dismantled and the eastern was rebuilt. At the same time, new rooms were added to the building, which significantly increased its area to 236m². Another open courtyard was created in the northeast corner of the house. In this way, the area of both courtyards together came to 70m², which made up 30% of the total space of the building.

After this reconstruction, the entrance into the house remained in its former place. The well continued to function. For its part, the cellar began to be used as a trash pit. The surface of the courtyard was paved with pebbles and small flat stones. In all of this, the correspondence between the levels of the courtyard and of the floor of the interior space remained as it was, owing to the repeated clay coating of the latter (the overall thickness of which reached 0.10–0.15m).

The southern room retained its domestic-economic purpose during the second construction period. The interior of the northern room, however, changed substantially. In place of the stoves which had existed here earlier, an open hearth was built by the western wall; the hearth was constructed of the inverted upper halves of amphorae, coated with clay. An original heating and ventilation system was built into the eastern wall, the surviving lower parts of which consisted of a channel 0.40m wide cut into the floor a distance of 4.2m. The depth of the channel increased gradually in a southern direction, averaging 0.40–0.50m below the level of the floor. The channel was lined with flat stones placed on their sides, and was contained by mud-brick walls 0.40m wide, which have survived to a height of 0.15–0.20m above the floor. To the north, the channel connected to a small pisé stove.

These particular features of construction suggest that the channel was used as a means to vent smoke. The application of this kind of technique in dwellings in the northern Black Sea region was unknown up to that time. However, close analogies can be found in materials from Olynthus dating from the 4th century BC. Ventilation systems frequently found there differ from those on Berezan mainly in terms of their large size (Robinson and Graham 1938, 189–97). There are two possible interpretations of this kind of system: either as a modern fire-place (Robinson and Graham 1938,

196 Fig. 15), or as a ventilation chamber separate from the rest of the interior space, especially when ventilation openings are found in the upper part of the wall (Robinson and Graham 1938, 191 Fig. 14). Berezan builders probably applied the latter type. In the opinion of scholars who have studied Olynthus, systems like these were typical features of kitchen areas (Robinson and Graham 1938, 192–4), and so might they be in this case as well.

The presence of a heating and ventilation system is directly related to any volumetric assessment of the whole space. There are two possible spatial interpretations: the building had either one or two floors. It is worth noting here that the presence of a second floor over the interior space is not precluded by the type of leveling and the thickness of the exterior walls, which (as at Olynthus: Robinson and Graham 1938, 227–8), measured 0.45m. Nevertheless, I will first consider the single-floor interpretation.

In this case, calculating the lowest possible height of a room formed by the following measurements: depth of the floor from the top of the leveling was 0.6–0.7m, and the height of the old doorway was not less than 1.7m, and would have reached at least 2.6m. The ceiling spans of rooms were originally 3.5–3.7m. Using the single-sided roof interpretation, and taking into account the tendency of Olbian and Olynthian houses to pitch their roofs at an inclination of 170–210 (Robinson and Graham 1938, 236; Kryzhitskii 1971, 89), the greatest possible height of the building above the level of the floor would have been 3.5m. To be sure, the buildings in question could have had the same outward appearance even during the first construction period.

A single-floor interpretation of the northern interior space also makes little sense given the presence of a heating and ventilation system, which (as in houses at Olynthus) may have been designed not only to vent smoke from the building, but also to provide heat to room on the upper floor. Warm air would have passed from the kitchen into a flue through openings in the mud-brick walls, and also from stoves placed in the building's northern end. The warm air would have then risen along a ventilation shaft, warming the walls of the upper floor before being vented outside.

In the two-floor interpretation of room's block, the height of the second floor was probably 3/4 that of the first;[39] that is, 1.9–2m. In the likely event that there was a two-sided (gabled) roof, the height of the rooms would have ranged from 1.7–2.3m, and the height of the entire block would have reached 4.7–4.8m above the level of the courtyard.

Installing a heating-ventilation system evidently required changes in the location of the entry into the northern building, which can now be found only in the northern wall. The only way to pass from this building to the courtyard was through a narrow passageway (0.90m wide) with one earthen step (0.20m high) reinforced with flat stones. This passageway separated the group described above from a newly-built block of rooms, the construction of which had involved dismantling the northern wall of the courtyard from the first construction period. Since neighboring houses built at this time in the northern half of the block tended to align their layout axes to the east, the whole block of new rooms was correspondingly turned as well, to be

---

[39] It is known that such an assumption does not contradict the principles of ancient Greek architecture (Vitr. 6.3.9).

parallel to existing exterior walls. Thus the new block was not built directly onto those walls (as often happened in ancient construction) but on the contrary was separated from them by a narrow passageway 0.50–0.80m wide.[40]

In order to clarify more precisely what seems to me a rather atypical design, there are two possible interpretations: first, neighboring homeowners may not have wished to use shared walls;[41] second, the block of new buildings may have consciously been kept separate, for some other, as yet unclear reasons. Thus I would like to discuss the characteristics of these premises in greater detail.

The western room measured 12m² in area. By the walls its floor was covered with limestone pebbles, and in the center with pottery fragments. The eastern walls of the space (which was shared with the neighboring room) was a little narrower than others (0.20m) and was built of well-dressed stones arranged in a single-layer, embedded system. As a result of its poor state of preservation, the location of the ancient doorway is unclear.

The eastern room, with an area of 34.5m², possessed mud-brick walls on three sides (each 0.30–0.35m wide). The northern and southern walls were built partially of stone. The clay-and-straw (pisé) floor was set at the level of the courtyard and 0.10m higher than the floor of the western room. A pisé stove measuring 1.5 × 2 m was located on the eastern side of the room. A doorway 0.80m wide was also located here, with a threshold built of three stone slabs; the threshold led to small courtyard, 10.0m² in area, which abutted the wall of a neighboring house. On the southern side of this little courtyard another room 12.0m² in area opened up. This latter room probably had a household purpose.

In this way, the new, northeastern part of House 2 was composed of an isolated group of premises with its own separate small courtyard. It was possible to pass from the large courtyard to this area only through a doorway with a stone threshold set into the southern wall of the eastern room. In front of the entry into this space (just as in front of the entry to the house itself) there was a small squarish landing measuring 1.30 × 1.30m, built of smoothly-fitted flat stones. Pieces of the stone coupling from a ship's anchor was used in the construction of this small landing.

The house in question was apparently subdivided by function in the following way: the western premises was residential, the eastern was used as a kitchen and for other domestic purposes, the southern room was a household annex, and an inner courtyard.

From a volumetric standpoint the most likely interpretation is that the space in question occupied a single floor, with a two-sided (gabled) roof above the western and eastern rooms and a single (ungabled) sloping roof above the southern household annex. In both cases the roofs were built of adobe. A number of facts provide evidence in support of this interpretation: the mud-brick walls and the size of the bay of the eastern room (4.5m), and the presence of a post-hole 0.30m in diameter located along

---

[40] The presence of blank walls surrounding the block of new premises on three sides, together with the opening toward a large courtyard with which one of the premises connected via a stone-threshold doorway, undoubtedly provides evidence that the entire group of new constructions belongs only to House 2, and not to one of the neighbouring buildings.

[41] See, for example, Vitr. 1.1.10.

the longitudinal axis of the entire block of rooms. In this case, additional supports could have been arranged along the longitudinal axis of the eastern room, since the length of the gable purlin measured 8m. Furthermore, post-holes for support columns of smaller diameter were found in the floor in the northeast corner of the western room and at the northern end of the plinth of its western wall. It is reasonable to assume that such supports could have been set up on the southern side of the room as well. In that case, there may have been a loft space above,[42] supported by these columns. Then the height of the room from floor to ceiling would have been about 2m, and so the height of the highest point of the roof above the level of the courtyard may have exceeded 2.8m, but if we increase the supposed pitch of the roof to 210 then the height would have reached 3.3m (*cf.*: Kryzhitskii 1971, 89).

Another room which appeared in this house as a result of its reconstruction was the area which occupied its southeast corner and apparently opened only outward, to the street. This room had an area of 10.5m². The roof over the previously-mentioned household annex probably was extended to cover this area as well. The purpose of areas which occupied such a peculiar, isolated position in a house, with an exit only onto the street, is well known from finds at Olynthus: they were small shops (Robinson and Graham 1938, 211–2). A similar interpretation is entirely possible in regard to the room described above. However, in this case it is not possible to substantiate the hypothesis with corresponding diagnostic material.

Having concluded a description of House 2 during the second construction period, there is sufficient basis to assert that, but for a few secondary details (such as the placing of windows and, in some cases, doorways), the evidence allows a clear interpretation of the layout and design of the dwelling. There are two possible interpretations: as a single-floor or (more likely for a number of reasons discussed above) two-floor group of premises. This interpretation stands despite the absence of direct evidence of the existence of stairs between the first and second floors.

Another house[43] in the same block (Fig. 53), located next to the one just described (the two buildings shared one side wall), was built at the end of the 6th century BC; that is, during the reconstruction of House 2. This house ceased functioning during the first third of the 5th century BC. House 4 measured 181m² in area, and consisted of five rooms arranged in an L-shape around a courtyard located in the south-western part of the building. The area of the courtyard was 54m², which represented 30% of the entire area of House 4. The entrance into the house was evidently set into the blank southern wall of the courtyard.

The stone plinths from the walls of this building have been partially preserved. The plinth footings measured 0.45–0.50m in width and 0.60m in height, and rested on a foundation consisting of a single row of limestone slabs 0.60m wide and 0.10m high. The plinths themselves were laid down in a two-faced, single-row, double-level embedded spoon-style system which mimicked (except on the front) isodomic leveling (Fig. 54). The plinths themselves were laid out in a two-front, one-row, two-level embedded arrangement, mirroring (except on the front), the pattern outside. Small stones, which were close in size, well prepared, slightly rounded on the obverse side,

---

[42] This may have substantially improved the heat-retaining properties of the entire room.
[43] In the course of excavation, this house was designated No. 4.

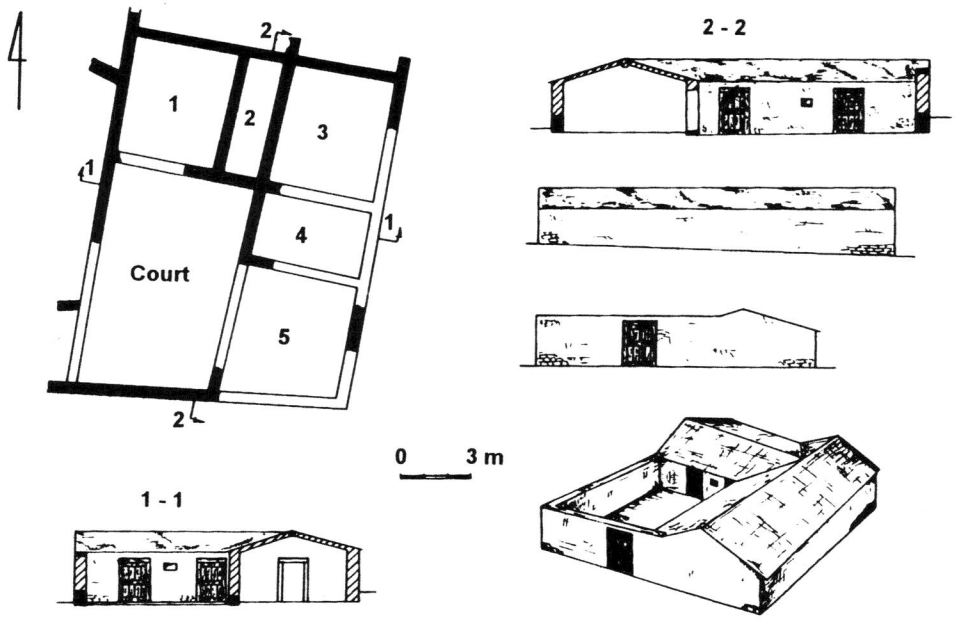

Fig. 53. House 4.

Fig. 54. North façade of House 4.

and carefully fitted into place, were used for this purpose. The upper part of the walls was evidently constructed of mud-bricks.

The northern part of House 4 consisted of two rooms: the eastern one, with an area of 24m², and the western, with an area of 32m². The latter was soon divided into two smaller rooms. Two more rooms adjoined the courtyard from the east. The first of these occupied an area of 13m², and the second 27m².

A volumetric interpretation of House 4 may be figured in the following way. The building evidently had one floor. Since the height of the ceiling span of the northern rooms was 5.2 and 5.3m, and of the eastern rooms – 4.5–4.8m, the likeliest assumption is the use of a pitched-gable type of roof, probably of adobe (given the absence of remnants of tile). Taking into consideration the prevalence among ancient residential buildings of roofs with a pitch of 170–210, the altitude of the highest point of the roof above the level of the courtyard (which was 0.1–0.15m lower than the floors of the rooms) would have been 3.3m. The rooms of House 4 (with only one exception, in the southeastern corner) apparently opened onto the courtyard, although the exact locations of the door embrasures have not been found. Due to the paucity of data the rooms cannot be functionally differentiated.

Having finished examining the particular characteristics of two residential houses of the Berezan settlement in the Late Archaic period, it is worthwhile to focus attention on the peculiar layout of House 2 in the second construction period. The building was distinctive for its isolated group of rooms with a separate courtyard. The western premises seems to have been the most significant. It is important to emphasize that the layout design of House 2 included two distinct principles of spatial relations among its rooms: there was an equivalence of placement of some rooms, and a hierarchical relationship among others.[44]

It is worth noting that a volumetric interpretation of Berezan dwellings also has its own distinctive features. In developing the vertical height of the buildings, the inhabitants not only worked to perfect techniques of aboveground construction but also developed methods to lower the level of the floor in some places. In the subsequent, Classical period this tendency led to the creation of separate basement areas (Kryzhitskii 1982, 27).

Of major interest is one other building of the Berezan settlement during the time in question: House 8, which was partially excavated in 1991. One may assert reliably that this is the first private building with elements of architectural order of the Late Archaic period in the northern Black Sea region.[45] It was built at the end of the third quarter of the 6th century BC. Included in the building's layout design was a four-columns portico opening onto the courtyard. This was probably a *prostas*, which was built in front of the northern group of residential premises. The columns of the portico,

---

[44] Without question, this fact places in doubt the hypothesis (put forward by S.D. Kryzhitskii: 1982, 30, 152) that home architecture in the Lower Bug region in the Archaic period relied exclusively on the design principles of residential buildings, in which the rooms and the inner courtyard had an equivalent spatial relationship (*i.e.*, equivalent area).

[45] It is usually believed that the appearance of elements of architectural orders in private residential construction in the northern Black Sea dates to the 4th century BC (Kryzhitskii 1982, 74*ff*; 1993, 60*ff*).

Fig. 55. House 8.

Fig. 56. Stone column base in House 8.

which were probably made of wood, rested on stone bases, three of which (preserved *in situ*) were spaced 1.95m apart (Solovyov 1992a, 6; 1994, 90).

All these distinctive features of Berezan residential buildings make them a highly valuable resource for studying the early stages in the evolution of ancient dwellings in the northern Black Sea. In addition, these constructions provide an excellent

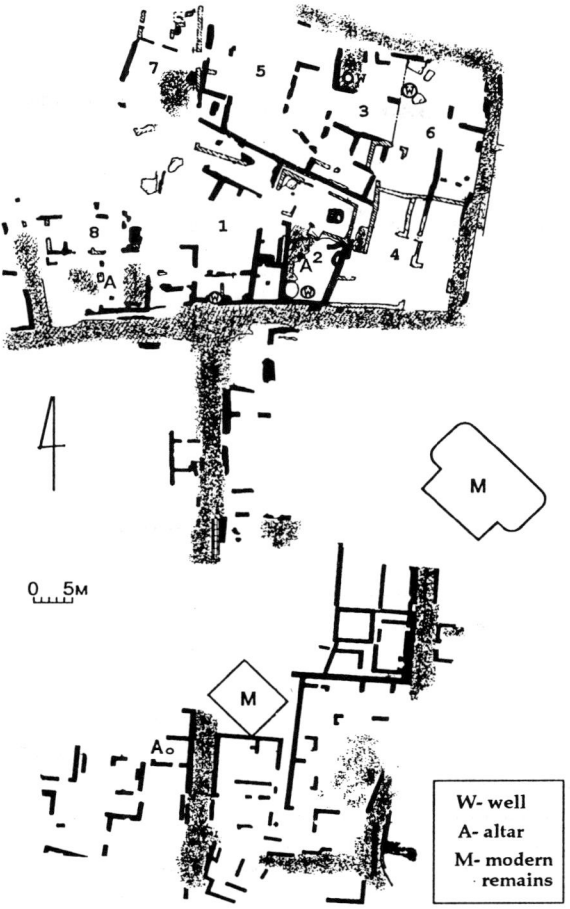

Fig. 57. Blocks of houses in the Northwest Sector.

example of a pre-set urban Greek residential building plan imported to the Lower Bug region.[46] Further, the architectural design of aboveground houses on Berezan clearly indicates their urban character; very few Berezan buildings of this type and time show features characteristic of ancient rural dwellings, which were formerly expressed mainly by the large area of the inner courtyard.

It has become clear that all the residential buildings of the Berezan settlement, irrespective of their external appearance, were grouped in blocks of eight or more houses (Fig. 57). The area of such a block of houses was close to 2000m². The size

---

[46] Given certain of their characteristics, such as the quality of the construction work, dimensions, the well-developed design and layout, the Berezan buildings may be placed in one group together with residential houses of the 5th century BC to the southwest of the Athenian Agora and at the northern foot of the Areopagus (Thompson and Wicherly 1972, 173–9 Figs. 41, 42).

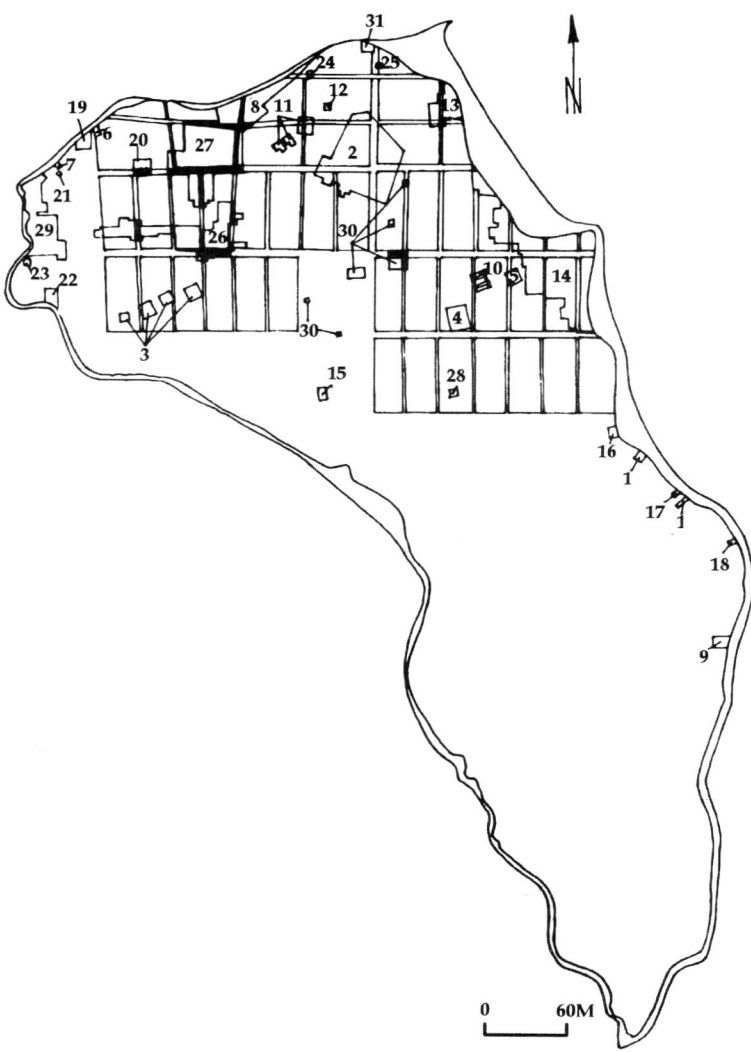

Fig. 58. Reconstructed scheme of the Late Archaic town-planning.

and position of the blocks were regulated by a well-developed network of streets (Fig. 58), which was evidently set up from the beginning according to a more or less regular plan. That plan was probably close to an orthogonal one, and probably took into account the particular topographical features of the ancient peninsula. The width of the streets was probably determined by their importance for local inhabitants. The widest streets (with a width up to 5m), of which there were not fewer than two, evidently served as main civic thoroughfares. These streets divided the ancient city into at least two parts, the layouts of which were determined by other, smaller streets (which measured up to 3.5m in width). The final element in the overall street network were alleys (up to 1.2m wide) which ran between blocks of buildings, and which were included in some sort of smaller planned subdivision of the layout of ancient Berezan. This regulation of the area of the settlement occupied by aboveground buildings evidently did not extend to outlying areas, where dugout construction continued right up to the beginning of the 5th century BC (although to a significantly lesser extent than before).

Today it has become clear that the urbanization of the Berezan settlement, which was carried out in such a short period of time, could not have been implemented without the occurrence of a mass immigration of Greeks.[47] At the present time few doubt an Ionian (predominantly Milesian) origin of the colonists.[48] That the new inhabitants of Berezan possessed a political organization of the city-state type also seems difficult to doubt (Solovyov 1993, 41).

By the beginning of the 5th century BC, the area of the Berezan settlement had reached its greatest historical dimensions. There is an impression that most of the territory of the settlement which was allotted to aboveground construction was opened up practically all at once at the very start of the period of time we have been examining. According to materials from excavations in the northwestern area of the island (Fig. 59), at the end of the 6th century BC the planning of city blocks and most of the houses included in them underwent substantial changes, which probably affected other areas of the settlement in a similar fashion; however, this did not entail a cardinal re-planning of the settlement as a whole. It is worthwhile to point out that in a number of cases this reconstruction took place quickly, and even included reducing quality standards for construction; nevertheless, it was under just these conditions that construction work on Berezan reached its peak, which undoubtedly gave it the characteristic features of an ancient city (Kryzhitskii *et al.* 1986, 9*ff*; Kryzhitskii 1987, 17–21; Domanskii *et al.* 1989, 37; Solovyov 1989, 9–10; 1993, 41).

The necropolis of Berezan gives interesting material to support this.[49] From the second half of the 6th to the first half of the 5th century BC 89% of burials were inhumations in simple pits of rectangular or oval shape. Most of the bodies were

---

[47] In my opinion, the earlier inhabitants of the Berezan settlement abandoned the peninsula in a peaceful way, not owing to any violence on the part of the Greeks, possibly upon the conclusion of an agreement between colonists and native leaders (Vinogradov Y. G. 1989, 40). Such an agreement may have included payment of redemption fees or some other obligation for the land granted to the Greek colonists, probably for an unlimited period of time. In all likelihood, only a very small number of the former inhabitants of Berezan remained living on the peninsula. These people were possibly involved in construction work at the new city or had some other relationship with the new inhabitants.

[48] The opinion that the first contingent of Greek colonists on Berezan was predominantly from Rhodes, recently put forward by A. Wasowicz in a paper delivered at the conference dedicated to 200 years of study of Olbia, seems to me still insufficiently substantiated. Relying mainly on the known facts of regular construction at the Berezan settlement in the second half of the 6th century BC (which also serves as Wasowicz's main argument for the participation of people from Rhodes in the colonization of Berezan), this assumption is certainly not supported by most of the archaeological material found on the island. The proportion of Rhodian imports among this material is far from the greatest, and a much more significant share of imports were from the cities of northern Ionia (Kopeikina 1986, 32).

[49] For a brief description of the burials dating from the second half of the 6th – first half of the 5th century BC, see: Domanskii and Vinogradov 1989, 38*ff*; Vinogradov J. and Domanskij 1996, 294*ff*.

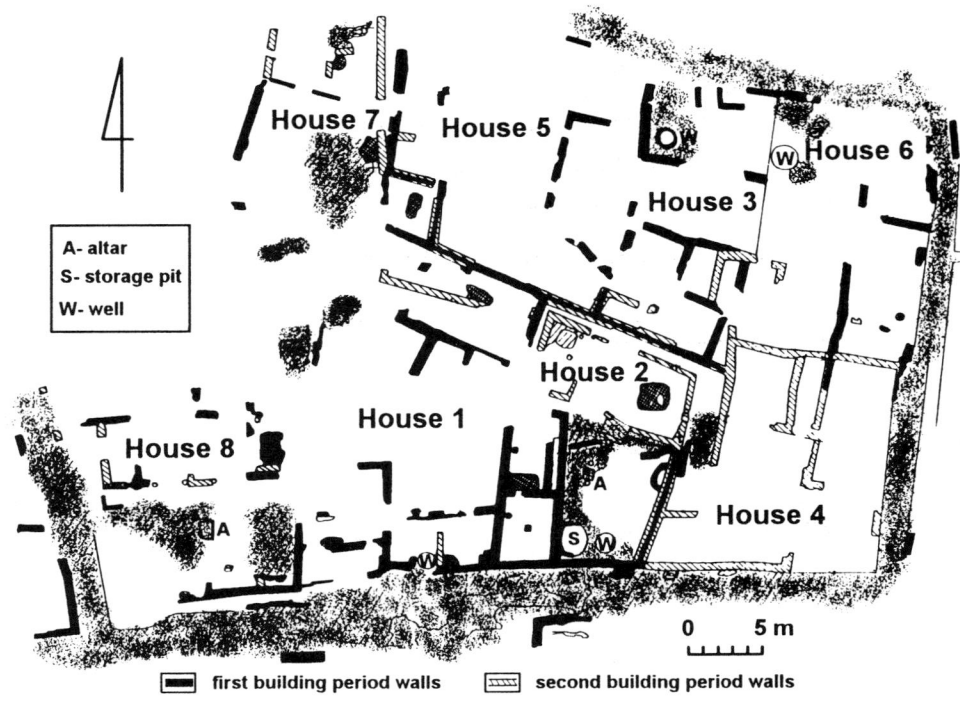

Fig. 59. Plan of houses' rebuilding in the Northwest Sector.

lying on their backs oriented, as a rule, to the northeast or northwest (Figs. 60–61), but 33% were on their side in a crouched position (Fig. 62). It is possible to attribute these to the local population.[50] About 7% of burials opened in 1982–90[51] were of children (Fig. 63), often in large ceramic vessels (Vinogradov J. and Domanskii 1996, 295). As a rule, amphorae and (less frequently) pithos-shaped urns were employed (Fig. 64). Cremations comprised no more than 4% of Berezan burials (Vinogradov J. and Domanskii 1996, 295).[52]

The burial offerings were inexpensive and diverse but, as a whole, composed of fairly standard subjects.[53] They included amphorae (Fig. 65), plain and painted jugs and kraters (Figs. 66–68), cups (Figs. 69–70), lekythoi (Figs. 71–73), askoi (Figs. 74–75), lydia (Fig. 76) and gutti. Other categories of offerings were also found in graves: stone and metal tools; bronze, iron and glass adornments; terracotta statuettes and

[50] The question of the ethnic identity of the crouched burials found in the necropoleis of the Greek cities of the northern Black Sea littoral is still unresolved. Some scholars think they belong to Greeks; others, to the local population (Lapin 1966, 90–4; Kadeev 1973, 108–16; 1981, 111–20; Zubar 1993).
[51] Skadovskii found 154 burials in amphora (Kaposhina 1956, 220) – that is about 19% of all Berezan burials.
[52] Skadovskii noted more than 100 cremations (Fabritsius 1951, 58)
[53] Of all the Berezan graves only two were notable for their richness: Grave 371 of the 1900 excavation (Kaposhina 1956, 220–1) and Grave 98 of the 1984 excavation (Vinogradov Y. G. 1994).

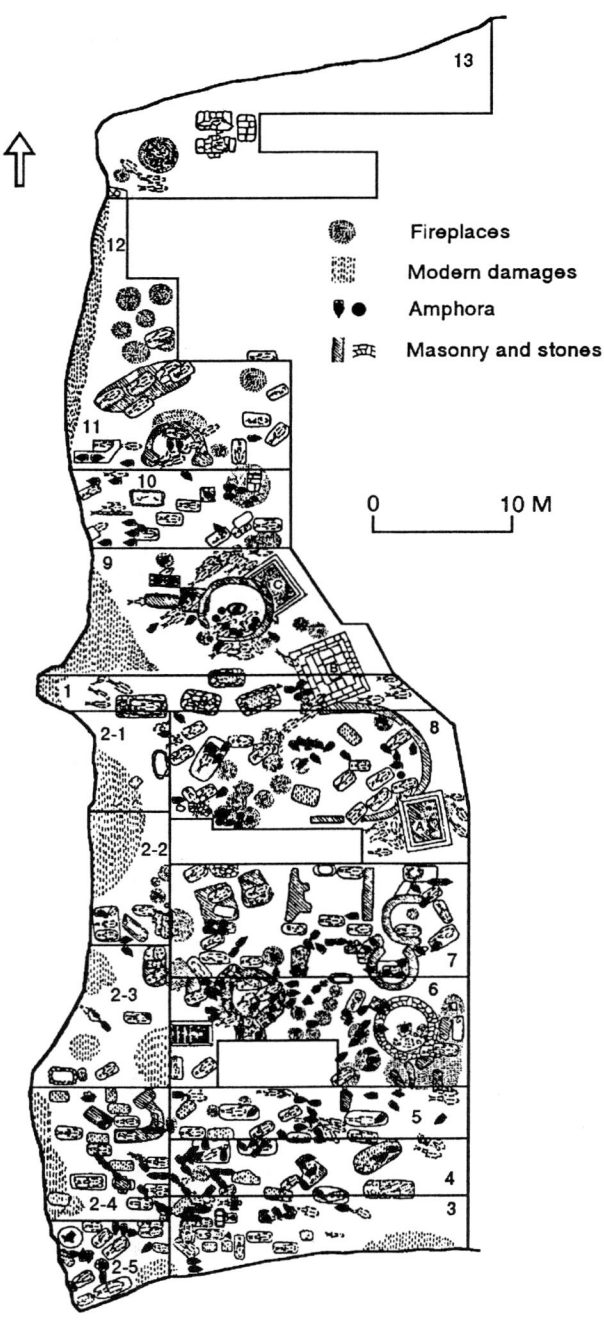

13

12

Fireplaces

Modern damages

Amphora

Masonry and stones

0   10 M

11

10

9

1

2-1

8

2-2

2-3

7

6

5

2-4

4

3

2-5

Fig. 60   Berezan necropolis, exacavated by G.L. Skadovskii (after Lapin 1966).

Grave 118
1
2
3
1 Lekythos
2 Cup
3 Amphora
0 50 sm

Fig. 61. Berezan necropolis, grave 118 (1984).

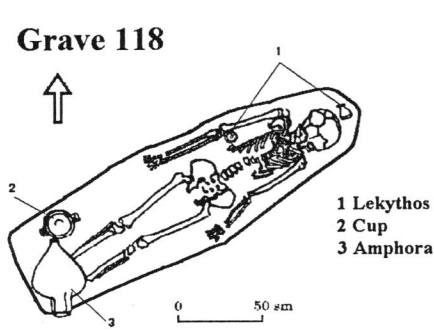

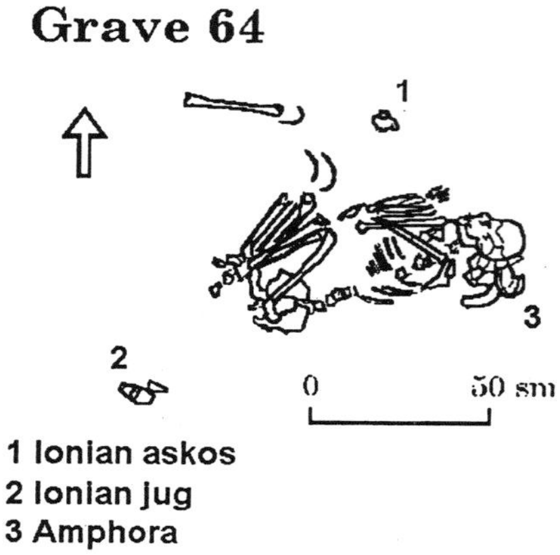

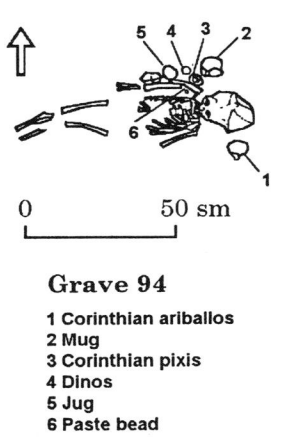

Grave 64
1
2
3
0 50 sm
1 Ionian askos
2 Ionian jug
3 Amphora

Fig. 62. Berezan necropolis, grave 64 (1982).

5 4 3 2
6
1
0 50 sm
Grave 94
1 Corinthian ariballos
2 Mug
3 Corinthian pixis
4 Dinos
5 Jug
6 Paste bead

Fig. 63. Berezan necropolis, grave 94 (1983).

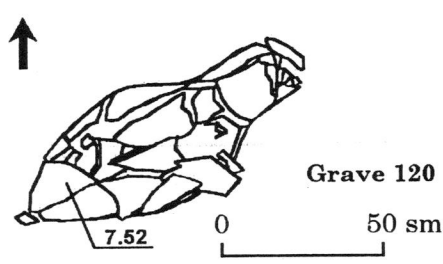

Grave 120
7.52
0 50 sm

Fig. 64. Berezan necropolis, grave 120 (1984).

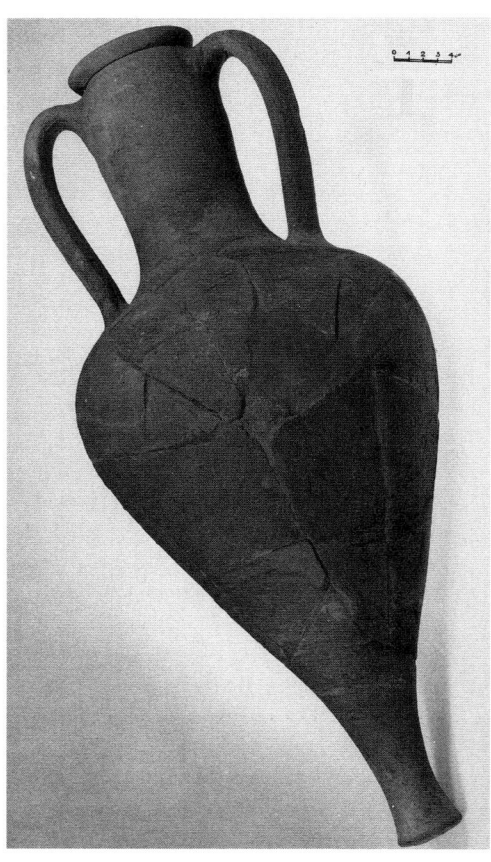

Fig. 65. Ionian amphora of the 5th century BC (B.85.347).

Fig. 66. The handle of an Attic black-figure column-krater, mid-6th century BC (B.90.61).

Fig. 67. Attic red-figure column-krater, mid-5th century BC, side A (B.88.41).

Fig. 68 . Attic red-figure column-krater, mid-5th century BC, side B (B.88.41).

Fig. 69   East Greek cup, mid-6th century BC (B.84.28).

Fig. 70. Attic black-figure cup, last quarter of 6th century BC (B.82.125).

faience figure vessels (Fig. 77); and copper coins. Occasionally weapons, mainly arrow-heads, were found. All of these features were typical of any Greek necropolis in the northern Black Sea littoral and the Berezan necropolis of the second half of the 6th – first half of the 5th century does not stand out archaeologically.

As before, the main economic activities of the colony were probably trade and handicrafts. This interpretation is supported not only the evidence of archaeological materials from Berezan and its surrounding areas, but also by epigraphic finds on the island, for example, the well-known letter of Achillodorus (Vinogradov Y. G. 1971, 64–7; 1971a, 98*ff*; *cf*: Bravo 1974; Yailenko 1974; 1975). A new and very recent scholarly understanding of the political status of the Berezan settlement (Kryzhitskii and Otreshko 1986, 12*ff*; Vinogradov Y. G. 1983, 378*ff*; 1989, 32*ff*; Solovyov 1993, 39*ff*) may require certain corrections in the interpretation of particular parts of the Achillodorus letter; it is possible to suggest something new about the letter's addressee.

Fig. 71. Samian lekythos, third quarter of 6th century BC (B.82.69).

Fig. 72. Attic black-figure lekythos, third quarter of 5th century BC (B.89.111).

Fig. 73. Ionian askos, second half of 6th century BC (B.86.44).

Fig. 74. Attic black-figure white-ground lekythos, first quarter of 5th

Fig. 75. Ionian askos, second half of 6th century BC (B.82.151).

Fig. 76. Ionian lydion, third quarter of 6th century BC (B.82.68).

Fig. 77. Egyptian faience figure vessel, late 6th century BC (B.82.315).

In all likelihood, the Berezan settlement was one and the same place as that named in the letter, and was where the addressee evidently lived. Considering the absence of any clear traces of urban construction at Olbia in the 6th century BC (Kryzhitskii 1985, 57*ff*), that city can hardly claim to be the place mentioned. The letter's destination as Olbia, or more precisely, as the small Greek settlement which existed at that time on the site of the future city, probably indicated something different: the settlement may have been an outer northern post of a city-state populated by Greek colonists. In addition, this population centre was also a place for honouring the highest divine patron and protector of the city-state – Apollo the Healer (Rusyaeva 1986, 60*ff*), formerly also the defender of the northern borders. It is likely that this is the meaning of the "Northern Apollo" mentioned in an inscription on a bone plaque from Berezan (Rusyaeva 1986, 28).

Possibly, other deities in the Berezan pantheon were also endowed with similar functions as defenders of the borders of the city-state – Achilles, Cybele, and Herakles. It is known that the largest share of dedications to Achilles were found in the far western part of Berezan's outlying areas; specifically at the Beikush settlement, where this divine hero was apparently honored for his chthonic hypostasis (this interpretation is supported by the symbolism of votive offerings found here: Kryzhitskii *et al.* 1989, 84*ff*Fig. 32; Rusayeva 1992, 70*ff*). For their part, altars of the Great Mother-Goddess and Herakles were located at Hylaea, *i.e.*, on the eastern territory of the city-state. Owing to their distance from the center these places became easy booty for raiders, as the so-called letter of an Olbian priest indicates (Rusyaeva 1987, 146*ff*; Rusjaeva and Vinogradov 1991). All these sources suggest that such cults of divine defenders of the borders of the state probably played a significant rôle in the world-view of local citizens, especially in the early period of opening up the new homeland, when danger from outside surely seemed especially pronounced, and even more terrifying for being so unknown.

In addition, the broad development of trade between residents and the cities and hinterland suggests a rather stable local and foreign political situation in the region. This stability is also evidenced by the indisputable facts of the ceramic complex found in residential buildings and in the cultural level of the settlement in the last quarter of the 6th through the first third of the 5th centuries BC. At that time, as before, amphorae remained the dominant form of pottery. To be sure, the composition of amphorae itself changed significantly; the majority of such finds at the settlement became amphorae from Lesbos (both red- and grey-clay types), Chios, and the so-called proto-Thasian amphorae (Zeest 1960, Tabl. 6, 15b, g).[54] There can be little doubt that, at the time, northern Ionian cities were the primary suppliers of wine to the Berezan market.

Meanwhile, in the same period the main exported tableware in the Lower Bug region was Athenian (Figs. 78–88). If during the last quarter of the 6th century BC the only competitors able to withstand Athenian trade interest were those very same northern Ionian pottery workshops (Fig. 89), then after the full takeover of Ionia by the Persians at the beginning of the 5th century BC there was probably no one left who could seriously compete with the Athenians in the markets of the northern Black Sea (Brashinskii 1963, 26–34). As a result, even the serious economic difficulties which beset the Athenians during the course of the Greek-Persian wars would not have posed a problem. In the first half of the 5th century BC, Attic pottery imports (all types of which had grown in scale) penetrated not only into coastal Greek cities and the rural areas surrounding them, but also into

Fig. 78. Attic black-figure amphora of the middle of 6th century BC (B.90.44).

deeper regions of the Scythian steppe and its settlements. Without a doubt, the inhabitants of Berezan played a major rôle in these trading operations.

Artisanry and handicraft work remained, as before, one of the main activities of the people of Borysthenes at that time. However, unlike in the earlier period, this artisanry was oriented mainly toward meeting the demand of the inhabitants of the city (and its surrounding areas) themselves; in fact, the work had the all characteristics of home production. Several factors suggest the prevalence of this: there were, for

---

[54] Recently, V. V. Ruban (1991) made a rather unsuccessful attempt to present this type of amphora as a further development of a known form of earlier Milesian amphora. Such an identification seems to me highly eclectic and, to a lesser extent, artificial. No morphology and no technology of such amphorae, which are well represented in the archaeological material of the Berezan settlement, provides any basis for associating these two fundamentally different kinds of amphora.

Fig. 79. Attic black-figure krater of the third quarter of 6th century BC (B.91.226).

Fig. 80. Attic black-figure cup of the last quarter of 6th century BC (B.84.125).

Fig. 81. Attic black-figure cup of the last quarter of 6th century BC (B.90.68).

Fig. 82. Attic black-figure cup of the late 6th century BC (B.84.139).

Fig. 83.1. Attic black-figure cup of the late 6th century BC (outside) (B.82.127).

Fig. 83.2. Attic black-figure cup of the late 6th century BC (inside) (B.82.127).

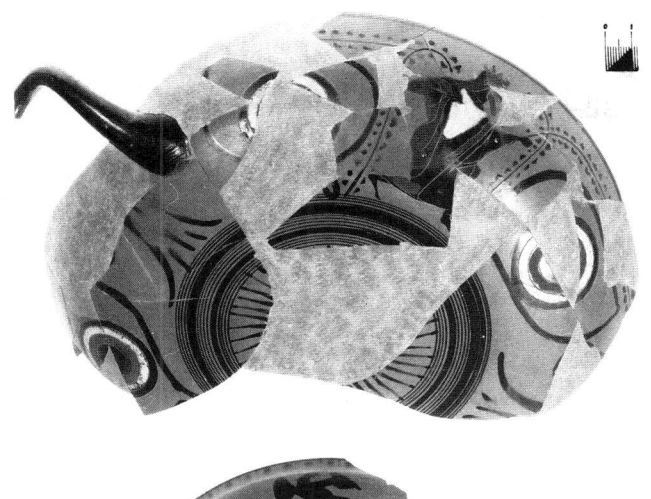

Fig. 84. Attic black-figure cup of the late 6th century BC (B.90.67).

Fig. 85. Attic black-figure cup of the late 6th century BC (B.90.77).

Fig. 86. Attic black-figure cup of the first quarter of 5th century BC (B.87.76).

Fig. 87. Attic black-figure cup of the first quarter of 5th century BC (B.87.78).

Fig. 88. Attic black-figure cup of the first quarter of 5th century BC (B.88.39).

Fig. 89. Ionian cup of the early 5th century BC (B.89.91).

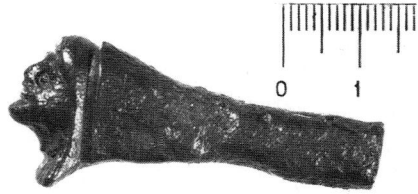

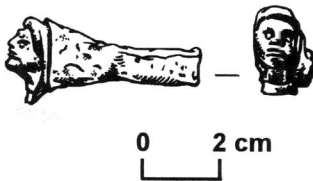

Fig. 90.1. Late Archaic bronze stamp   *Fig. 90.2. Late Archaic bronze stamp*
(B.86.311).   *(B.86.311).*

instance, copper-smelting and bronze-casting workshops set up inside some Borysthenes houses,[55] and many women occupied themselves with spinning and weaving. Traditional male occupations included hunting[56] and fishing, activities which yielded a large portion of the foodstuffs consumed by local residents. Traces and finds of tools and equipment connected to all these activities are found very frequently at excavations on the island (Figs. 90–96).

Starting in the second half of the 6th century BC a new economic trend emerged at Borysthenes: the direct exploitation of the fertile lands surrounding the city, in order to build up some marketable agricultural production. Although up to the present day there have been few data directly supporting the presence of a *chora* at Borysthenes, few could seriously doubt that that the inhabitants were engaged in agricultural activities, especially tilling and raising livestock.[57] The only remaining question is the form and extent of agricultural production.

Since there are very few data of the type required, at the present time it is difficult to provide answers to these questions. In addition, it is becoming more and more clear that one direct consequence of the activities of the Greek colonists (not only in trade, but also in agriculture) was to involve the local, indigenous population in the process of opening up the coast of the Dnieper-Bug estuary[58] and possibly in creating

---

[55] One very special find in one of these workshops of the end of the 6th century BC was of a bronze die-stamp (Fig. 90) for making gold or silver sewn-on medallions in the form of a male human mask. Although waste products from jewellery were not found in this place, it is still reasonable to assume that the owner of this bronze-casting workshop (a major one, judging from the large amount of bronze-casting waste found in a household pit and in the courtyard) was also a jeweller.

[56] Judging from osteological material, which is numerous among other finds on Berezan, hunting occupied a rather small place in the economy of the settlement. However, even a small number of finds related to hunting make it possible to determine the variety of wild animals which lived in areas surrounding the settlement. It has been established that among these animals were those living in the steppe and forest-steppe zones of the northern Black Sea region in the Archaic period (Zhuravlyov 1983).

[57] Evidence for this conclusion is provided by well-known, although numerically small, finds of agricultural tools on Berezan (Lapin 1963; Otreshko 1987). The large amount of osteological material, mentioned earlier (Zhuravlyov *et al.* 1990), also supports this interpretation.

[58] The appearance of a whole network of rural settlements on the coast of the Bug and Dnieper estuaries in the last quarter of the 6th century BC (more than 150 settlements of that time have been counted in the area) could hardly have been under the control of the Borysthenes or Olbia, or even both of them together (Marchenko 1991, 20–3). Otherwise, the population of these cities would have grown to an improbable size (by ancient standards), clearly exceeding the size of the modern population of the area (according to Kryzhitskii *et al.* 1989, 36). In addition, there have been attempts to resolve these complicated demographic issues with simple mathematical calculation, but also ignoring well-known and widely-accepted archaeological methods. These attempts are not so much unconvincing as unscientific, or more exactly, fantastic.

Fig. 91. Late Archaic louteria (B.85.332,334).

Fig. 92. Late Archaic grey wares (B.85.133,141).

Fig. 93. Late Archaic mug (B.85.134). *Fig. 94. Late Archaic lopas (B.91.190).*

Fig. 95. Late Archaic iron Greek sword (B.91.211).

Fig. 96. Late Archaic Scythian sword (B.86.255).

control-points for managing the acquired territory. The previously-mentioned Greek settlement located on the site of the future Olbia may have been one of these points, for the settlement undoubtedly existed by this time. Very soon after, not later than the end of the 6th century BC, by virtue of its geographical and topographical merits this point on the right bank of the Bug River estuary became the center of a new city-state – Olbia.[59]

Today we can only guess at how the citizens of the city-state were organized, whether as a result of a one-time appearance by new Greek colonists, or in the course of a permanent, spontaneous, and mass influx of immigrants to the Lower Bug region.[60] It is worth noting, however, that the archaeological and epigraphic data of this region[61] clearly indicate that Berezan and Olbia developed separately and distinctively, as did most of their outlying rural settlements. The data thus tends to support the first supposition, emphasizing the impulsive, spontaneous character of colonization in the Lower Bug region (Vinogradov Y.G. 1989, 32*ff*).

In any case, there is good reason to believe that by the last quarter of the 6th century BC a social conflict began to develop between the pioneers and the newcomers. If we adhere to Rusyaeva's interpretation of the key epigraphic document from that time it appears that the conflict (which developed as a religious dispute between worshippers of Apollo the Healer and those of Apollo Delphinios: Rusyaeva 1986, 25*ff*; 1992, 41–2) was quickly settled with the help of the mother-city, Miletus, which evidently had a strong interest in keeping its colonial areas developing calmly and without conflict. It is even possible to believe that the dispute was resolved by creating a new city-state on territory which had formerly been under the control of Borysthenes[62] (*i.e.*, of the Berezan settlement). In all likelihood, the residents of Olbia were the petitioners in this case and probably received the famous Didyma oracle, the leitmotiv of which in this case may have been to consider the phrase "Peace to

---

[59] Significant and substantial changes which took place in the culture of Olbia at the end of the 6th century BC (clearly reflected in archaeological evidence), compel agreement with the opinion of certain academics that the Olbia was founded at this time, and not earlier (Kryzhitskii 1985, 174; Kryzhitskii and Otreshko 1986, 9).

[60] This question has been sharply disputed in recent years in view of the appearance in the literature of a new conception of Greek colonization in the northwestern Black Sea. However, the basic positions underlying this new conception (Buiskikh 1986, 17–28; 1990; Kryzhitskii and Buiskikh 1988, 1–8; Kryzhitskii *et al.* 1989, 12–41), completely overlook the opinion formulated earlier by Lapin on the character of colonization in the northern Black Sea (Marchenko 1994, 92–9).

[61] For instance, Didyma oracle (Rusyaeva 1986).

[62] It is reasonable to propose that the Adzhigol riverbed may have served as the border between Borysthenes and Olbia during the first third of the 5th century BC. Strange as it may seem, the slopes of this large, broad riverbed, which was deeply wedged into the right bank of the Bug floodplain and which divided it into two roughly equal parts, was completely devoid of permanent settlements in the Archaic period, with the exception of temporary stopping places (Kryzhitskii *et al.* 1989, 25 Fig. 3) used by herdsmen and nomads (the reader is reminded that the Maritsin funeral site investigated by M. Ebert [1913], which had clearly Scythian burial-rite features, relates specifically to this region). Major cultural centres which were more or less firmly settled in the area in the Late Archaic period were located to the north and south of the riverbed. According to new and recent data accumulated from the Archaic sites in the Lower Bug area, the specific cultural characteristics of the northern and southern regions have become clearer (Marchenko 1985; Vinogradov Y. A. *et al.* 1989). It has been established that the rural territory to the north of Adzhigol was characterized by fixed, almost uninterrupted (it is difficult to detect the borders between distinct settlements) construction along the entire coast of the estuary. In the particular

the Olbia *polis.*" It would also be tempting to see echoes of these events in the wide-scale reconstruction of Berezan's residential blocks at the end of the 6th century BC.[63]

No long after the conflict was settled, these events were followed by the growth of both the Borysthenes and Olbia economies, which led to the full opening up of the Lower Bug region and to a further deepening of interaction between the Greeks and the indigenous population across a wide zone. The Berezan settlement was at the height of its economic and political development at this time. Berezan's stable forward development was disturbed, however, at the end of the first third of the 5th century BC.

---

features of their building and types of hand-made pottery, the rural settlements in this region were by and large quite similar to Scythian sites of the right-bank central Dnieper region. The settlements located to the south of the Adzhigol riverbed, however, look quite different. Here the settlements are spaced much farther apart, and in architectural appearance and the technical characteristics of their hand-made pottery these areas are by and large reminiscent of Scythian sites of the middle Dneister region. Today it is becoming more evident that, in the Late Archaic period, each of these Lower Bug regions had its own historically-shaped economic and political centre. To the north of Adzhigol was Olbia, and to the south Borysthenes (*cf:* Otreshko 1979, 156).

[63] It is worthwhile to note the curious fact established by archaeology that fires and conflagrations in two of the houses in the northwest section date to precisely this time.

PART 4

The Berezan Settlement in the Classical Period

Until very recently, our understanding of the Berezan settlement in the Classical period was based primarily on the rather contradictory opinions of V.V. Lapin and L.V. Kopeikina. According to Lapin (1966, 108, 121; 1978, 94*ff*), in the 5th century BC the settlement reached the peak of its social, economic, and demographic development, and gradually slid into decline by the end of this period. This assertion is based on the results of Lapin's excavations on the eastern shore of Berezan island, which rather persuasively demonstrated that the settlement functioned uninterruptedly and with few changes during the entire 5th century BC (and even much later). Furthermore, excavations in this part of the island indicated that the transition to building aboveground houses of the general Greek type occurred at the beginning of the 5th century BC, and was accompanied by the construction of public buildings (Lapin 1966, 109, 119; Kryzhitskii 1987, 20–1).

In Lapin's opinion, all this makes it possible to assume that changes in other parts of the Berezan settlement were similar in appearance and timing. In other words, Lapin saw good reason to assert that there was a structural uniformity, functional integrity, and chronological unity behind the evolution of the site during the Classical period (Lapin 1978, 72). Another factor involved at least indirectly in the formation of this opinion was probably Lapin's desire to synchronize fully the historical development of Berezan with that of Olbia; this goal resounds insistently in Lapin's work, and created an illusion of unity between these two highly important sites (Lapin 1966, 146; 1978, 383).

There are many scholars today who share Lapin's opinion (Vinogradov Y. G. 1976, 80–2; 1989, 67–8; Kryzhitskii and Otreshko 1986, 14*ff*; Kryzhitskii *et al.* 1989, 22, 38–40). Essentially, they do not see substantive differences (excepting naturally economic ones: Otreshko 1979, 156–7; 1994, 119; Nazarov 1994a, 97–8) between the Berezan settlement in the Archaic period and its successor city-state in the 5th and 4th centuries BC. These academics are persuaded both by older archaeological material, and by those found on the island more recently. Recent excavations on the eastern part of Berezan discovered the ruins of aboveground residential buildings from the time in question. It has been established that in erecting these constructions the builders relied on principles of planning and construction which date back to the previous period. This generates the overall outward appearance of a settlement existing serenely during the entire period in question, of its organic inclusion at a particular time in the Olbian state, and of Berezan inhabitants participating fully in the final creation of the Olbia as a city-state.[64] For its part, the economic decline of Berezan is supposed to be seen as part of a general crisis which gripped the Olbian city-state at the beginning of the 3rd century BC (Kryzhitskii *et al.* 1980, 8–12; 1989, 99–100).

Meanwhile, in the 1970's L.V. Kopeikina turned her attention toward the contraction of the area of the residential zone of Berezan, which occurred at the beginning of the 5th century BC (Kopeikina 1975, 193–4; 1979, 111). This was a significant event; one could even say it was catastrophic, especially in terms of its consequences for the future fate of the settlement. Excavations carried out in the northwestern part of the island provided the basis for the observation that there had indeed been such a large-scale construction. It has been established that solid, well-constructed aboveground residential buildings existed in the northwest area during the Late Archaic period; for unknown reasons these buildings were quickly abandoned by their residents (who took with them practically all the household goods). This fact gave Kopeikina good reason to take issue with Lapin's earlier deductions, and to propose instead a different course for the historical development of the Berezan settlement in the 5th century BC.

In Kopeikina's opinion (1979, 109–11; 1981a, 206–8), at the beginning of the century the settlement slid into decline due to a number of external circumstances. This decline affected practically all facets of life, and led to a significant reduction in the number of inhabitants. Outwardly this process was manifested first by a reduction in the area of the residential zone and by a decline in living standards for the remainder of the population. Internal changes in Berezan's social and political structure were probably even more profound (although Kopeikina did not study these questions). In addition, Kopeikina justifiably proposed that the main consequence of all these changes was the transformation of the settlement into a minor trade and transit point on the northern coast of the Black Sea and in the Olbian system. In this way, according to Kopeikina, the 5th century BC was a period of deep crisis in the history of Berezan, especially against the background of its former prosperity.

Admittedly, right up to the present day very little has changed in the positions of scholars on both sides of this debate on the history of Classical Berezan. Their argument, as before, is based on scanty archaeological data which have hardly been augmented at all since the 1970s (Rusyaeva 1986b, 301); it is known that these data included the very fragmented and uncoordinated (with rare exceptions) remains of

---

[64] These kinds of buildings suggest that the Berezan settlement played a rôle as one of the transmitters of a process of *synoikismos* in the Lower Bug region, which some scholars believed (Lapin 1966, 176; Ruban 1977, 43–4; *cf*: Marchenko 1980, 142) was the main reason that the Olbia took the form it did in the 5th century BC (the form in which Herodotus found it). Not all scholars refer to this process directly, often calling it a blending or merging process among Greek settlements which arose spontaneously on the shores of the Borysthenes and Hypanis Rivers, with the aim of creating a single urban centre – Olbia – and structuring its outlying areas (*chora*) (Kryzhitskii and Rusyaeva 1978, 24; Rusyaeva 1979, 107; Rusyaeva and Skryzhinskaya 1979, 27–8; Kryzhitskii and Otreshko 1986, 15; Kryzhitskii *et al.* 1989, 95). Given this, certain academics believe that some part of the Berezan population, having abandoned familiar areas, participated directly in building the demographic potential of Olbia itself. Other scholars propose the opposite – a merger of some of the rural inhabitants with the urban population of Borysthenes (the Berezan settlement). Clearly, there is a wide spectrum of opinions on the subject. To what extent each of these different points of view is justified will become clearer upon further examination of the material from the Berezan settlement brought to light in the present Part of this book.

aboveground buildings and of various types of depressions in the cultural level of the settlement: most often household pits, more rarely wells and cisterns (Lapin 1966, 107; Gorbunova 1969, 16–8).[65] Without exaggerating, it is possible to assert that none of these sites have become subjects of special study. This inattentive treatment of the archaeological complexes in question has probably resulted from their highly unsatisfactory state of preservation. A further matter in this regard is that studying these old materials is particularly difficult because the field documentation on one or another complex is often incomplete, and because the collections of materials themselves are often uncoordinated and fragmentary (not to mention that some parts of the collections have been irreplaceably lost),[66] except for only one dwelling discovered by Lapin in 1961–61 in the eastern part of the settlement (Lapin 1978, 165; Kryzhitskii 1982, 27 Fig. 4, 4).

According to the graphic volumetric-layout interpretation proposed by Lapin and his co-author Kryzhitskii, this building was completely typical of Greek residential building. It consisted of an open interior courtyard surrounded by residential and household premises, one of which was a half-basement and two others of which had lower floors. The area of the building was close to 70m², but its height was hardly more than that of ordinary single-floor buildings of the time. Unfortunately, it remains unclear how the building was connected to other constructions in that area of the settlement, which makes it difficult to make judgments about its layout in the 5th century BC. However, information has recently been gained about the features of construction in a neighboring area of the settlement (where a group of aboveground residential buildings dating from the 5th-4th centuries BC was partially excavated)[67]. Taking this information into account, it is reasonable to propose that the eastern part of the Berezan settlement at that time had a regular layout, the main principles of which were close to those which were used in the Late Archaic period.

The building mentioned in the third section of this book, dating to the first half of the 5th century BC and discovered by Lapin (1978, 174–7) on the eastern coast of

---

[65] Most of these constructions date to the 4th century BC (and not even to the beginning of that century). Nevertheless, all of them are, to one degree or another, characteristic of the Berezan settlement during the Classical period. A different type of material from that time was found in significantly greater amounts – mainly pottery, primarily (of course) fragments of amphora, and also pieces of Attic black-glazed vessels (Lapin 1967; 1968; 1972; 1978, 153*ff*. It is important to note that a significant part of all these materials was found on the eastern coast of the island, which undeniably supports the opinion of L.V. Kopeikina. However, there remain a few supporters of Lapin's point of view.

[66] This inattentive treatment of the archaeological complexes in question has probably resulted from their highly unsatisfactory state of preservation. In any case, this approach will change in the near future, as a result of growing interest in the history of Olbia in the Classical period and given the recent appearance of new data regarding Berezan in the 5th century BC (Solovyov 1995a).

[67] Unfortunately, it is impossible to say anything more definite about these buildings. The sites were excavated at the beginning of the 1980s, but up to the present day have not been any proper publication of them. It is known only that these were probably typical medium-sized urban houses with many functionally-differentiated rooms possessing different kinds of interior amenities, especially stone paving, drains, stoves, cisterns, and possibly wells and house altars. All of these buildings had the same orientation, and were set right against each other along both sides of a street, 3.0m wide, which extended from north to south. It is also known that later investigation at this site was stopped and has not not been resumed, although it is entirely possible that continuing the work would reveal a new page in the history of the Classical Berezan.

the island in 1963–65, represented an entirely different type of construction. The building was aligned longitudinally and was preserved to a length of 20m and a width of 5.4m; it consisted of at least three premises, the most northerly of which was finished with slate 2.7m in radius. The territory adjoining the building to the west was paved in places with stones and pottery and was enclosed with a mud-brick wall set on a stone plinth. Judging from particular features of the building's design, it could hardly have served as a dwelling and was probably used instead for official or religious purposes. Still, no objects have been found, either in the building itself or alongside it, which might have indicated what purpose the building served. In my opinion, at the present time a more detailed analysis of this site, which is interesting and unique for the northern Black Sea region, is impossible owing to the lack of detailed publications describing it.

Summing up the small amount of data accumulated earlier about Classical Berezan, it is worth noting that all the facts clearly suggest that the *polis*-type structure of the settlement was maintained during the whole 5th century BC, and possibly a even little later. It is also evident that in the 5th century, as opposed to the previous period, basic principles of urban building were followed only in a small part of the territory: the former residential zone (that is, primarily the eastern and northeastern areas of the settlement). Another part of the territory, that which occupied practically the entire central and northwest regions of the ancient peninsula, was abandoned by its former residents and either remained empty during the whole period of time in question, or was used for some other purpose.

In recent years, archaeological work on the island has substantially broadened our understanding of the history of Berezan in the Classical period. Research conducted in the northwestern part from 1987 to 1991 opened an entirely new page in the life of the settlement in the 5th and 4th centuries BC. The reason for this was the unexpected find of a whole series of building complexes and storage pits, along with a large quantity of contemporaneous material finds (mainly pottery) (Domanskii *et al.* 1989, 38; 1991, 12–3). Considering the importance of this discovery for studying the Berezan settlement, it is worthwhile to describe its particular features in greater detail.

Without exception, the building complexes consisted of full dugouts; *i.e.*, dwellings dug into the ground, the construction of which had already stopped on Berezan long before (at least 25 to 30 years). As indicated above, buildings of this type predominated at the settlement during the first three quarters of the 6th century BC, and faded out not later than the beginning of the following century. Therefore, the discovery of new dugouts in an area formerly occupied by houses built aboveground was an extremely unexpected event.[68]

---

[68] Moving a little ahead, it is important to note that similar instances of analogous shifts in building traditions, and which took place almost at the same time, have been observed in a few other places on the northern shore of the Black Sea – in the vicinity of Olbia (Marchenko 1985a; Marchenko and Solovyov 1988a; Kryzhitskii *et al.* 1989, 147), Panticapaeum (Tolstikov 1992, 71), and Myrmekion (Vinogradov Y. A. 1991; 1991a; 1994, 59). Very different explanations for these events have been given; however, with but one exception (Marchenko and Solovyov 1988, 53), all the explanations have shared the view that these changes are attributable to Greek population of the northern Black Sea colonies.

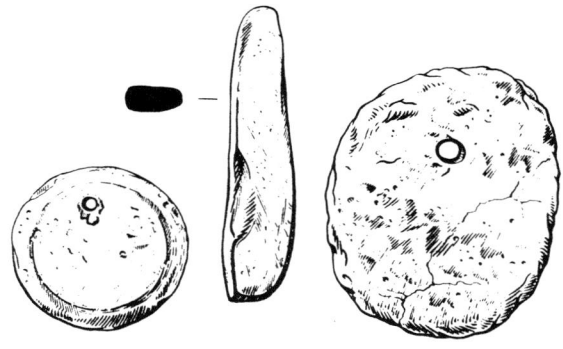

Fig. 97. Late Archaic weights and hone.

Fig. 98. Classical dugout dwelling 72 (Northwest Sector).

Dugout 72 had a rectangular form aligned north to south, and an area of 14m² (Figs. 97–99).[69] The depth of its trench easily surpassed 1m. The sides of the trench were vertical, and all four sides were reinforced with stone walls, which served also as a plinth for the mud-brick walls which held up the roof of the building. The leveling of the stone plinth was done irregularly, in an embedded system, and on one face small tightly-packed stones were used. On the front side, the plinth was coated with clay. The thickness of the plinth and walls did not exceed 0.35m.

The entrance into the building was set into its northern side – the northeast corner. From here a three-step staircase of large flat stones led into the dwelling. A large stove was located in the northwest corner of the building; the stove was set into the

---

[69] My numeration of the building complexes corresponds to the documentation composed during their excavation (Solovyov 1992a, 6).

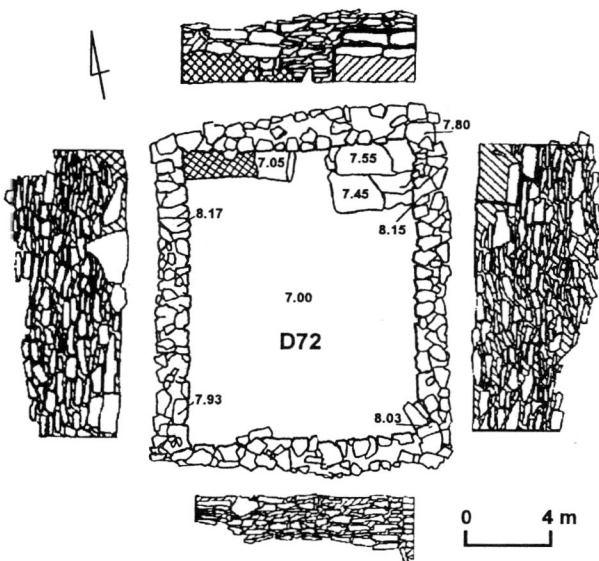

Fig. 99. Plan of dugout 72.

northern side of the building deeply enough that its flue could be built into the stone plinth. Smoke was vented outside through an opening in the ground located just outside the building.

The stove itself consisted of two horizontally-arranged parts, with an ashpit located to the right of the fire-box. The part of the stove which projected from the walls into the interior space of the dwelling was built of clay and straw (pisé). Its footing was also pisé, with a foundation consisting of pottery fragments and small stone slabs arranged on a bed of sea sand and shells.

The floor of the building was covered with a clay coating, which was repeatedly re-done as household trash accumulated. The surface of the floor and of the walls was in places scorched, or covered with black soot. Apparently, portable braziers or lamps were located in these places.[70]

The roof of the dugout was probably a two-sided, gabled one, supported by a gable balk and mud-brick walls the height of which (considering the steep pitch of the roof) could not have been very great.[71] The roof itself was most likely thatched

---

[70] I have provided such detailed descriptions of this and subsequent building complexes in order to demonstrate the solidity, durability, and high quality of the buildings, as well as to show the thoroughness with which these buildings were constructed. Based on these very same points, I would like to warn against the appearance in the literature of baseless attempts to interpret these buildings as temporary dwellings. Indisputably, the particular features of these buildings provide evidence that people lived in them for long periods of time, possibly their entire lives. The residents were probably seeking stability, and were not striving to put these buildings up quickly and with shoddy or superficial construction (as they would have done if building temporary dwellings). Finally, the extended functioning of these dwellings (which occupied not less than a quarter-century in each particular case) speaks for itself.

[71] I have in mind here the side walls, not end walls, of the building.

with reeds and held together with clay; its pressure on the walls corresponds neatly with the thickness indicated above.

Dugout 52 looked somewhat different (Fig. 99), although this building too had a stone wall reinforcing the sides of the trench to their greatest depth (1.1m).[72] This dugout had a rounded shape with a diameter of 4.1m. However, in all senses its construction seemed exceedingly modest, especially as far as its interior and living conditions were concerned. Thus, the front of the masonry was coated with clay, the pisé floor was repeatedly re-done, and the overall thickness of the floor-levels and of the levels of trash between them reached 0.20m. Traces of depressions of various types and sizes were found in the floor; these were primarily of a conical shape. Some of these were apparently used in supporting the roof, and the remainder evidently had an interior use, possibly for furniture and other household items set up inside the dwelling.

The particular features of the construction and layout of dugout 52 permit us to make some judgments about how the building was designed. Given the rounded shape of the building, the roof was probably conical. It is believed that two types of roof were possible here: braced and unbraced. However, it is very difficult to support either one of these interpretations over the other. In the second (unbraced) interpretation, the edge of the roof would have rested on the aboveground mud-brick part of the walls (which as shown before was reinforced by the sides of the trench) and on additional supports built around the sides. With either of the two roof types, the height of the mud-brick levels must have varied depending on the pitch of the roof itself. In the braced-roof interpretation, the pitch may have reached 40–50°, but in that case the construction of aboveground walls would have been pointless. At the same time, the most rational construction of the entrance (at the expense of interior space, which was precisely the principle applied in this case) must have been linked to the unbraced type of roof. Using this type of construction, the height of the roof would have been 1.8m, and its maximum height above ground level using a minimal pitch 170–210 would have been 2.7m. It is important to add that the absence of a hole for a central support column (such a column being required the unbraced type of roof) should not be seen as negating the layout proposed here, since it is impossible to exclude the possibility that a stone footing was used instead for the central support pole.

Although it cannot be proved conclusively that dugout 52 functioned as a residence, this is very likely the correct interpretation. The hypothesis that it was a residence is supported by a number of indirect factors: the solid and meticulous construction, the interior finish and regular renovation of the floor (and, indeed, the fact that the level of the floor rose over time due to the formation a level of household rubbish, including cinders and other traces of daily living), and also pits for holding vessels. All of these indicators distinguish dugout 52 from the already well-known buildings which had a more household purpose.

---

[72] This was, more precisely, the stone plinth or footing of a mud-brick wall, as was the case in dugout No. 72. The thickness of the plinth was 0.35–0.40m, and on one side it was built in a double-layer embedded system breaking up the evenness of the layering. The frontal side was built of stone, sometimes boulders, of various (but mainly medium) sizes. The second layer, which adjoined the side of the foundation trench, was composed of small stones with clay. In one place (where the plinth rests on the loose fill of an earlier earthen building), the layer was reinforced with an adobe wall built of one brick and set on a foundation of large, undressed limestone slabs. This additional wall was 0.42m wide.

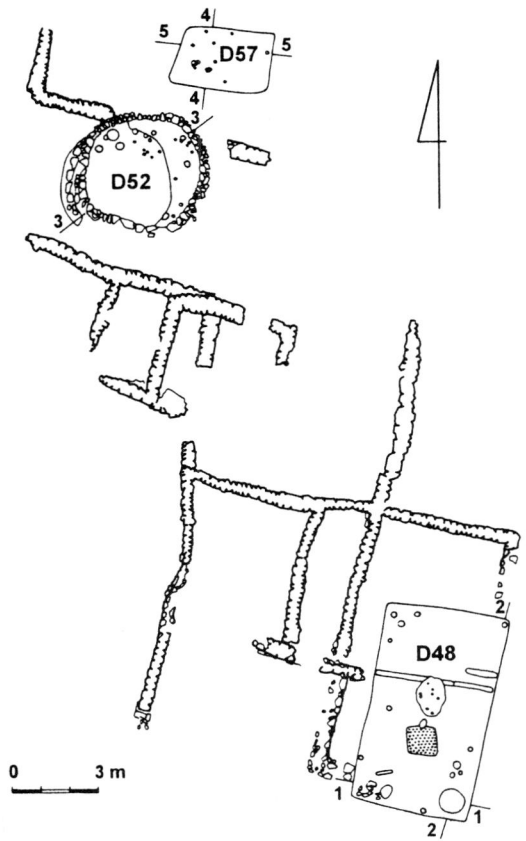

Fig. 100. Plan of the settlement with the Classical dugouts 52, 57 and 48 (Northwest Sector).

There is one additional building of the same period, located not far from the one just described above, which may serve to support the conclusion that dugout 52 had a residential purpose. Dugout 57 (Figs. 99; 100, 5–6), unlike 52, had a roughly rectangular form measuring 2.3 × 3.3m, and the building was oriented latitudinally. The depth of the trench apparently did not exceed 1.0m. The corners of the building were rounded, and its sides vertical. There was no coating on the walls or floor. A slipshod and haphazard layout, very simple interior finish, and an almost total lack of detailing in the interior are all typical indicators of a household building, and all were characteristic of dugout 57. Furthermore, the remains of portable braziers were found in the building's fill. Considering the position of holes in the floor (two of which held stone rubble), the building probably had a single-sloping (ungabled) roof inclined to the north. Therefore its entrance was evidently on the southern side.

Finally, one more building ought to be mentioned: dugout 48 (Figs. 100–102), which also had a rectangular shape (measuring 7.3 × 4.1m), and which was aligned north-northeast to south-southwest. This building was dug into the cultural level 1.1m deep below the level of ancient soil surface. The sides of the trench (which had cleanly-cut right angles) were strictly vertical, and in some places on them a clay coating was preserved. The floor of the building turned out to be composed of clay and straw (pisé).

Dugout 48 consisted of two premises divided by a wall of interwoven tree branches. The foundation of this wattle fencing was buried 0.15m into the floor. The two spaces differed not only in size but also in their interior detail. In the larger, southern room, which had an area of 18.5m², there was an open-style pisé hearth in the center of the space, a pear-shaped household pit in the northeast corner, and a pisé "table" with stone edging (found in extremely poor condition) in the southwest corner. The single major interior detail found in the smaller northern room (10m²) was a wattle fence in the southwest corner. The fenced-off area, which measured about 5m², seems to

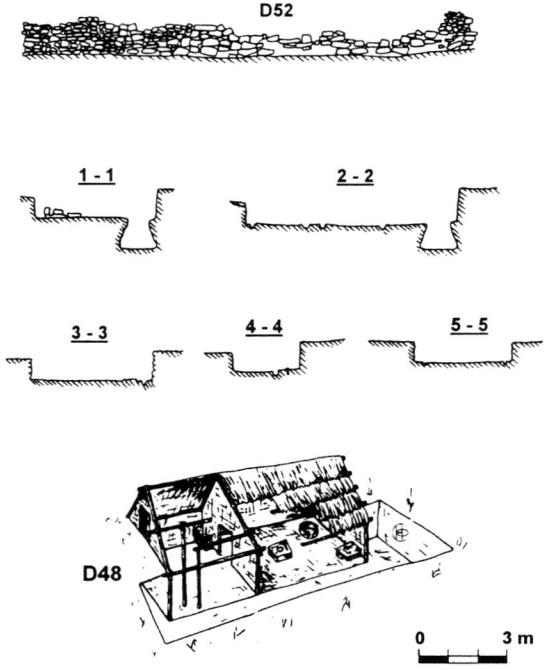

*Fig. 101. The Classical dugouts: sections (48, 52, 57)
and reconstruction (48).*

have been used to keep small domestic animals. Aside from all this, it is worth mentioning one further detail – the floor of the northwest corner of the room was slightly scorched, indicating that a portable clay brazier may have stood there.

The differences between the interiors of the northern and southern parts of dugout 48 are evidently related to their different functions as working and living areas. The embrasure of the door between the two premises, about 1.0m wide, was located in the middle of the wattle fence. In this layout design, the entry into the dugout must have been located in the blank northern end of the building. Interior space was used in building the entry.

This description of the ruins of dugout 48, supplemented by data on the location of support-holes in its floor used in building its roof, makes it possible to present a general view of the building's external appearance. There can be little doubt that in this case the unbraced type of gabled roof was used; the roof included a level of trusses along the gable purlin and along the edges of the trench, and also used additional support posts set up in the corners of the building. The central purlin rested on two columns in the southern room and on the northern aboveground end-wall built of mud-bricks, the collapse of which filled in the entire nearby portion of the trench. Taking into account the possible height of the door embrasure, the pitch of the roof probably approached 40^0.

In determining the time during which this building complex functioned, a stratigraphic analysis of the site and an examination of material from the fill inside the trench were used. It has been established that all four buildings were located on that part of the settlement which had earlier been built up with aboveground mud-brick residential houses. These houses were abandoned by their inhabitants not later than first third of the 5th century BC, and it is now clear that in constructing the dugouts the stone plinths of the walls and the courtyard paving of the aboveground houses were partially dismantled. Some part of this material was apparently used to erect stone constructions inside the dugouts themselves. Furthermore, there is little doubt that by the time the latter were built, the aboveground houses had already been destroyed and covered over with levels of mud-brick rubble and household

Fig. 102. The Classical dugout 48.

rubbish. From this it is easy to determine the *terminus post quem* for erecting the new dugout buildings. There remains only the unresolved question of the precise date of construction in each particular case, inasmuch as there is good reason to propose a more or less prolonged interval between the abandonment of the aboveground houses and the construction of the dugouts. The resolution of this question will no doubt depend on the results of an analysis of material found *in situ* and in the fill of the foundation-trenches.

In one of the support-holes in dugout 52, a large fragment of Attic black-glazed cup was found; this may be dated to 450–430 BC (Sparkes and Talcott 1970, Pl. 19, 413). Among the finds from the fill of the foundation-trench, even more suggestive were fragments of Attic black-glazed vessels, mainly cups, and also pieces of red-clay amphorae from Chios, Thasos and Mende. These materials date from the second and third quarters of the 5th century BC. Thus, it is possible to assert that dugout 52 was constructed literally just a few years after the desertion of the aboveground house, and in the third quarter of the same century it had already ceased functioning.

Most likely the life of dugouts 57 and 72 was confined within the same period of time. This is indicated not only by the similar stratigraphy, which was laid down as a result of the construction of a household building, but also by a complex of finds chronologically quite like those described above. According to an analysis of material from dugout 72, the building functioned at the same time as dugout 52 or possibly slightly later. Even more indicative in this regard were two cast copper coins, shaped like dolphins, with the letters ΘY on one side (Fig. 104). Such coins circulated in the Lower Bug region in the second half of the 5th century BC (Karyshkovskii 1988, 36–7).[73]

The stone plinths of the walls of an aboveground house were also dismantled in the construction of dugout 48. The house had been abandoned by its inhabitants at

---

[73] According to V.A. Anokhin (1989, 17), these coins could be dated 430–410 BC.

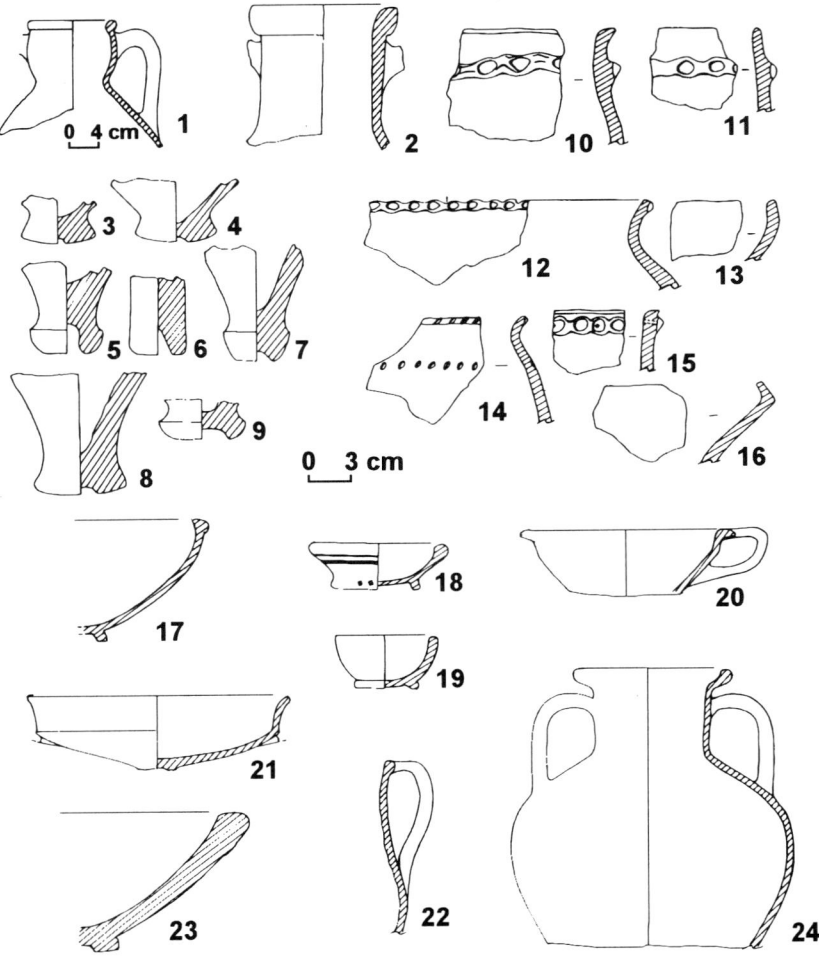

Fig. 103. Finds from the Classical dugouts.

the end of the first third of the 5th century BC. However, unlike the other dugouts already described, the construction of this one took place much later, in the last quarter of the 5th century BC (and even more probably at the very end of that century). This is indicated by the dating of a large mass of material from the fill of the trench, which included numerous fragments of amphorae from Chios, Thasos, Mende, and Heraklea, and also fragments of kitchen- and tableware. In addition, finding Olbian copper coins of 385–365 BC (Fig. 105) in the fill of the dugout's foundation-trench serves as a definite *terminus post quem non* (Karyshkovskii 1978, 99). Consequently, considering all the dates discussed above relating to dugout 48, it is reasonable to believe that the building functioned in the later years of the 5th century BC and in the first two decades of the following century.

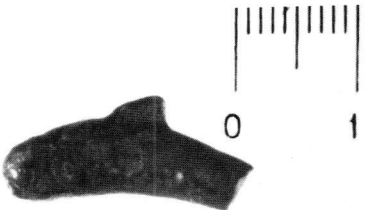

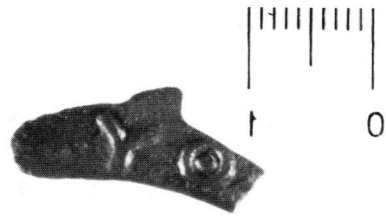

Fig. 104.1. Copper coin from dugout 72 (B.90.269).

Fig. 104.2. Copper coin from dugout 72 (B.90.269).

The data shown above regarding building on Berezan in the 5th century BC surely change our conception of the dynamics involved in the cultural and historical development of the site. First of all, it is important to note that the territory of the settlement which was abandoned by its inhabitants apparently did not remain empty very long. After just a short time the area was repopulated. There is good reason to believe that the length of the interval between these events could have been minimal. It is also clear that the renewed building differed fundamentally from that which had taken place before in all key elements of construction: in the layout

Fig. 105. Olbian copper coin from dugout 48 (B.87.261).

of the dwellings, in the planning and regulation of the overall structure of the settlement, and in the scale of construction. On this basis, one may assume that the return to dugout construction after an almost 60–year period of building aboveground houses of stone and mud-bricks, and maintaining a civil structure for the settlement, was in no way connected to the Greek part of the Borysthenes population.

Such an assumption becomes even more appropriate if the building complexes under discussion here can be placed into one evolutionary set along with Berezan dugouts of the Late Archaic period. A very small number of the latter were still functioning at the beginning of the 5th century BC in outlying areas of the residential zone.[74] Without a doubt the construction of full and partial dugouts was in many ways a more primitive endeavor than aboveground building with mud-bricks and stone, not to mention other distinctions which come to light when comparing the two types of construction practice: social and psychological (Solovyov 1989, 12–4).[75]

---

[74] In this regard, it is important to remind the reader that aboveground residential building of the Greek type was widespread on Berezan after the end of the 6th century BC, and that after the start of the 5th century BC this type of construction also spread widely at Olbia and in many other settlements in the Lower Bug region (Kryzhitskii 1987).

[75] This approach to studying aspects of culture, including building and its various traditions (and not only in the area of technique), can be very productive. However, this approach also takes us into scholarly fields related to archaeology – anthropology, and even further into cultural studies – fields which have successfully and for a long time addressed these questions. Still, the presumed linkage of these fields with archaeology is a question which used to evoke keen discussion. This is an issue which will have to be decided on the level of theory.

Following from this, it is justified to raise the issue of the ethnocultural identity of the creators of the dwellings described above.

It is thought that the construction of dugouts on Berezan in the second half of the 5th through the beginning of the 4th centuries BC may have resulted from at least three factors. These will be discussed below in increasing order of probability.

First, in the second quarter of the 5th century BC for some reason a harsh and abrupt impoverishment of the population took place, including a decline in living conditions – irrespective of ethnocultural identity. If we assume that this event occurred with the Greek colonists, it is completely unclear how they differed from the inhabitants of the northeastern part of the ancient peninsula, an area which followed Hellenic principles of urban construction during the entire 5th century BC and even much later. Furthermore, for the non-Greek population of Borysthenes dugout buildings and the way of life associated with them were familiar, even traditional. Thus it seems unlikely that economic considerations could have a significant rôle in explaining the aforementioned changes in Classical Berezan's building activities.

Arguments about social organization also do not seem very convincing. The only reasonable theory, proposing the settlement in Borysthenes of a new, large group of colonists not possessing full civic rights, does not stand up to the well-known fact that Miletus ceased its colonial activities after it was taken by the Persians in 494 BC. Of course, there is little doubt that socially independent population groups did exist in the Lower Bug region, including the non-Greek population above all. The latter circumstance can help to resolve the question, but only in the event that the shift of cultural, architectural, and building traditions is seen as the result of one ethnic group replacing another; or if, more simply, the heterogeneous indigenous population of the Berezan periphery and the culturally homogeneous Greek colonists are considered one and the same. And this, finally, is the third and most probable reason for the appearance on Berezan of the dugout structures described above.

Admittedly, at the present time it is unlikely that the last assertion can be supported by some substantive material, mainly because of a lack of sufficient data on the period of time in question. The complex of hand-made pottery from those dugouts which have been studied has also revealed very little.[76] As expected, the complex was dominated by vessels of a Scythian steppe appearance; these were broadly distributed across the entire northern Black Sea region from the beginning of the 5th century BC (Marchenko 1988, 122).

Recent material from the Borysthenes necropolis, however, may be more valuable (Domanskii *et al.* 1989, 38*ff*). Here, burials of the 5th century BC possess a series of graves containing bones in distorted positions, which may be attributed to the non-Greek population of the peninsula. Also attributable to the non-Greeks, and found in the upper levels of the necropolis, are numerous uninventoried burials of people in distorted poses. However, it must be said that this material has, thus far, not been studied sufficiently to work out the issues posed above. In order to resolve these

---

[76] I also note that the proportion of hand-made pottery found in the dugouts did not exceed 10% (of course, not including amphorae). The ceramic complex found in dwellings dating to the concluding phase of the Late Archaic dugout construction possessed quite similar characteristics.

issues the most helpful task at the present time would be to work out the history itself of the Lower Bug region in the first half of the 5th century BC.

At the end of the first third of the 5th century BC, cultural and historical conditions in the Dnieper-Bug region were changing in fundamental ways. Clarifying the reasons for these changes has created much scholarly activity in recent years.[77] Without delving too deeply into the details, it is important to note at least that which all academics concede: at the end of the first third of the 5th century BC, against the backdrop of real threat to the well-being of the Olbian state from the Scythians, there was a swift reduction in the size of the city-state's outlying areas. It is also evident that the rural, agricultural periphery of Borysthenes did not escape this fate, nor did its urban territory (which has been discussed above).

Unstable political circumstances in the steppe zone of the northern Black Sea apparently inflicted a serious blow on the Borysthenes economy; the traditional economic links between the city-state and the tribes of forest-steppe Scythia were destroyed. These links had constituted one of the most important conditions for Borysthenes' well-being. Furthermore, the growing external danger created a very real physical threat to the colonists; graves of those who perished from Scythian arrows and spears became quite common in the Berezan necropolis by the beginning of the 5th century BC (Domanskii *et al.* 1989, 56–60). The consequences of these and other negative factors for life at Borysthenes were irreversible. Ultimately, these factors led to economic collapse and reduced the size of the population; these problems, in turn, led a decline in the construction industry and brought about both an abrupt contraction of the area occupied by aboveground houses and an increase in the construction of dugouts. During the 5th century BC the Berezan settlement gradually lost its earlier urban characteristics and its political independence, becoming first a trading port of the Olbian state, and then an ordinary rural settlement of the Olbian periphery. Even the construction of a temple to the east of the settlement in the 5th century BC changed nothing regarding Berezan's status.

Olbia, which had broad potential for territorial and demographic growth (which distinguished this city advantageously from Berezan), became the political and economic centre of the Lower Bug region in the 5th century BC. During the confused period of ethno-political instability in Scythia, Olbia evidently became a refuge for the mixed population of its outlying regions. These people came together near the walls of Olbia and formed a small settlement there in the second quarter of the 5th century BC.[78] It is believed that at the time there may have been an overflow into

---

[77] Y. G. Vinogradov (1989, 81–7) provides the most detailed overview of different points of view on this issue. The single, fundamental difference between them consists in the fact that some scholars see the main source of these changes in the internal development of the Olbia, while others prefer foreign policy reasons for the observed transformations.

[78] Interpreting this as a temporary settlement of Greek immigrants (Kozub 1979, 3*ff*) is rarely supported by academics, most of whom lean toward the idea that the residents of this settlement were mainly indigenous people who were economically or (possibly) socially associated with the Olbia (Marchenko 1982; Vinogradov Y. G. 1989, 83). In this regard it is supposed that the main function of the settlement was to safeguard a basic nucleus of the agricultural population from the threat of physical destruction at the hands of nomads (Marchenko 1982, 134*ff*).

Olbia of part of the urban (and possibly rural) population of Borysthenes (Vinogradov Y. G. 1989, 82).[79]

It is therefore possible to assume that the appearance of dugout buildings in the western part of Berezan, on the outskirts of 5th century BC urban construction, was also linked to non-Greek inhabitants of outlying areas moving in. Having found themselves in an unpleasant and life-threatening situation, these people were apparently compelled to find protection near the Greek community – which itself, having declined in numbers by this time, was probably living with just the same fears. The abovementioned material from the Berezan necropolis provides evidence that such fears were hardly groundless. Nevertheless, judging from the high level of activity in the settlement in the second half of the 5th century BC, Berezan's location on a peninsula apparently provided its inhabitants with relative safety.[80]

As far as functioning is concerned, in my opinion, the indigenous settlement which existed on the outskirts of Berezan from the second quarter of the 5th to the first quarter of the 4th centuries BC[81] was very similar to the environs near Olbia of the same time. The fundamental features of building and the basic characteristics of material culture in the two places are very close. This assertion is supported by current conceptions of the social, economic, and cultural-historical character of these settlements.[82] Still, it would be remiss not to point out that the structural layout of the two settlements was not exactly alike. This latter observation cannot be used as a persuasive argument that the two were functionally dissimilar, and only provides evidence of the new settlements' originality. The reasons for this originality hinge on the ethnic and cultural heterogeneity of the rural population of the Lower Bug region, a phenomenon which to the present time remains very difficult to understand adequately.[83]

---

[79] In this instance, urban inhabitants of Borysthenes were probably accommodated inside the boundaries of the settlement. It is important to note, however, that the fixed outflow of Berezan residents may have been directed toward other nearby cities in the northwestern Pontus. One of these other cities, for instance, may have been Kerkinitis, where mass urban construction culturally reminiscent of the Olbia-Berezan region was begun in the second quarter of the 5th century BC (Kutaisov 1986, 95–6; 1990, 145–6). Above all, at Kerkinitis certain features of the layout and design, home-building, and interior spaces of residential buildings, and the monetary system, showed striking similarities with the same types of characteristic at Berezan and Olbia.

[80] Although defensive installations at Borysthenes have not been found, it is still reasonable to assume that such constructions may have been set up on the spit of land which in ancient times connected the island with the mainland.

[81] The date at which permanent habitation in the northwestern part of the settlement in the Classical period came to an end is provided by material found in household pits in the area. The pits were filled in by the second quarter of the 4th century BC, and probably closer to the beginning of that quarter-century.

[82] For all its attractiveness, the hypothesis that dwellings and household structures quite similar in basic features to those of the Olbian environs existed on Berezan in the 5th century BC requires much additional evidence, since the data we have at our disposal is clearly insufficient to make a fully persuasive case. However, one can hope that continuing archaeological excavations on Berezan will enable us to clarify the issue.

[83] Conceding the completely disordered character of dugouts Nos. 48, 52, and 72, it is important to note that many particular features of their construction still find close analogues in the building techniques of both previous and subsequent periods (Domanskii *et al.* 1989, 36; Marchenko and Solovyov 1988, 49–54).

Thus, the data available today on the Lower Bug region of the Classical period leave little other course but to concede that the serious internal and external stresses which determined the fate of the peoples of the northern Black Sea in the 5th century BC (Vinogradov Y. G. 1989, 81–7; Marchenko and Vinogradov 1989, 807*ff*) had different historical consequences for Borysthenes (Berezan) and Olbia. The former experienced total collapse, the latter an unprecedented flowering (Kryzhitskii 1985, 174–5; Vinogradov Y. G. 1989, 123). Despite the contraction of its outlying rural areas at the time, the Olbia city-state was able to achieve great success economically and politically (and, possibly, to eliminate a rival in the form of Berezan settlement). Indeed, it is thought that the inclusion of the Berezan settlement in the Olbian state represented a natural result of the region's historical development. In my opinion, all these successes became possible mainly thanks to the political flair and diplomatic flexibility of Olbian leaders, who were apparently able to find an optimal mean to co-exist peacefully with warlike nomads.[84] In this way, Olbia could provide relative safety for its citizens. Furthermore, having paid lip service to the authority of the Scythian king and providing him regular tribute,[85] Olbia was able not only to preserve its economic and human potential, but also to continue expanding. Olbia continued its expansion until such time (the end of the 5th century BC) when it became possible to re-consolidate the outlying areas which had formerly belonged to it (Vinogradov Y. A. and Marchenko 1985; 1991, 152*ff*; Golovacheva *et al.* 1991), and take in new areas as well, the northwest Crimea in particular (Vinogradov Y. G. and Shcheglov 1990, 313*ff*).

By the middle of the 5th century BC, the Olbia *polis* had become the sole political and economic, and primary religious, center in the Lower Bug region. By virtue of having taken in former Berezan residents, Olbia received the right to a second name: Borysthenes. This name apparently belonged to Olbia at the time the city was visited by Herodotus. His reference (Hdt. 4. 17–18, 24) to the demotikon "Olbiopolites" and to the "Borysthenes /*Borystheneiteon emporion*" toponym suggests that Herodotus probably had heard both names. Moreover, Herodotus (4. 17) also knew of the " Port of the Borysthenites", which can be interpreted in three different ways: as a nameless harbour in the Lower Bug area, as name for the Berezan settlement at that very time, or, finally, as a reminiscence of that settlement's ancient name (*Cf*: Dovatur *et al.* 1982, 222–3).

---

[84] Probably in the form of a protectorate over Olbia held by one of the Scythian leaders: *basileus* according to Herodotus (Hdt. 4. 78–80). These may have included Ariapeithes himself, father of Skyles and Oktamasades, a trusted friend of whom was Tymnes, who is known as one of Herodotus' informants in Olbia (Hdt. 4. 76).

[85] The possibility of existence in the 5th century BC of such attitudes between the Greek *poleis* and Scyth-nomads proves to be true (Solomonik 1987; *cf*: Vinogradov Y. G. 1989, 91).

PART 5

Berezan in the Hellenistic and Roman Periods

A. The Berezan settlement in the second half of the 4th through the 3rd centuries BC

The entire subsequent history of ancient Berezan is that of a group of agrarian and fishing settlements barely distinguishable among other population centres of the Olbian periphery.[86] The archaeological evidence available today from the Hellenistic period is so small that it does not allow us to draw a complete picture of the life of the settlement during that time. The volume and completeness of the information available in no way compares with the evidence we have from earlier periods. In fact, the data can be reduced to just a few separate, unrelated artifacts; these consist mainly of relatively few pieces of pottery, incidental scraps of walls, a few exceptional cases of distinct parts of rooms, and a few very rare structures preserved in their entirety (such as cisterns, wells, household pits and basements).[87] Even less is known about the spatial organization of the settlement during this time. Therefore, it is possible only to make the most general judgments about the character of the Berezan settlement in the Hellenistic period.

First of all, it is worth noting that the settlement's residential area was extremely small, and did not extend beyond the northeast corner of the ancient peninsula. The aboveground construction which did occur there was very similar in character to buildings of the well-known agrarian settlements of the Olbian periphery of the second half of the 4th through the first third of the 3rd centuries BC.[88] Like most of these settlements, Berezan was probably an urbanized settlement of the *chora* of Olbia. From the time that the indigenous settlement on the western outskirts of the settlement

---

[86] For the latest and most complete review of these archaeological sites, see: Kryzhitskii *et al.* 1989, 96*ff*.

[87] At excavations in the eastern section (especially its southern part) of the island in the 1970s, V.V. Lapin distinctly revealed the cultural level of the Hellenistic period (Lapin 1978, 207*ff*). The construction remains in that level were none other than the ruins of a entire complex of dwellings, some which were apparently of remarkable size (as Lapin reported in his field notes for 1971, the area of the courtyard of one of these buildings was greater than 60m²). It has been established that basement rooms were often used in these buildings, and that a layered foundation had been applied in the construction of one of the houses. Unfortunately, none of this material has been published, due to Lapin's unexpected death in 1980.

[88] The most recent information on the characteristics of building in the rural settlements of outlying Olbian areas in the 5th-3rd centuries BC can be found in the studies of the Ukrainian archaeologists (Kryzhitskii *et al.* 1989, 103*ff*). This work, unfortunately, suffers from vexing problems regarding many important sites in the Lower Bug region dating from that period, and unjustifiably disregards certain important features (especially dugout construction, which is widely represented at these sites: Marchenko and Solovyov 1988a; Golovacheva *et al.* 1991).

(which was described in a previous section) was abandoned by its inhabitants, the construction of dugout dwellings was apparently discontinued. That may or may not be the case, but in any event no evidence has yet been found on Berezan of dugouts dating to the second half of the 4th century BC. If that is the case, today it remains only to determine the reasons behind the fact that, during the Hellenistic period, the only houses put up were of the aboveground type.

There is even sparser data available today about the inhabitants of the settlement during the time in question. Practically nothing is known of their social and ethnic composition, or of their political and legal status within the Olbian state. It is known only that they worked mainly in agriculture and fishing, apparently receiving all the household supplies they needed from the centre of the *polis*. The fact that coins from this time are found but rarely indicates that not much coins were circulated through the Berezan settlement.

By the 4th century BC Berezan had already lost its importance as a trading harbour, although it regularly received overseas imports (mainly wine, which is evidenced by finds of amphorae and imported tableware). These materials were mainly products of Athenian workshops: tableware of various types, apparently the very cheapest; and also ceramic jugs from Heraklea, Sinope, Crimean Chersonesus, Chios, and (to a lesser extent) Thasos. It is thought, however, that all these goods wound up at Berezan from Olbia itself, as a result of intermediary trading. From Olbia a large mass of simple table- and kitchenware of gray and red clay must have been brought to Berezan, since the settlement's pottery industry was practically nonexistent (with the exception, of course, of hand-made pottery, which was probably produced here).

It is likely that the Berezan settlement stopped playing any sort of significant rôle in the Olbian state by the second half of the 4th century BC. References or even allusions to Berezan are completely absent in written sources from that time. At the end of the first third of the 3rd century BC, the unfortunate fate of the remaining Olbian outlying areas befell Berezan as well.[89] Like all the many settlements in the area, Berezan was abandoned by its inhabitants, who evidently did not have the strength to withstand the pressure exerted by the nomads, and probably took refuge behind Olbia's walls. Weak, barely detectable traces of permanent living on Berezan at the end of the 3rd century BC were probably linked to a very brief, periodic revival of the *chora* of Olbia, a revival which was already concluded by the beginning of the following century (Marchenko 1991, 32–3).

---

[89] In regard to the time that habitation came to an end in the rural settlements of the Olbian outlying region the dating proposed by K. K. Marchenko (1991, 291*ff*) is to be preferred over that proposed by S. D. Kryzhitskii and his colleagues (1989, 100) – the middle of the 3rd century BC. Marchenko's dating is also preferable to that proposed by V. V. Ruban (1985, 43) – the beginning of the third quarter of the 3rd century BC. In these two instances, the date given is clearly too high, and is not supported by the archaeological material of the Olbian rural settlements themselves. The fact that the abandonment of the *chora* of Olbia coincided with similar events in other areas of the northern Black Sea indicates indisputably that these changes had a global character. These shifts can probably be attributed to the recurrent, broad-scale destabilization of the Scythian steppe zone in the 3rd century BC, which was linked primarily to the westward expansion of the Sarmatians (Vinogradov Y. A. and Marchenko 1991, 153). This overall destabilization brought about substantial changes in the arrangement of military and political forces in the northern Black Sea; these shifts were in turn directly reflected in the economies of the coastal Greek cities, including Olbia.

A major lacuna exists in contemporary data on the subsequent history of the Berezan settlement. This gap of information extends over, practically the entire post-Hellenistic period. Many years of excavations on the island have revealed no building ruins which can be reliably dated to these times, although a few material finds (mainly pottery) are known. Either there was no fixed settlement on Berezan in the 2nd century BC through the 1st century AD[90], or the absence of traces could be a consequence of destructive natural forces having ruined even minor remains of a settlement (Lapin 1978, 75). The future will tell. The archaeologically demonstrable fact is that permanent living on the island resumed only sometime in the middle of the 2nd century AD. To be sure, before that time the island had managed to become, though not for long, something completely different.

B. The Berezan settlement in the first centuries AD

Starting even in 19th century, research on Berezan island and in its surrounding areas came across inscriptions, most of them on marble slabs. The content of these inscriptions indicated their direct connection to the cult of one of the most revered heroes of ancient Greece: Achilles (Otreshko 1979a; Shelov-Kovedyaev 1990; Rusyaeva 1992, 70–83). The main sanctuary of Achilles was the island of Leuke (the modern island Zmeinyi), located not far from the mouth of the Dniester River. It is known from written sources that for a long time this sanctuary was under the protection of Olbia, which accorded the Achilles cult official status (Vinogradov Y. G. 1994, 19–21).

Archaeological material from both Berezan and Olbia provide direct evidence that Achilles had been a highly-revered deity in the Lower Bug region since the Archaic period (Rusyaeva 1987, 140*ff*; 1992, 71; Kryzhitskii *et al.* 1989, 88). In the minds of the inhabitants of the area he was endowed with a variety of capabilities, most important of which was his connection to the underworld and to water elements, etc. All these capabilities of the immortal hero were embodied during Roman times in the state cult of Achilles, mainly in his two incarnations: Hero and Pontarches. In one form or the other Achilles was probably worshipped throughout the territory of the Olbian state. However, just as in the Archaic period, his primary domain probably extended to the west of Olbia, which is made indisputably clear by the geographic distribution of finds of dedicatory inscriptions to him (Otreshko 1979a; Rusyaeva 1992, 77–80).

At the present time, 43 dedications to Achilles are known. Of these, 28 are dedicated only to Pontarches (Shelov-Kovedyaev 1990, 49–50). These inscriptions were addressed to the deeply-revered hero of the Olbia people in the names of leading

---

[90] This was a very difficult period in the history of Olbia, filled with economic problems and social and military conflicts (Vinogradov Y. G. 1989, 228*ff*). One of these conflicts ended tragically for the city (its crushing defeat by the Getae under the leadership of Burebista). By this time the inhabitants of Olbia hardly had the strength to support the functioning of its inner *chora*. And if anyone at this time recalled Berezan, it was fishermen who from time to time visited the island for a more or less extended period. Only in the 1st century AD was there some noticeable activity, in areas rather distant from the city. It is believed that fortified settlements began to appear at that time – future settlements of the Roman period (Buiskikh 1991, 102*ff*).

citizens: *archontes, agoranomoi, strategoi,* and priests (*i.e.,* primarily from representatives of the highest levels of the city magistracy). It is important to note that one-third of these finds were created on Berezan, which supports the opinion of those academics who hold that the island was a centre of worship for Achilles in Olbia after her defeat by the Getae (Shelov-Kovedyaev 1990, 61*ff; cf.:* Rusyaeva 1992, 80–1; Vinogradov 1994, 21). Scholars believe that the appearance of a sanctuary on Berezan at the time was a measure compelled by the loss of Olbia's control over the Greek sanctuary of Achilles on Leuke (Rusyaeva 1992, 79–80).

To a significant extent, such propositions are supported by one of the dedicatory inscriptions recently found at Berezan (Fig. 106). In the justified opinion of the scholar who published it (Shelov-Kovedyaev 1990), this inscription is a unique example of local poetry glorifying Achilles Pontarches, who had received possession of the island. The latter point is one of the most important pieces of documentary evidence indicating that that event had taken place not long before the creation of the inscription. Another important feature of the document is that it indicates unambiguously that at the time Borysthenes (Berezan) was an island, which supports the information provided by Roman authors that there were two islands of Achilles in the Black Sea and refutes the widely-held opinion that Berezan remained a peninsula until nearly the very end of antiquity (Shilik 1978, 78; Agbunov 1985, 116–26, 160). Finally, this inscription, which the publisher dates to the second half of the 1st century AD, also corroborates the words of Dio Chrysostom (36. 9, 14, 25) – who visited Olbia at around this time – regarding the special reverence for Homer and his immortal epic *The Iliad* among the Olbiopolites, who knew the work by heart (Shelov-Kovedyaev 1990, 58).

Unlike the previous inscription, two other dedications to Achilles (found in 1989) appear to be traditional, rather terse formulations (Vinogradov Y. G. 1994, 20–1). In one case (Fig. 107), the dedicator was probably a collegium of *agoranomoi;* in the other case (Fig. 108), a priest of the hero cult.

It is important to pay particular attention to the conditions under which these inscriptions were found. According to data from the excavations themselves, all were discovered in dugouts of the next period of permanent living on the settlement. It has been established that in that period the dedications were not used for their original purpose. For instance, the slab with the previously-mentioned poetic hymn served as a base for the central support column holding up the roof of the dwelling.[91] Two other slabs, were apparently used as steps for the entry. There is an impression that the spirit of Hellenic culture and its religious values were alien to the inhabitants of these dwellings, which also differed from Olbiopolites in their way of life. All of this strikes the eye immediately, especially in regard to the archaeological material from the Berezan settlement in the 2nd and 3rd centuries AD.

Until recently, almost all the information we have about the settlement in Roman times came from excavations on the eastern coast of the island. Traces of life and activity were found there by Lapin; these traces comprised a well-articulated cultural level of the 2nd-3rd centuries AD, containing numerous building remains and material finds (mainly pottery). Research on Roman Berezan was conducted most actively in

---

[91] In the article of F.V. Shelov-Kovedyaev (1990, 49) the archaeological context of the finding of the inscription is described incorrectly.

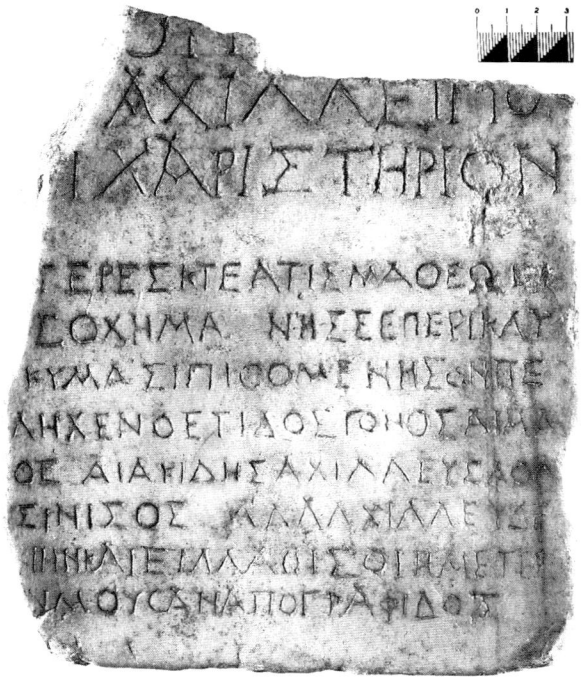

Fig. 106. Marble slab with hymn to Achilles Pontarches of the second half of 1st century AD (B.88.149).

Fig. 107. Marble slab with the dedication to Achilles Pontarches of the early 2nd century AD (B.89.376).

Fig. 108. Marble slab with the dedication to Achilles Pontarches of the first half of 2nd century AD (B.89.375).

the late 1970s (during the final years of Lapin's life), and unfortunately much of the work was left unfinished. The buildings found by Lapin seemed to be small, rather disordered houses of many rooms, not particularly distinguishable in appearance from the well-known rural buildings of outlying Olbian areas during the time in question.[92] The owners of these buildings were probably Greek peasants and artisans, citizens of the Olbian state.

The one exception found up to the present time is a building recently unearthed by a Ukrainian expedition on a site located a not far west of Lapin's excavation. Rectangular in form and possessing a large area, this building was single-chambered. Its main layout axes were oriented along the cardinal compass directions – lengthwise along a north-south line (where two stone bases for support columns were situated), and transversely east-west. In the opinion of V. V. Nazarov (1994, 89–90), who excavate this complex, the building was not used as a residence but possibly had some kind of social (probably cult) purpose.[93]

The aboveground buildings of Roman times on Berezan evidently made up an irregular and disorderly conglomeration. From this, and also from the absence of a continuous, uninterrupted cultural level from Roman times, Lapin (1968, 155) drew the conclusion that layout and planning had been "scattered and incoherent" in the 2nd and 3rd centuries AD.

In recent years excavations in the western part of the island have revealed a different kind of evidence about life at the settlement in the 2nd and 3rd centuries AD (Solovyov 1994, 93; 1995b). In the northwest area, about ten dugout dwellings from that time

---

[92] See, for instance: Burakov 1976, 16*ff.* The fullest presentation of building in the Olbian region in Roman times can be found in the writings of Ukrainian archaeologists (Kryzhitskii *et al.* 1989, 162*ff.*).

[93] Agreeing completely with the view that the building's function could not have been residential, there are insufficient grounds to interpret it as a building intended for social purposes. The coins and red-glazed pottery found in the building, which form the basis for Nazarov's suppositions, can also be seen as an indication of some other use; for example, as a storehouse or trading room.

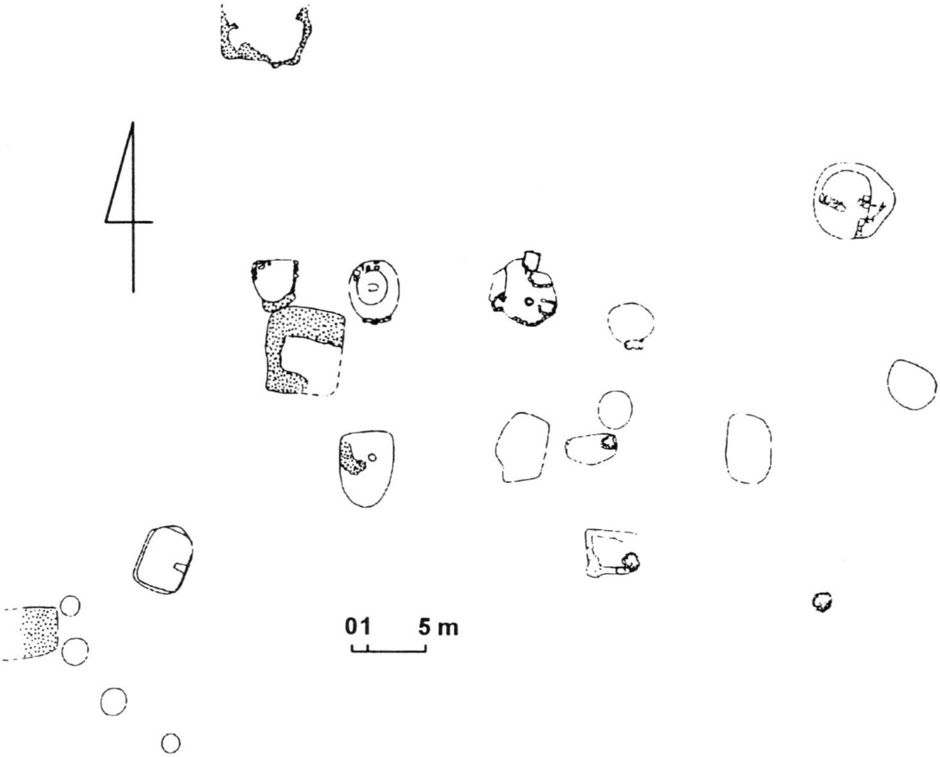

Fig. 109. Plan of Roman Berezan with dugout dwellings (Northwest Sector).

Fig. 110. Dugout of the Roman period.

were unearthed (Fig. 109). The area of the buildings varied little, from 10 to 18m², and as a rule the depth of their foundation-trenches exceeded 1m (Fig. 110). All these dugouts were rectangular (or close to it) in form. Judging from the frequent absence of pits in the floor for support columns and of the remains of mud-brick walls, one cannot exclude the possibility that a braced type of gabled roof was used, supported by the edge of the trench. In one case, the remains of fence-type walls, coated with clay, were found around the perimeter of a dwelling. The use of stone in the construction of dugouts was evidently episodic, and was usually connected with reinforcing separate parts of the sides of a trench or with building aboveground stone walls. One feature characteristic of the interior of earthen dwellings on Berezan in Roman times was a two-part stove (Fig. 111), divided vertically and built into the side of the foundation-trench. The base and sides of the stove were set with stone slabs, the arch was coated with a thick level of clay, and the footing was built of pisé. In addition to this, open-style pisé hearths were also found in these dugouts.

These particular features of dwellings in the western part of the settlement make it necessary to distinguish their inhabitants from the rest of the Berezan population in Roman times These differences may be explained by the ethnic and social heterogeneity of Olbian society, especially in its outlying regions, which included a variety of economically and socially dependent groups. These groups consisted primarily of representatives from native areas, which at the time may have included the descendants of those members of the multi-ethnic rural Olbian population of Late Hellenistic period who survived the Getic invasion; nomads who had settled; Scythians and Sarmatians who had moved into outlying Greek settlements (including

Fig. 111. Oven of 2nd – 3rd centuries AD.

Borysthenites)[94]; and those who wound up under the strong influence of a more advanced Hellenic culture (Kryzhitskii *et al.* 1989, 215–7).

Recent excavations have shown that, in Roman times, residential construction on Berezan was carried out primarily in the coastal regions of the island, on both the northern and eastern shores. Objects of household use and purpose were probably located here: pits and cisterns. It is now believed that dugout construction dominated on the northern coast, and aboveground building on the eastern. However, it is important to point out that a clearly-marked delineation between these two types of building has not been observed. Instead it is possible to refer to the predominance of one the other type of building in separate areas of the settlement. In addition, there are already strong grounds to assert that the extensive building seen in coastal areas of Berezan in the 2nd and 3rd centuries AD occurred largely spontaneously and in an unregulated, disorderly fashion.

As nearly all scholars on the Berezan settlement have noted, the cultural levels of the Roman period was remarkably rich with material finds. However, up to the present time the only published material has been some pottery from the excavations of Russian expeditions, and those only from the period 1962–1979 (Xenophontova 1984). Since these materials came from different, sometimes widely separated areas of the settlement, it is reasonable to assume that these finds sufficiently represent the entire ceramic complex of Roman Berezan (Figs. 112–113). To my knowledge, the composition of finds from the past ten years of expeditions on the island does not contradict data published earlier; still, the composition contains some differences which, on the whole, concern the percentage ratios of certain categories of archaeological material from the 2nd and 3rd centuries AD.

As established earlier and corroborated today, the overall mass of ceramic finds from the Roman period is represented by numerous fragments of imported amphorae. The proportion of these pieces in the ceramic complex of the time ranges from 80–95%. Most of the amphorae were evidently large red-clay vessels with wide necks, a ribbed, keg-shaped body and a complex arrangement of rims and handles. The remaining amphorae were small, narrow-necked, and made of light-colored clay, with ribbed handles and a fluted surface on the body. All these vessels were made in various Greek pottery-industry centres in the Pontus region, and were widely known in the Mediterranean and (even more so) Black Sea regions in the 2nd and 3rd centuries AD (Xenophontova 1984, Pls. 1–5).

In numerical frequency terms, the second group of Roman pottery was, as a rule, wheel-made table- and kitchen-ware. On Berezan this material usually makes up 5 to 15% of pottery finds. In composition, this category of ware is most often imported (mainly of Pergamenian and Samian manufacture), red-glazed, occasionally decorated in relief (Fig. 114). There are also local pieces of this kind, mainly of Olbian production, consisting of red and grey-clay tableware represented at Berezan by fragments of jugs, bowls, plates, dishes and lamps. It is thought, justifiably, that pottery imports reached Berezan thanks exclusively to Olbia's trading as middleman (Xenophontova 1984, 144 Pls. 6–9).

---

[94] The island is mentioned in the Roman written sources under this name (Latyshev 1887, 24, 56–61; Agbunov 1992, 184–7).

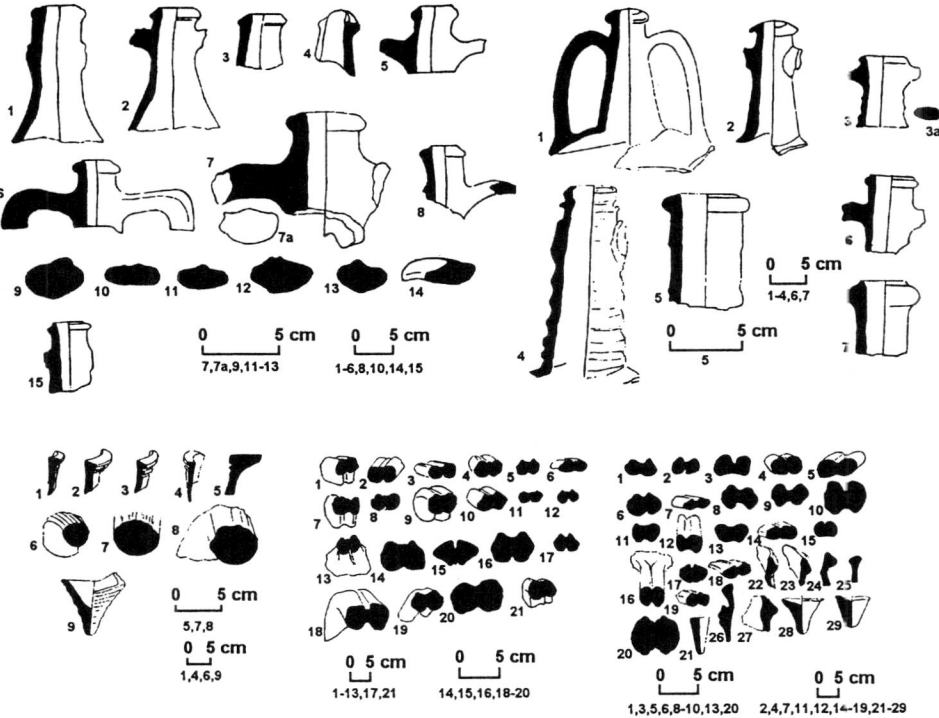

Fig. 112. Roman amphorae (after Xenophontova 1984, 140).

Other materials came to Berezan as well, apparently not without Olbia's help – works of metal (bronze and iron), for instance. These objects were first of all work tools, including various kinds of iron inplements: axes, adzes, hoes, also nails. Wares of non-ferrous metals included mainly buckles and clasps, fibulae, pins, and bracelets (Fig. 115). Rare finds included medical instruments (Fig. 116) and votive offerings (such as the lead model of a ship anchor (Fig. 117), found in the settlement and probably dedicated to Achilles).

Still, even today it is difficult to judge the extent to which trading operations between the Berezan settlement (peripheral point) and Olbia (the centre of the *polis*) were provided with financial support. Finds on the island of coins from this period of time are not very rare;[95] as a rule, such coins are copper Olbian ones of low face-value. On one side are images of Roman emperors, on the reverse is the Olbian state seal. However, some of the coins found were imported, including copper and silver provincial Roman coins, and copper coins from Greek cities of the Black Sea region. Representatives of these more distant places may have wound up accidental guests on Berezan owing to some unforeseen circumstance, such as a storm.

---

[95] A special article, devoted to coins of Berezan, has been prepared by the late A.I. Gilevich and will appear in: *Northern Pontic Antiquities from Collections of the Hermitage* (*Colloquia Pontica* 6).

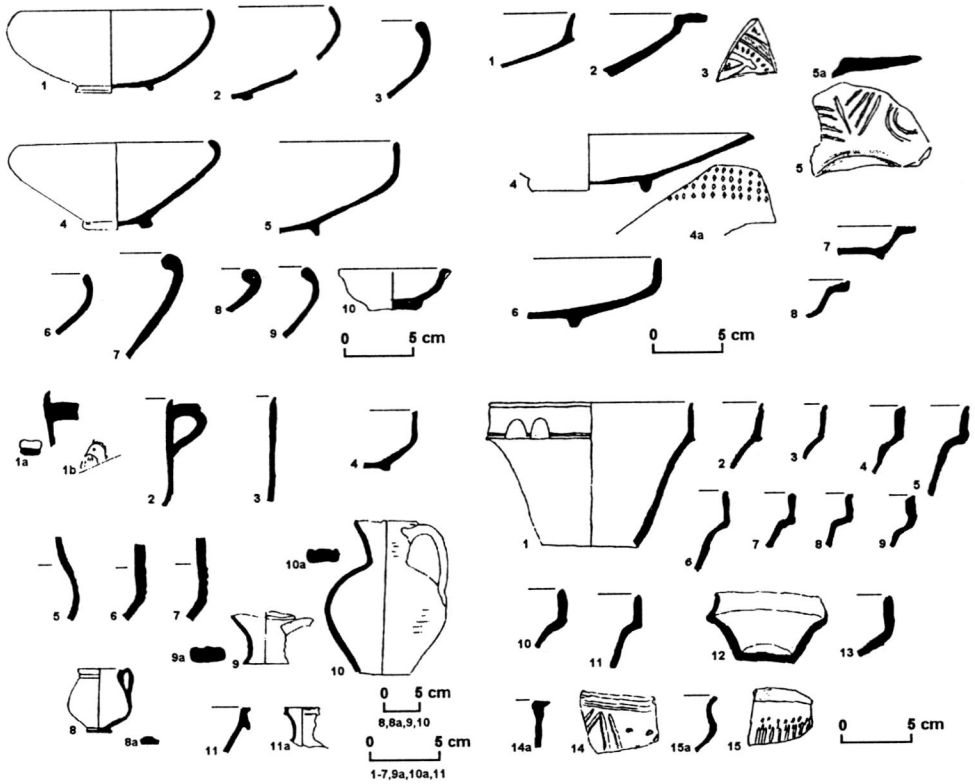

Fig. 113. Roman red-glazed pottery (after Xenophontova 1984, 140–1).

Some part of the inhabitants of Berezan in Roman times surely consisted of representatives from indigenous areas in the Black Sea region, who existed alongside the Greek population. This conclusion is supported by finds of hand-made pottery of the first centuries AD, the share of which ranged from 0.5–1.5% of the ceramic complex of the cultural levels of the settlement. The proportion of hand-made pottery increased substantially in the composition of finds from dugout dwellings of the time, occasionally reaching 6–7%, which comprised 23–27% of all pieces of ceramic vessels found in the dugouts (not counting amphorae). Furthermore, in terms of quantity, as a rule, hand-made pottery was almost half as frequent as kitchenware made on a potter's wheel. This fact may be seen as evidence that certain distinct elements of Hellenic culture had penetrated deeply into the everyday lives of the local population. Further evidence of this influence is the fact that the complex of hand-made pottery from Roman times turned out to be highly limited typologically: excavations turned out exclusively fragments of pots, pans, and rarely bowls. Nevertheless, despite the potential strength of cultural spread from the Hellenic colony, Hellenization of the local population occurred just on the surface, and did not reach the deeper foundation

Fig. 114. Fragment of the relief on the red-glazed vessel of the first half of 3rd century AD (B.89.141).

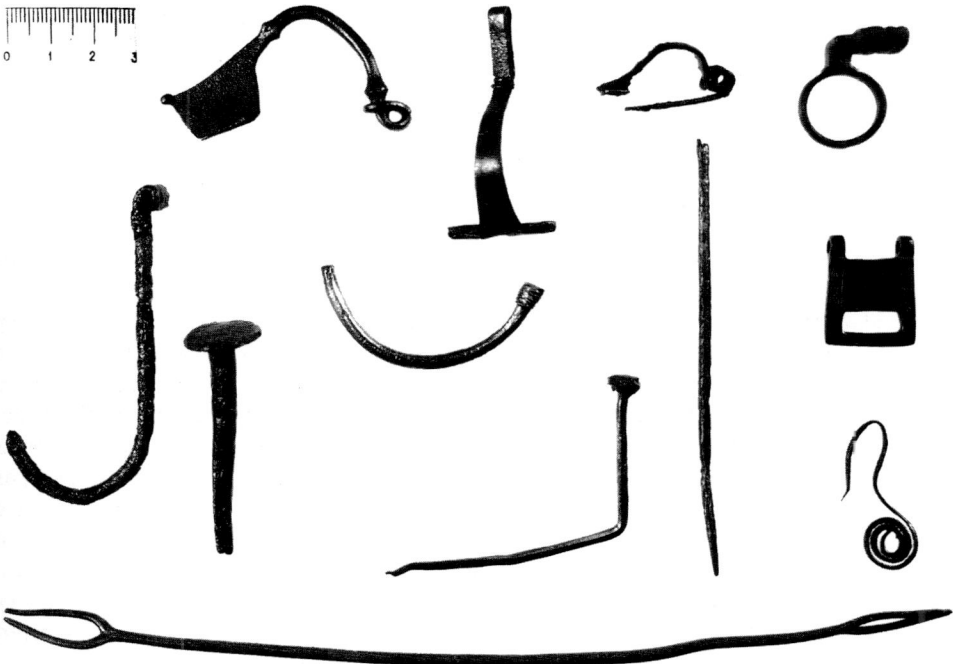

Fig. 115. Roman bronze items.

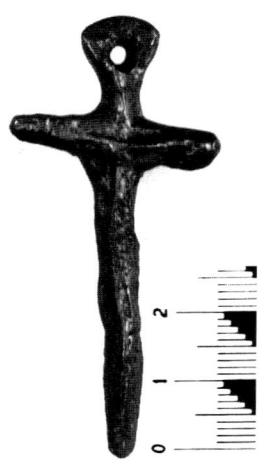

Fig. 117. Roman lead votive copy of anchor (B.91.31).

Fig. 116. Bronze medical instrument of the Roman period (B.88.100).

of the ethnic culture of the local population. Hellenic culture did, however, leave a noticeable impression on the culture of the people who settled in the northwest Black Sea in the 2nd-3rd centuries AD.

It is believed, and not without reason, that the second half of the 2nd through the first half of the 3rd centuries AD was a time of very intensive development for the Berezan settlement (Xenophontova 1984, 144; Nazarov 1994). It is also supposed that this development was connected exclusively to the overall economic growth of the Olbian state, which at the time was under the protection of the powerful Roman Empire. In turn, the cessation of life on Berezan evidently coincided with the complete collapse of the *chora* of Olbia and the downfall of Olbia itself as a consequence of the first Gothic invasion (Kryzhitskii *et al.* 1989, 155–6; Krapivina 1993, 153–4).

The chronological framework describing the concluding stage of the Berezan settlement can be further subdivided, but not by much. The beginning of this final stage is sometimes placed at the end of the 1st or in the first half of the 2nd century AD (Xenophontova 1984, 144). The latter date seems completely realistic and can be further supported by material finds (although those are, to be sure, very few in number). These finds can also be attributed to that period of Berezan history when the island was the main centre of Achilles worship and a haven for his pilgrims.

The latest finds of ancient objects on the island usually date to the 4th century AD. Like the very earliest ones, these materials are also very few in number. The appearance of these later objects on the island was probably due to infrequent, possibly seasonal, visits by local fishermen to Berezan's empty patches of dry land.

On this note, it is possible to conclude this nearly one thousand-year general history of the oldest ancient colony on the northern shore of the Pontus.

Conclusions

The formal, academic system of historical periodization (which was followed here in examining the archaeological material which has appeared in the past 10–15 years of excavations at ancient Borysthenes) can be summarized; in this way, we can say that the history of Berezan knew only two basic periods, which were divided by the 5th century BC. Everything which took place before that time furthered the growth of Berezan's economic and political influence, first in the Lower Bug region, and later in the northwest Black Sea. The 5th century BC turned out to be a critical period for the fate of Borysthenes. Everything which took place after that time represented a loss for the settlement's former economic position and total political oblivion.

During its existence, the Berezan settlement, unlike any other ancient colony on the northern coast of the Black Sea, endured a host of transformations which affected different sides of its life. The first appearance (in my opinion, at the end of the 7th century BC) of a permanent settlement at the estuary of the two largest rivers of Scythia – the Borysthenes and the Hypanis – was determined in part by the many positive properties of the region's geography. The way had also been paved by the earlier course of colonization. The Greeks were familiarizing themselves with this region (that process may have extended through nearly the whole second half of the 7th century BC), and that activity encouraged them to create firm and stable links with the indigenous peoples of forest-steppe Scythia. Those Scythian populations were gradually drawn into permanent economic (mainly trading) contacts with the Greeks. Finds of ancient imported pottery in Scythian settlements of the forest-steppe zone (located mainly in the area between the Lower Bug and Dniester rivers) and in steppe-Scythian burial sites serve as firm evidence of the interest local inhabitants must have had in maintaining and extending this kind of interaction. (The evidence provided by these finds is sound and fully representative, despite its relatively small quantity).

The archaeological material of the Berezan settlement of the second half of the 7th century BC is even more clear in this respect. The gradual and objective increase in the proportion of ancient imports to Berezan during this period of time indicates a continuing development of contacts (primarily trading) between the Greeks and the local populations. In the course of this process, the indigenous peoples, who had led a mainly semi-nomadic way of life, were ever more strongly drawn into the realm of Greek economic and cultural influence. In addition, it must be noted that Hellenic culture could not interact deeply with the large mass of the indigenous population, probably because of its traditionalism, and also because of inadequate strength and depth of the relationship, especially in the early stage.

As it turned out, the social group most receptive to the influence of Hellenic culture was the tribal leadership of the forest-steppe Scythians. This group consisted of the nomadic aristocracy – chiefs and their warriors (Vinogradov Y. A. and Marchenko 1991, 148). Apparently, in their environment imported Greek wares and objects like expensive, elegant metal and decorated vases[96] found a different, non-utilitarian value, not at all like ordinary goods, which gradually became an indicator of the special position of their owners in local society. The establishment of the Greek colony on Berezan at the end of the 7th century BC was brought about by a whole set factors, among which the continued development of Greek interaction with the local population by no means occupied last place.

From the time that a permanent settlement was erected on Berezan, the place became its own kind of magnet, which with its growing strength attracted representatives of local tribes (or their smaller subdivisions) into the Lower Bug region. The first fixed settlements began to appear on this territory in the first half of the 6th century BC. One of these – the settlement of Shirokaya Balka, located to the south of Parutino[97] – can be called the second settlement in the region, and its main features closely resembled those of Berezan. In my opinion, the parallels between the two ancient settlements can be extended even further: in both cases the settlement structure included a Greek trading station (Fig. 118, 1).

The simple fact that a Greek colony of this type existed in the Lower Bug region is not surprising. What is interesting to note is that this settlement of Greek traders was not isolated from the local population around it.[98] Moreover, Greek dwellings in their external appearance differed little from the traditional houses of the indigenous people; that is, full and partial dugouts. The Greek ones stood out among the natives' dwellings only by their large size and more advanced architecture, and by the fact that in the local climate the Greeks relied more often than the natives on stoves and hearths (it is known that, in the past, the climate in the area was cooler than it is today, and it was cool as well in comparison with the Mediterranean climate).

The archaeological material from Berezan shows that there were other results of the close proximity of the Greeks and the native population. Above all, a broad import industry (mainly of wine and pottery) settled on the peninsula, and products were distributed to many places in the Lower Bug and northern Black Sea areas. In most other respects, the Berezan settlement of the first three quarters of the 6th century BC was probably a quite ordinary trading-centre for both Greeks and natives. In exchange for imported Greek wares, the people of Berezan may have provided fish and agricultural products, and possibly processed raw materials for ironworking industries.

The Berezan settlement was fundamentally transformed by the establishment of a city-state (*polis*) on the peninsula, which took place at the end of the 6th century

---

[96] Surely it was these objects, along with a few other goods, which became the basis of early imports into the northern Black Sea, as shown by the archaeological material from practically all the Greek settlements in the region and of the Scythian settlements of the forest-steppe (Fabritsius 1951; Onaiko 1966).

[97] An area on the right bank of the Lower Bug.

[98] Later Bosporan merchants acted in a similar way, living on the Elizavetovskoe site in Don delta – one of the largest Bosporan *emporion* in steppe-Scythia (Brasinskij and Marcenko 1984; Marchenko *et al.* 1988, 67–8).

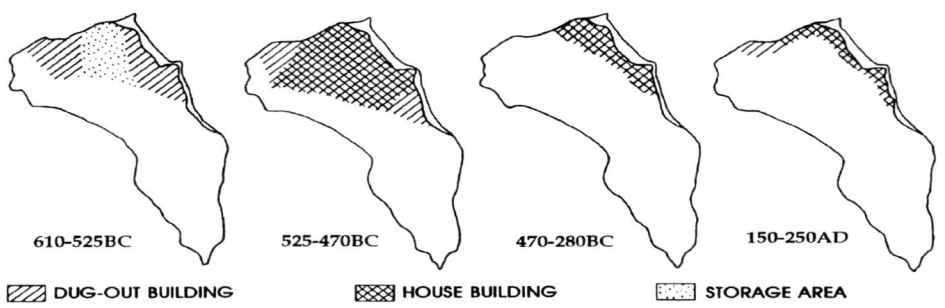

Fig. 118. Scheme of the development of the ancient Berezan settled area.

BC. The earlier settlement's past is remembered only by a few pitiful remains of dugout buildings found on the periphery of the Greek city which arose on the site of the former settlement (Fig. 118, 2). The city was laid out onetime, and built over very quickly with typical Greek aboveground, residential houses arranged in blocks. The city's plan was formulated on the basis of an orthogonal network of streets, the basic principles of which differed little from typical colonial construction in the Mediterranean and Black Sea regions (*Cf.*: Ward-Perkins 1974; Wasowicz 1982).

This transformation touched the cultural face of Berezan as well. Starting at the end of the third quarter of the 6th century BC, Hellenic traits and traditions began to dominate. Thereafter, Hellenic characteristics came to define practically all sides of life at Borysthenes. In everyday life this Hellenic influence was noticeable especially in the composition of household utensils (of course, that part which has survived to the present day: the pottery complex, small ornaments and decoration, and the tools of domestic industries). Unlike the previous period, the religious life of the Borysthenites became essentially Hellenic, although the organization of the main cults, the emergence of their specific features, and the appearance of Greek religious tendencies in the region probably began much earlier – even in the first half of the 6th century BC (Rusyaeva 1992, 219*ff*).

Without a doubt, the social and political aspects of these transformations were even more fundamental. Excavations have revealed that the formation and development of the civil structure of the settlement was fully subordinate to state institutions, which in turn determined the social organization of Borysthenes. Archaeological and written sources show that that organization included different categories of citizens, some with full civil rights and other completely dispossessed of those rights. Among the latter both Greeks and members of the native population, possibly the inhabitants of Borysthenes' outlying regions, may have been included.

Today much is still unclear about the interaction between Borysthenes and Olbia, that other major Greek city of the Lower Bug region. This lack of clarity hinges on two unresolved issues: the date of the establishment of the Olbia city-state, and the character of early Olbia itself. I am sure that new archaeological material which has appeared in recent years (Rusyaeva 1991; 1994; Kryzhitskii 1994; Kryzhitskii and Krapivina 1994), and which has shed some light on particular aspects of life of Olbia in the Archaic period, will in the very near future compel us to re-examine certain conceptions about the initial stage of development of the Olbian state.

Nothing similar is necessary now regarding the Berezan settlement in the Classical period. Archaeological excavations of the past ten years have discovered the ruins of an indigenous settlement of the second half of the 5th through the first quarter of the 4th centuries BC; all of its features show a remarkable similarity to the native settlement near Olbia of the same time. However, unlike the Olbian case, for Borysthenes the appearance of a native settlement on the outskirts of the city's buildings at a time of general instability in the northern Black Sea marked the beginning of the *polis'* economic and political decline. The contraction of the city's population, the reduction of the territory of both urban and outlying areas, the impossibility of maintaining economic and political independence – these were the main reasons for the gradual desertion of the settlement during the Classical period. A just end to all this was Berezan's transformation into a small agricultural and fishing settlement of the *chora* of Olbia, as it evidently remained during the Early Hellenistic period (Fig. 118, 3).

The next page in Berezan's history was very short, but unquestionably bright. This brief period took place when the centre of worship of Achilles in the northwest Black Sea was transferred to the island, an event which occurred in the 1st century AD. If the remains of the temple to this immortal and favourite hero of the Olbiopolites are not found, at least the number of finds of lapidary items dedicated to him totals nine, among which there is a unique example of Olbian poetry of that time.

The concluding period of the history of ancient Berezan occurred in the Roman period; more precisely, in the second half of the 2nd through the first half of the 3rd centuries AD (Fig. 118, 4). The revival of the settlement at that time was probably made possible by an overall improvement in the political climate of the northwest Black Sea and above all in the Lower Bug region; this political improvement was brought about by the inclusion of the area into the Roman province of Lower Moesia, and by the stationing at Olbia of a garrison of Roman forces under the Emperor Antonius Pius. The settlement which arose on the island consisted of two parts: Greek and native, which were rather weakly delineated territorially. Apparently, the population of the settlement was mostly mixed, and ethnic differences among inhabitants probably arose only in regard to religious and spiritual culture, possibly in the two groups' separate relationships with Hellenic religion and its priests. The heterogeneous composition of the Berezan population during Roman times is also indicated by variations in construction techniques, which at this time became a combination of aboveground and dugout building.

As unusual as the history of ancient Berezan was, the future fate of the island turned out to be just as unusual. During its long historical oblivion, the place occasionally became a temporary haven for fishermen and brigands (most of whom were Slav), and then for Cossack fighters who pillaged coastal Byzantine and Turkish cities. It is important to note that people lived permanently on the island for a long time, during the 10th-13th centuries. On the island's eastern coast some of their buildings are known – dugouts, in which Slav hand-made pottery, imported wheel-made glazed vessels, works of bronze and bone, and coins have been found (Boltenko

1947; Solovyov 1992a). On the western part of the island, there was a necropolis dating from the same time. As before, among the interred one often encounters those who died violently, as is indicated by iron arrowheads embedded in their bones.

Later on, in the 18th through the beginning of the 20th centuries, Turkish and then Russian military forces chose this ancient island as an object for their activities. As a result, recent and contemporary military works and fortifications found themselves close by the ancient building remains, and sometimes in the same place. (For some reason we have not reproached them for this.) Nevertheless, in the final analysis damage to the ancient site caused by military construction cannot be compared with that resulting from the action of nature, which continues to demolish the island today. Owing to this threat, today the problem of saving and preserving the cultural legacy of the past acquires special significance and relevance.

Abbreviations and Bibliography

Abbreviations

ACSS   *Ancient Civilizations from Scythia to Siberia* (Leiden).

AIU   *Arkheologicheskie Issledovaniya na Ukraine* (Archaeological Investigations in the Ukraine. Kiev).

AO   *Arkheologicheskie Otkrytiya* (Archaeological Discoveries. Moscow).

ASGE   *Arkheologicheskii Sbornik Gosudarstvennogo Ermitazha* (Archaeological Collections of the State Hermitage. St Petersburg).

AV   *Arkheologicheskie Vesti* (Archaeological News. St Petersburg).

CGA VMF   Central'nyi Gosudarstvennyi Arkhiv Voenno-Morskogo Flota Rossii (Central State Archive of the Russian Navy. St Petersburg).

DHA   *Dialogues d'histoire ancienne.*

IAK   *Izvestiya Imperatorskoi Arkheologicheskoi Komissii* (Bulletin of the Imperial Archaeological Commission. St Petersburg).

IGAIMK   *Izvestiya Gosudarstvennoi Akademii Istorii Material'noi Kul'tury* (Reports of the State Academy of the History of Material Culture. Moscow).

KSIA   *Kratkie Soobshcheniya Instituta Arkheologii Akademii Nauk SSR* (Brief Reports of the Institute of Archaeology, USSR Academy of Sciences. Moscow).

KSIIMK   *Kratkie Soobshcheniya Instituta Istorii Material'noi Kul'tury* (Brief Reports of the Institute of History of Material Culture. Moscow).

MASP   *Materialy po Arkheologii Severnogo Prichernomorya* (Materials on the Archaeology of the Northern Black Sea Littoral. Odessa).

MIA   *Materialy i Issledovaniya po Arkheologii SSSR* (Materials and Studies on the Archaeology of the USSR. Moscow).

OAK   *Otchety Imperatorskoi Arkheologicheskoi Komissii* (Reports of the Imperial Archaeological Commission. St Petersburg).

PAV   *Peterburgskii Arkheologicheskii Vestnik* (St Petersburg Archaeological Herald).

RA   *Revue archéologique.*

RosArc   *Rossiiskaya Arkheologiya* (Russian Archaeology. Moscow).

SA   *Sovetskaya Arkheologiya* (Soviet Archaeology. Moscow).

SAI   *Svod Arkheologicheskikh Istochnikov* (Collection of Archaeological Sources. Moscow).

SGE   *Soobshcheniya Gosudarstvennogo Ermitazha* (Reports of the State Hermitage. St Petersburg).

TGE   *Trudy Gosudarstvennogo Ermitazha* (Proceedings of the State Hermitage. St Petersburg).

VDI   *Vestnik Drevnei Istorii* (Journal of Ancient History. Moscow).

VOKK   *Vestnik Odesskoi Komissii Kraevedeniya* (Journal of Odessa Committee of Regional History).

WZ   *Wissenschaftliche Zeitschrift des Universität Rostock.*

ZOAO   *Zapiski Odesskogo Arkheologicheskogo Obshchestva* (Notes of the Odessa Archaeological Society).

ZOOID   *Zapiski Odesskogo Obshchestva Istorii i Drevnostei* (Notes of the Odessa Society of History and Antiquities).

Bibliography

AGBUNOV, M.V. 1985: *Pontus Euxinus Puzzles* (Moscow) (in Russian).

AGBUNOV, M.V. 1992: *Ancient Geography of the Northern Black Sea Coastline* (Moscow) (in Russian).

ALEKSEEV, A.Y. 1992: *Scythian Chronicles* (St Petersburg) (in Russian).

ANOKHIN, A.V. 1989: *Coins of Ancient Cities of the North-West Black Sea Littoral* (Kiev) (in Russian).

ARTAMONOVA, O.A. 1940: The Earliest Settlement on Berezan Island. *KSIIMK* 5, 100–17 (in Russian).

BOLTENKO, M.T. 1930: Concerning the Dating of the Appearance and Name of Ancient Ionian Settlement on the Banks of the Borysthenes. *VOKK* 4–5 (Archaeological Section), 35–9 (in Ukrainian).

BOLTENKO, M.T. 1947: The Ancient Slavs in Berezan. *Arkhaeologiya* 1, 39–53 (in Ukrainian).

BOLTENKO, M.T. 1949: Excavations on Berezan Island in 1946. *Archaeological Sites of Ukraine* (Kiev) 2, 31–8 (in Ukrainian).

BOLTENKO, M.T. 1953: A New Inscription in Honour of Achilles Pontarches. *VDI* 4, 132–5 (in Russian).

BOLTENKO, M.T. 1960: The Historical Fate of Berezan Island. *ZOAO* 1(34), 38–46 (in Russian).

BOLSHAKOV, A.O. and ILYNA, Y.I. 1988: Egyptian Scarabs from Berezan Island. *VDI* 3, 57–67 (in Russian).

BRASHINSKII, I.V. 1963: *Athens and the Northern Black Sea Littoral in the 6th-2nd Centuries BC* (Moscow) (in Russian).

BRASHINSKII, I.V. and SHCHEGLOV, A.N. 1979: Some Problems of Ancient Greek Colonization. In Lordkipanidze, O. (ed.), *Problems of Greek Colonization of the Northern and Eastern Black Sea Littorals* (Tbilisi), 29–46 (in Russian).

BRASINSKIJ, I.V. and MARCENKO, K.K. 1984: *Elisavetovskoje:Skythische Stadt im Don-Delta* (Munich).

BRAVO, B. 1974: Une lettre sur plomb de Beresan. *DHA* 1, 111–74.

BRAVO, B. 1994: Some Remarks on the Foundation of the *Polis* of Olbia and the Early Stages of its History. In Kryzhitskii, S.D. (ed.), *Olbia-200* (Abstracts of Papers of Jubilee Conference) (Nikolaev), 23.

BROMLEI, Y.V. 1983: *Essays on the Theory of Ethnos* (Moscow) (in Russian).

BUISKIKH, S.B. 1987: Armour. In Kryzhitskii, S.D. (ed.), *Archaic Culture of Olbia and its Environs* (Kiev), 127–31 (in Russian).

BUISKIKH, S.B. 1991: *Fortifications of the Olbian State (First Centuries AD)* (Kiev) (in Russian).

DOMANSKII, Y.V. 1961: From the History of the Population of the Lower Bug Region in the 7th-4th Centuries BC. *ASGE* 2, 26–44 (in Russian).

DOMANSKII, Y.V. 1970: Notes on the Character of Trade Relations between Greeks and Natives in the Northern Black Sea Littoral in the 7th Century BC. *ASGE* 12, 47–53 (in Russian).

DOMANSKII, Y.V. 1979: Concerning the Character of Greek Colonization and the Post-Colonization Period in the Northern Black Sea Littoral. In Lordkipanidze, O. (ed.), *Problems of Greek Colonization of the Northern and Eastern Black Sea Littorals* (Tbilisi), 81–8 (in Russian).

DOMANSKII, Y.V. 1985: Berezan Expedition Excavation. *AO 1983*, 272–3 (in Russian).

DOMANSKII, Y.V. and MARCHENKO, K.K. 1975: Some Questions of the Ancient History of the Lower Bug Region. In Karyshkovskii, P.O. (ed.), *150th Anniversary of the Archaeological Museum in Odessa.* (Abstracts of Papers) (Odessa), 120–1 (in Russian).

DOMANSKII, Y.V., SOLOVYOV, S.L. and VINOGRADOV, Y.G. 1989: Main Results of the Berezan Expedition. In Smirnova, G.I. (ed.), *Main Results of Archaeological Expeditions of the State Hermitage* (Leningrad), 33–60 (in Russian).

DOMANSKII, Y.V., SOLOVYOV, S.L. and VINOGRADOV, Y.G. 1991: Results of Excavation on Berezan Island. *Results Forum of the State Hermitage. Abstracts of Papers* (Leningrad), 11–5 (in Russian).

DOMANSKII, Y.V., VINOGRADOV, Y.G. and SOLOVYOV, S.L. 1986: The Berezan Archaeological Expedition in 1982. In Smirnova, G.I. (ed.), *Ancient Cultural Monuments on the Territory of the USSR* (Leningrad), 24–36 (in Russian).

DOVATUR, A.I.. KALLISTOV, D.P. and SHISHOVA, I.A. 1982: *Peoples of Our Country in the "Histories" of Herodotus* (Moscow) (in Russian).

DZIS-RAIKO, G.O. 1959: Hand-Made Pottery of the 7th-6th Centuries BC from Berezan Island. *MASP* 2, 37–40 (in Ukrainian).

EBERT, M. 1913: Ausgrabungen auf dem Gute Maritzyn, Guov. Cherson (Sud. Rußland). *Prahistorische Zeitschrift* 5(Leipzig) .

ENMAN, N.A. 1911: Naucratite Chalice from Berezan Island. *IAK* 40, 142–58 (in Russian).

FABRITSIUS, I.V. 1951: *The Archaeological Map of the Ukrainian Black Sea Littoral* (Kiev) (in Russian).

FAREWELL 1911: *Farewell to E.R. von Stern* (Odessa) (in Russian).

FARMAKOVSKII, B.V. 1898: Results of Excavation in the Olbia Necropolis and on Berezan Island. *OAK 1896*, 200–12 (in Russian).

FYODOROV, P.V. 1978: *Pleistocene of Ponto-Kaspii* (Moscow) (in Russian).

GOLOVACHEVA, N.V., MARCHENKO, K.K., POGOV, E.Y. and SOLOVYOV, S.L. 1991: The Ancient Settlement Kozyrka-12 (Classical Period). *KSIA* 204, 66–70 (in Russian).

GORBUNOVA, K.S. 1964: The Black-Figured Krater by Lydos. *SA* 3, 297–301 (in Russian).

GORBUNOVA, K.S. 1966: The Samian Amphorae with Comasts. *SGE* 27, 35–8 (in Russian).

GORBUNOVA, K.S. 1967: Investigations on Berezan Island. *AO 1966*, 206–7 (in Russian).

GORBUNOVA, K.S. 1968: The Votive Inscription in Honour of Achilles Hero from Berezan Island. In Gaidukevich, V.F. (ed.), *Ancient History and Culture of the Mediterranean and Black Seas* (Leningrad), 96–9 (in Russian).

GORBUNOVA, K.S. 1968a: The Berezan Necropolis. *AO 1967*, 207–8 (in Russian).

GORBUNOVA, K.S. 1969: *Ancient Greeks on Berezan Island* (Leningrad) (in Russian).

GORBUNOVA, K.S. 1969a: The Berezan Expedition of the State Hermitage. *AO 1968*, 272–3 (in Russian).

GORBUNOVA, K.S. 1970: The Chalice with Comasts from Excavations on Berezan in 1966. *SA* 4, 199–201 (in Russian).

GORBUNOVA, K.S. 1970a: The State Hermitage Expedition's Excavation on Berezan Island. *AO 1969*, 247 (in Russian).

GORBUNOVA, K.S. 1971: The Berezan Expedition of the State Hermitage. *AO 1970*, 272–3 (in Russian).

GORBUNOVA, K.S. 1972: Archaeological Investigations on the Northern Shore of the Black Sea in the Territory of the Soviet Union. 1965–1970. *Archaeological Reports* for 1971–1972, 48–59.

GORBUNOVA, K.S. 1973: Onothes from Excavations on Berezan. *Archeologia Polonja* 14, 79–85 (in Russian).

GORBUNOVA, K. 1973a: Les fragments des ceramiques attiques de la première moitié du 6 siècle av J.C., provenant de l'ile de Berezan. *RA* 2, 195–202.

GORBUNOVA, K.S. 1974: Les fouilles archeologiques du musée de L'Ermitage sur les bords de la Mer Noire. *Academie Inscriptions et Belles-lettres* (Paris), 439–44.

GORBUNOVA, K.S. 1976: Fragments of Attic Black-Figured Vases by the Tleson Painter from Berezan Island. In Sokolskii, N.I. (ed.), *Artistic Culture and Archaeology of the Ancient World* (Moscow), 94–6 (in Russian).

GORBUNOVA, K.S. 1982: Attic Black-Figured Pottery from Excavations 1962–1971 in Sector

G of Berezan Island. In Boriskovskaya, S.P. (ed.), *Artistic Productions of Ancient Craftsmen* (Leningrad) 36–49 (in Russian).

HIND, J.G.F. 1984: Greek and Barbarian Peoples on the Shores of the Black Sea. *Archaeological Reports* for 1983–1984, 71–97.

IEVLEV, M.M. 1987: The Paleogeographical Situation in the Steppe Regions of the Northern Black Sea Littoral in the 7th-5th Centuries BC. In Chernenko, E.V. (ed.), *Cimmerians and Scythians. Abstracts of Papers* (Kirovograd) 1, 64–6 (in Russian).

IEVLEV, M.M. 1992: Natural Conditions and Economic Activity of the Olbian State in the 7th-5th Centuries BC. In Pankov, S.V. (ed.), *Ancient Production on the Territory of the Ukraine* (Kiev), 129–41 (in Russian).

ILINA, Y.I. 1987: The Black-Figured Skyphos from the Excavation in the Berezan Necropolis. *SGE* 52, 31–3 (in Russian).

ILINA, Y. I. 1994: Antiquities from Berezan. In *Great Art Treasures of the Hermitage Museum. St Petersburg* (New York), 268–79.

ILINSKAYA, V.A. and TERENOZKIN, A.I. 1983: *Scythia in the 7th-4th Centuries BC* (Kiev) (in Russian).

KADEEV, V.I. 1973: On the Ethnic Identity of Crouched Graves from Chersonesus Necropolis. *VDI* 4, 108–16 (in Russian).

KADEEV, V.I. 1981: *Tauric Chersonesus in the First Centuries AD* (Kharkov) (in Russian).

KAPOSHINA, S.I. 1956: From the History of Greek Colonization of the Lower Bug Region. *MIA* 50, 211–54 (in Russian).

KARYSHKOVSKII, P.O. 1978: From the History of Coinage in Olbia in the First Half of the 4th Century BC. In Karyshkovskii, P.O. (ed.), *Archaeological Investigation in the Northwestern Black Sea* (Kiev), 83–99 (in Russian).

KARYSHKOVSKII, P.O. 1988: *Coins of Olbia* (Kiev) (in Russian).

KOBYLINA, M.M. 1948: The Bear Statuette from Berezan Island. *VDI* 3, 163–6 (in Russian).

KOHLER, H.K.E. 1826: Memoire sur les iles et les course consacrées à Achile dans le Pont-Euxin. *Memoires* 10, 531–819.

KOPEIKINA, L.V. 1968: The Group of East Greek Amphorae from Berezan Island. *SGE* 29, 44–7 (in Russian).

KOPEIKINA, L.V. 1970: Peculiarities of the Development of East Greek Pottery in the First Half of the 6th Century BC. *VDI* 1, 93–106 (in Russian).

KOPEIKINA, L.V. 1970a: Fragment of an East Greek Plate from the Berezan Excavation. *SA* 3, 197–208 (in Russian).

KOPEIKINA, L.V. 1970b: Orientalizing East Greek Pottery from the Berezan Excavation. *WZ* 8, 559–66 (in Russian).

KOPEIKINA, L.V. 1970c: Peculiarities of the Development of Some 6th Century BC East Greek Pottery Groups and Questions of their Origin. *VDI* 1, 93–106 (in Russian).

KOPEIKINA, L.V. 1973: The Earliest Pattern of Decorated Ancient Greek Pottery from Berezan Island. *SA* 1, 240–4 (in Russian).

KOPEIKINA, L.V. 1974: The Northern-Western Sector of the Berezan Settlement. *AO 1973*, 290–1 (in Russian).

KOPEIKINA, L.V. 1975: New Data about the Place of Berezan and Olbia in the Archaic Period. *SA* 1, 188–99 (in Russian).

KOPEIKINA, L.V. 1975a: The Western Boundary of the Berezan Settlement. *AO 1974*, 297–8 (in Russian).

KOPEIKINA, L.V. 1976: Residential Blocks of the Berezan Settlement. *AO 1975*, 340–1 (in Russian).

KOPEIKINA, L.V. 1977: The Assemblage of Archaic Terracotta Statuettes from Berezan. *VDI* 3, 92–104 (in Russian).

KOPEIKINA, L.V. 1977a: The Berezan Expedition of the State Hermitage. *AO 1976*, 309 (in Russian).

KOPEIKINA, L.V. 1978: Excavations of the Berezan Settlement. *AO 1977*, 334–5 (in Russian).

KOPEIKINA, L.V. 1979: Peculiarities of the Development of the Berezan Settlement during the Colonization Process. In Lordkipanidze, O. (ed.), *Problems of Greek Colonization of the Northern and Eastern Black Sea Littorals* (Tbilisi), 106–13 (in Russian).

KOPEIKINA, L.V. 1979a: The Development of the Black-Figured Style in Clazomenian pottery. In Gorbunova, K.S. (ed.), *From the History of the Northern Black Sea Littoral in Antiquity* (Leningrad), 7–25 (in Russian).

KOPEIKINA, L.V. 1981: Local Features in the Culture of the Berezan Settlement in the Archaic Period. In Lordkipanidze, O. (ed.), *The Demographic Situation in the Black Sea Littoral in the Period of Greek Colonization* (Tbilisi), 163–74 (in Russian).

KOPEIKINA, L.V. 1981a: Peculiarities of the Development of the Berezan Settlement in the Archaic Period (According to Excavation Results from the Northern-Western Sector of the Site). *SA* 1, 192–208 (in Russian).

KOPEIKINA, L.V. 1981b: Results of the Berezan Expedition. *AO 1980*, 263–4 (in Russian).

KOPEIKINA, L.V. 1982: 7th century BC East Greek Pottery and its Importance for the Study of the Initial Stage of the Berezan Settlement. In Boriskovskaya, S.P. (ed.), *Artistic Productions of Ancient Craftsmen* (Leningrad), 6–35 (in Russian).

KOPEIKINA, L.V. 1982a: Black-Figured Amphorae from Excavations on Berezan Island. *SGE* 17, 39–41 (in Russian).

KOPEIKINA, L.V. 1986: Archaic Painted Pottery from Ancient Sites in the Lower Bug Region as a Source for Studying Trade and Cultural Connections. *ASGE* 27, 27–47 (in Russian).

KOSHELENKO. G.A. and KUZNETSOV, V.D. 1990: The Greek Colonization of Bosporus. In Lordkipanidze, O. (ed.), *The Black Sea Littoral in the 7th-5th Centuries BC* (Tbilisi), 30–47 (in Russian).

KOVALEVSKII, T.M. 1906: Berezan Island: a Military and Historical Essay. *ZOOID* 26, 48–52 (in Russian).

KOVPANENKO, G.T., BESSONOVA, S.S. and SKORYI, S.A. 1989: *Scythian Antiquities from the Forest-Steppe Dnieper Region* (Kiev) (in Russian).

KOZUB, Y.I. 1979: The Environs of Olbia. *Arkheologiya* 29, 3–33 (in Ukrainian).

KRAPIVINA, V.V. 1986: Archaic Weights of Berezan and Olbia. In Rusyaeva, A.S. (ed.), *Olbia and its Environs* (Kiev), 105–11 (in Russian).

KRAPIVINA, V.V. 1993: *Olbia. The Material Culture of the 1st-4th Centuries AD* (Kiev) (in Russian).

KRYZHITSKII, S.D. 1982: *Domestic Dwellings of the Ancient Cities of the Northern Black Sea Littoral* (Kiev) (in Russian).

KRYZHITSKII, S.D. 1985: *Olbia. Historiographical Study of Architectural and Building Complexes* (Kiev) (in Russian).

KRYZHITSKII, S.D. 1987: Town Planning. In Kryzhitskii, S.D. (ed.), *Archaic Culture of Olbia and its Environs* (Kiev), 17–27 (in Russian).

KRYZHITSKII, S.D. 1989: Concerning the History of the Colonization of the Lower Bug Region. *Arkheologiya* 3, 40–50 (in Ukrainian).

KRYZHITSKII, S.D. 1993: *Architecture of Ancient States of the Northern Black Sea Littoral* (Kiev) (in Russian).

KRYZHITSKII, S.D. 1994: Brief Results of Archaeological Investigations in Olbia (1972–1994). In Kryzhitskii, S.D. (ed.), *Olbia - 200* (Abstracts of Papers of Jubilee Conference) (Nikolaev), 6–16 (in Russian).

KRYZHITSKII, S.D. and BUISKIKH, S.B. 1988: The Structure of Archaic Settlement Patterns in the Lower Bug Region. *Arkheologiya* 63, 1–8 (in Ukrainian).

KRYZHITSKII, S.D., BUISKIKH, S.B., BURAKOV, A.V. and OTRESHKO, V.M. 1989: *Rural Surroundings of Olbia* (Kiev) (in Russian).

KRYZHITSKII, S.D., BUISKIKH, S.B. and OTRESHKO, V.M. 1990: *Ancient Settlements of the Lower Bug Region (Archaeological Map)* (Kiev) (in Russian).

KRYZHITSKII, S.D. and KRAPIVINA, V.V. 1994: Archaeological News from Olbia and its *Chora. ACSS* 1(1), 40–4.

KRYZHITSKII, S.D. and OTRESHKO, V.M. 1986: Concerning the Problem of the Formation of Olbia. In Rusyaeva, A.S. (ed.), *Olbia and its Environs* (Kiev), 3–17 (in Russian).

KRYZHITSKII, S.D. and RUSYAEVA, A.S. 1978: The Earliest Dwellings of Olbia. *Arkheologiya* 28, 3–26 (in Ukrainian).

KUTAISOV, V.A. 1986: Concerning the Numismatics of Kerkinitis in the 5th Century BC. *VDI* 2, 94–7 (in Russian).

KUTAISOV, V.A. 1990: *The Ancient City of Kerkinitis* (Kiev) (in Russian).

KVASOV, D.D. 1975: *The Late Quaternary History of Large Lakes and Inland Seas in Eastern Europe* (Leningrad) (in Russian).

LAPIN, V.V. 1961: Excavations of the Settlement on Berezan Island in 1960. *KSIA of the Academy of Sciences of the Ukrainian SSR* 2, 43–52 (in Russian).

LAPIN, V.V. 1963: The Character of the Economy of the Berezan Settlement. In Boltunova, A.I. (ed.), *Ancient City* (Moscow), 31–9 (in Russian).

LAPIN, V.V. 1966: *Greek Colonization of the Northern Black Sea Littoral* (Kiev) (in Russian).

LAPIN, V.V. 1967: Excavations of the Ancient Greek Settlement on Berezan Island in 1966. *AIU 1965–1966* 1, 145–9 (in Russian).

LAPIN, V.V. 1968: Investigations of the Ancient Greek Settlement on Berezan Island. *AIU 1967* 2, 150–5 (in Ukrainian).

LAPIN, V.V. 1972: Investigations on Berezan Island in 1969. *AIU 1969* 4, 157–60 (in Ukrainian).

LAPIN, V.V. 1975: Problems of Genesis of the Culture of the Northern Black Sea Littoral. In Karyshkovskii, P.O. (ed.), *150th Anniversary of the Archaeological Museum in Odessa. Abstracts of Papers* (Odessa), 100–2 (in Russian).

LAPIN, V.V. 1977: *The Results of the Berezan Archaeological Expedition in 1977* (Kiev, Archive of Expeditions of the Institute of Archaeology of the Ukrainian Academy of Sciences), 1977/98 (in Russian).

LAPIN, V.V. 1978: *Berezan and Problems of the Genesis of the Culture of the Northern Black Sea Littoral* (Kiev, Archive of the Institute of Archaeology of the Ukrainian Academy of Sciences, Group 24) (in Russian).

LATYSHEV, V.V. 1887: *Studies on the History and State Structure of the City of Olbia* (St Petersburg) (in Russian).

MANTSEVITCH, A.P. 1927: The Amphorae from Berezan. *IGAIMK* 5, 283–95 (in Russian).

MARCARYAN, E.S. 1983: *The Theory of Culture and Modern Scholarship* (Moscow) (in Russian).

MARCHENKO, K.K. 1976: Hand-Made Pottery of the Second Half of 7th-6th Centuries BC from Berezan and Olbia (According to material from excavations of 1953–1970). In Sokolskii, N.I. *et al.* (eds.), *Artistic Culture and Archaeology of the Ancient World* (Moscow), 157–65 (in Russian).

MARCHENKO, K.K. 1980: Model of Greek Colonization of the Lower Bug Region. *VDI* 1, 131–43 (in Russian).

MARCHENKO, K.K. 1982: Concerning the So-Called 'Suburb' of Olbia. *VDI* 3, 126–36 (in Russian).

MARCHENKO, K.K. 1985: Comparative Analysis of Two Late Archaic Settlements in the Lower Bug Region: Staraya Bogdanovka-2 and Kutsurub-1. In Kryzhitskii, S.D. (ed.), *Problems of Study of Olbia. Abstracts of Papers* (Parutino), 50–1 (in Russian).

MARCHENKO, K.K. 1985a: Investigations of the Staraya Bogdanovka-2 Settlement. *AO 1983*, 312–3 (in Russian).

MARCHENKO, K.K. 1988: *Barbarians Among the Population of Berezan and Olbia* (Leningrad) (in Russian).

MARCHENKO, K.K. 1991: *Greeks and Barbarians in the Northern-Western Black Sea Region in the 7th-1st Centuries BC.* Abstract of Doctoral Dissertation (Leningrad) (in Russian).

MARCHENKO, K.K. 1994: "Spontaneous Trend" of Greek Colonization or Concerning the Formation of the Rural Population in the Late Archaic Northwestern Black Sea Littoral. *VDI* 4, 92–9 (in Russian).

MARCHENKO, K.K. and DOMANSKII, Y.V. 1981: The Ancient Settlement of Staraya Bogdanovka-2. *ASGE* 22, 62–75 (in Russian).

MARCHENKO, K.K. and DOMANSKII, Y.V. 1986: The Ancient Settlement of Kutsurub-1. *ASGE* 27, 48–61 (in Russian).

MARCHENKO, K.K. and SOLOVYOV, S.L. 1988: The New Group of Late Archaic Hand-Made Pottery from Lower Bug Region. *Arkheologiya* 63, 56–60 (in Russian).

MARCHENKO, K.K. and SOLOVYOV, S.L. 1988a: Concerning the Typology of the 4th Century BC Building Complexes in the Lower Bug Region. *KSIA* 194, 49–54 (in Russian).

MARCHENKO, K.K. and VINOGRADOV, Y.A. 1989: The Scythian Period in the Northern Black Sea Region (750–250 BC). *Antiquity* 63 (241), 803–13.

MARCHENKO, K.K., ZHYTNIKOV, V.G. and YAKOVENKO, E.V. 1988: Elizavetovskoe Settlement – the Greek and Barbarian Trading Post in the Don Delta. *SA* 3, 63–78 (in Russian).

MAZARATI, S.N. and OTRESHKO, V.M. 1987: Semi-Dugout and Dugout Dwellings. In Kryzhitskii, S.D. (ed.), *Archaic Culture of Olbia and its Environs* (Kiev), 8–17 (in Russian).

NAZAROV, V.V. 1990: Investigations on Berezan in 1989. In Abikulova, M.I. (ed.), *Archaeological Problems of the Northern Black Sea Littoral. Abstracts of Papers* (Kherson), 82–3 (in Russian).

NAZAROV, V.V. 1994: About the Roman Period in the History of the Berezan Settlement. In Kryzhitskii, S.D. (ed.), *Olbia – 200* (Abstracts of Papers of Jubilee Conference) (Nikolaev), 89–90 (in Russian).

NAZAROV, V.V. 1994a: Concerning the Marine Experience of Olbiopolites. *Arkheologiya* 2, 94–102 (in Ukrainian).

NUDELMAN, D.I. 1946: The Ancient Greek Settlement on the Northern Black Sea Littoral. *Academic Notes of the Moscow State Pedagogical Institute* (Moscow) 37(3), 21–42 (in Russian).

OKHOTNIKOV, S.B. and OSTROVERKHOV, A.S. 1993: A Scarab from Berezan. In Okhotnikov, S.B. (ed.), *Ancient Black Sea Littoral* (Odessa), 69–74 (in Russian).

OKHOTNIKOV, S.B. and OSTROVERKHOV, A.S. 1993a: *The Sanctuary of Achilles on Leuke Island* (Kiev) (in Russian).

OLGOVSKII, S.Y. 1980: Precious Metals from Berezan. *SA* 4, 190–200 (in Russian).

OLGOVSKII, S.Y. 1987: The Social and Economic Rôle of the Kamenskoe Settlement. In Chernenko, E.V. (ed.), *Scythians of the Northern Black Sea Littoral* (Kiev), 48–52 (in Russian).

OLGOVSKII, S.Y. 1992: Copper and Bronze Work of the 6th-1st Centuries BC in the Lower Bug Region. In Pankov, S.V. (ed.), *Ancient Productions on the Territory of the Ukraine* (Kiev), 72–8 (in Ukrainian).

ONAIKO, N.A. 1966: *Ancient Greek Imports of the 7th-5th Centuries BC in Dnieper and Bug Regions.* (Moscow, *SAI* D1–27) (in Russian).

OSTROVERKHOV, A.S. 1978: Ancient Glass Workshop of the Yagorlyk Settlement. *Arkheologiya* 25, 41–9 (in Ukrainian).

OSTROVERKHOV, A.S. 1978a: Concerning the Iron Work of the Yagorlyk Settlement. *Arkheologiya* 28, 26–36 (in Ukrainian).

OSTROVERKHOV, A.S. 1979: Concerning to the Raw Material Basis of Handicraft Production in the Dnieper and Lower Bug Area. *VDI* 3, 115–26 (in Russian).

OSTROVERKHOV, A.S. 1989: Glass of Archaic Berezan. In Gudkova, A.V. (ed.), *Ancient Black Sea Littoral* (Odessa), 41–3 (in Russian).

OTRESHKO, V.M. 1979: Concerning the Problem of the Economic Differentiation of the

Lower Bug Region in the Archaic Period. In Lordkipanidze, O. (ed.), *Problems of Greek Colonization of the Northern and Eastern Black Sea Littorals* (Tbilisi), 151–8 (in Russian).

OTRESHKO, V.M. 1979a: Dedications to Achilles Pontarches as a Criterion of Determining the Olbian State Boundary. In Baran, V.D. (ed.), *Monuments of Ancient Cultures of the Northern Black Sea Littoral* (Kiev), 80–7 (in Russian).

OTRESHKO, V.M. 1987: Tools. In Kryzhitskii, S.D. (ed.), *Archaic Culture of Olbia and its Environs* (Kiev), 125–7 (in Russian).

OTRESHKO, V.M. 1994: Concerning the Fundamental Basis of the Berezan Settlement. *Arkheologiya* 2, 112–22 (in Ukrainian).

PARNIKI-PUDELKO, S. 1985: *Architektura Starozytnej Grecji* (Warsaw).

PASHKEVITCH, G.A. 1990: Structure of Culture and Plants from Excavations on the Olbian Rural Settlements. In Kryzhitskii, S.D., Buiskikh, S.B. and Otreshko, V.M., *Ancient Settlements of the Lower Bug Region (Archaeological Map)* (Kiev), 114–9 (in Russian).

PRENDEL, R.A. 1886: Archaeological Investigations on Berezan Island. *Proceedings of the VI Archaeological Congress in Odessa in 1884* 1 (Odessa), 216–9 (in Russian).

RABITCHKIN, B.M. 1951: A Settlement near Shirokaya Balka. *KSIIMK* 40, 114–24 (in Russian).

RADLOV, N.E. 1910: Two Fragments from Berezan Island. *IAK* 37, 81–6 (in Russian).

ROBINSON, D.M. and GRAHAM, J.W. 1938: The Hellenic House. In Robinson, D. (ed.), *Excavations at Olynthus* (Baltimore).

RUBAN, V.V. 1977: Some Aspects of Studying the Formation Process of Ancient Cities in the North-Western Black Sea Littoral. *Ancient Cities. Materials of Conference* (Leningrad), 42–4 (in Russian).

RUBAN, V.V. 1982: Concerning the Chronology of Archaic Settlements on the Bug Estuary (According to analysis of Chiot amphorae). In Telegin, D.Y. (ed.), *Material for Chronology of Archaeological Sites in the Ukraine* (Kiev), 96–113 (in Russian).

RUBAN, V.V. 1985: Problems of Historical Development of the *Chora* of Olbia in the 4th-3rd Centuries BC. *VDI* 1, 26–45 (in Russian).

RUBAN, V.V. 1990: About the Chronology of Red Clay Amphorae with Conical Feet of the 7th-5th Centuries BC. *KSIA* 197, 12–9 (in Russian).

RUBAN, V.V 1991: The Classification of So-Called Milesian Amphorae from the Low Bug Region. *SA* 2, 182–95 (in Russian).

RUSYAEVA, A.S. 1979: Some Features of the Cultural and Historical Development of the Northwestern Black Sea Region in the 7th-5th Centyries BC. *Arkheologiya* 30, 3–18 (in Ukrainian).

RUSYAEVA, A.S. 1984: Terracotta from the Berezan Settlement (V.V. Lapin's Excavations). In Kryzhitskii, S.D. (ed.), *Ancient Culture of the Northern Black Sea Littoral* (Kiev), 129–47 (in Russian).

RUSYAEVA, A.S. 1986: Miletus – Didyma – Borysthenes – Olbia. Problems of Colonization of the Lower Bug Region. *VDI* 2, 25–64 (in Russian).

RUSYAEVA, A.S. 1986a: Greek Colonization of the Northern Black Sea Littoral. In Artyomenko, I.I. (ed.), *Archaeology of the Ukrainian SSR* 2 (Kiev), 293–6 (in Russian).

RUSYAEVA, A.S. 1986b: Borysthenes (the Berezan Settlement). Necropolis. In Artyomenko, I.I. (ed.), *Archaeology of the Ukrainian SSR* 2 (Kiev), 297–304 (in Russian).

RUSYAEVA, A.S. 1987: Epigraphic Evidence. In Kryzhitskii, S.D. (ed.), *Archaic Culture of Olbia and its Environs* (Kiev), 134–53 (in Russian).

RUSYAEVA, A.S. 1991: Investigations of the Western Sacred Zone of Olbia (Preliminary Results). *VDI* 4, 123–39 (in Russian).

RUSYAEVA, A.S. 1992: *Religion and Cults of Ancient Olbia* (Kiev) (in Russian).

RUSYAEVA, A.S. 1994: Investigations of the Western Temenos of Olbia. *ACSS* 1(1), 80–102.

RUSYAEVA, A.S. and SKRYZHINSKAYA, M.V. 1979: Olbia *Polis* and Callipidae. *VDI* 4, 25–37 (in Russian).

RUSJAEVA, A.S. and VINOGRADOV, J.G. 1991: Der "Brief des Priesters" aus Hylaia. In Rolle, R. (Ed.), *Gold der Steppe. Archäologie der Ukrine* (Schleswig), 201–2.

SHCHEGLOV, A.N. 1965: Notes on the Ancient Geography and Topography of Sarmatia and Taurica. *VDI* 2, 107–13 (in Russian).

SHCHEGLOV, A.N. 1978: *The Northwestern Crimea in the Ancient Times* (Leningrad) (in Russian).

SHCHEGLOV, A.N. 1990: Northern Pontus Grain Trade of the Second Half of the 7th-5th Centuries BC: Littoral Sources and Archaeology. In Lordkipanidze, O. (ed.), *Black Sea Littorai in the 7th-5th Centuries BC* (Tbilisi), 99–121 (in Russian). (= O. Lordkipanidzé and P. Lévêque [eds.], *Le Pont-Euxin vu par les Grecs* [Besançon 1990], 141–60).

SHELOV-KOVEDYAEV, F.V. 1990: Berezan Hymn to the Island and Achilles. *VDI* 3, 49–62 (in Russian).

SHILIK, K.K. 1975: On the Palaeogeography of Olbia. In Kryzhitskii, S.D. (ed.), *Olbia* (Kiev), 51–91 (in Russian).

SHILIK, K.K. 1977: Major Change of Sea Level in the Late Holocene and Palaeotopography of Northern Black Sea Archaeological Sites in Ancient Times. In Kaplin, P.A. and Shcherbakov, T.A. (eds.), *Palaeogeography and Pleistocene Deposits of Southern Seas of the USSR* (Moscow), 158–62 (in Russian).

SHILIK, K.K. 1978: Evolution of Berezan Coastline Topography in the Holocene. *AIU 1976-77* (Uzhgorod), 77–8 (in Russian).

SMIDT, R.V. 1953: Archaic Greek Pottery of Myrmekion and Tyritake. *MIA* 25, 233–249 (in Russian).

SIDOROVA, N.A. 1962: Archaic Pottery from Panticapaeum (excavations of 1945-1958). *MIA* 103, 94–148 (in Russian).

SIDOROVA, N.A. 1992: Archaic Pottery from Excavations in Panticapaeum in 1965-1985. *Archaeology and Art of Bosporus (Bulletin of the Pushkin State Museum of Fine Arts, Moscow* 10). 131–72 (in Russian).

SKADOVSKII, G.L. 1900: *Field Notebook (Copy).* Archive of the State Hermitage, Fund 1, List 5, Book 37 (in Russian).

SKUDNOVA, V.M. 1955: Attic Black-Figured Chalices from Berezan. *SGE* 8, 35–7 (in Russian).

SKUDNOVA, V.M. 1957: Fragments of Black-Figured Vases by Sophilos from Berezan. *SGE* 12, 48–9 (in Russian).

SKUDNOVA, V.M. 1957a: Chiot Cups from Excavations on Berezan Island. *SA* 4, 128–39 (in Russian).

SKUDNOVA, V.M. 1960: Rhodian Pottery from Berezan Island. *SA* 2, 153–67 (in Russian)

SLAVIN, L.M. 1956: Ancient Greek Settlement on Berezan Island. *Historic Article Collection of the State University of Kiev* 7 (Kiev), 157–69 (in Ukrainian).

SMIRNOVA, G.I. 1978: New Studies of Archaeological Sites of Northwestern Scythia (Western Podolia Group of Monuments). In Lukonin, V.G. (ed.), *The Culture of the Orient* (Leningrad) 115–30 (in Russian).

SMIRNOVA, G.I. 1990: *Cultural and Historical Process in the Middle Dniester Area in the end of the 2nd - First Half of the 1st Millennium BC.* Abstract of Doctorate Dissertation (Kiev) (in Russian).

SOLOMONIK, E.Y. 1987: Two Ancient Letters from Crimea. *VDI* 3, 114–25 (in Russian).

SOLOVYOV, S.L. 1989: *Building Complexes of Archaic Berezan (Analysis of Architectural and Building Traditions).* Abstract of Dissertation (Leningrad) (in Russian).

SOLOVYOV, S.L. 1992: House-Building Peculiarities of the Lower Bug Region in the 6th - early 3rd Centuries BC in Connection with Greek and Barbarian Interactions in the Northwestern Black Sea Littoral. In Raev, B.A. (ed.), *Ancient Civilization and Barbarian World* (Novocherkassk) 3(1), 44–52 (in Russian).

SOLOVYOV, S.L. 1992a: Excavation on Berezan Island in 1991. *Annual Archaeological Meeting of the State Hermitage.* Abstracts of Papers (St Petersburg), 5–7 (in Russian).

SOLOVYOV, S.L. 1993: Concerning the Formation of the Urban and *Polis* Structures of the Berezan Settlement. *PAV* 3, 39–43 (in Russian).

SOLOVYOV, S.L. 1994: New Aspects of History and Archaeology of Ancient Berezan. *PAV* 8, 85–95 (in Russian).

SOLOVYOV, S.L. 1995: Hand-Made Pottery with Geometric Ornament from the Berezan Settlement. *ASGE* 32, 31–9 (in Russian).

SOLOVYOV, S.L. 1995a: New Data for the Typology of Berezan Dwellings in the Classical Period. *RosArk.* 1, 121–32 (in Russian).

SOLOVYOV, S.L. 1995b: Periodization of House-Building in Berezan during the Classical Period. *AV* 4 , 153–63 (in Russian).

SON, N.A. 1987: Handicraft Production. In Kryzhitskii, S.D. (ed.), *Archaic Culture of Olbia and its Environs* (Kiev), 118–25 (in Russian).

SPARKES, B.A. and TALCOTT, L. 1970: *The Black and Plain Pottery of the 6th, 5th and 4th Centuries BC* (Princeton, New Jersey) (*Athenian Agora* 12).

STERN, E.R. von 1900: Importance of South Russia Pottery Finds for the Studying of Cultural History of the Black Sea Civilization. *ZOOID* 22, 1–21 (in Russian).

STERN, E.R. von 1901: About the Recent Excavations in Akkerman Town and on Berezan Island. *ZOOID* 23, 88–91 (in Russian).

STERN, E.R. von 1904: About Preliminary Excavations on Berezan Island. *ZOOID* 25, 97–100 (in Russian).

STERN, E.R. von 1907: Excavations on Berezan Island. *OAK 1904*, 41–9 (in Russian).

STERN, E.R. von 1908: Excavations on Berezan Island. *OAK 1905*, 35–8 (in Russian).

STERN, E.R. von 1909: Excavations on Berezan Island. *OAK 1906*, 50–8 (in Russian).

STERN, E.R. von 1909a: Die griechische Kolonisation am Nordgestade des Schwarzen Meeres im Lichte archäologischer Forschung. *Klio* 9, 139–52.

STERN, E.R. von 1910: Excavations on Berezan Island. *OAK 1907*, 66–75 (in Russian).

STERN, E.R. von 1912: Excavations on Berezan Island. *OAK 1908*, 84–93 (in Russian).

STERN, E. von 1912a: Kulturleben und Geschichte des Schwarzmeergebietes. *Deutschen Monatschrift für Rußland* 5, 1–26.

STERN, E.R. von 1913: Excavations on Berezan Island. *OAK 1909–1910*, 105–17 (in Russian).

STERN, E.R. von 1913a: Graffiti. *Philologus* 72, 536–58.

STERN, E.R. von 1914: Results of Excavations on Berezan Island. *OAK 1913*, 76–108 (in Russian).

STITELMAN, F.M. 1956: Ancient Greek Settlements on the Lower Bug Area. *MIA* 50, 255–72 (in Russian).

TCHESNOV, Ya. V. 1979: Concerning Principles of Typology in a Traditional Culture. In Bromlei, Y.V. (ed.), *Problems of Typology in Ethnography* (Moscow), 189–203 (in Russian).

THOMPSON, H. and WYCHERLY, R. 1972: *The Agora of Athens. The History, Shape and Uses of an Ancient City Center* (Princeton, New Jersey) (*Athenian Agora* 14).

TOLSTIKOV, V.P. 1992: Panticapaeum – the Capital of Bosporus. In Koshelenko, G.A. (ed.), *Essays on Archaeology and History of Bosporus* (Moscow), 45–99 (in Russian).

TSALKIN, V.I. 1960: Domestic and Wild Animals of the Northern Black Sea Littoral in the Early Iron Age. *MIA* 53, 7–109 (in Russian).

TSALKIN, V.I. 1966: Cattle Breeding and Hunting of the East Europe Forest-Steppe Tribes. *MIA* 135, 9–107 (in Russian).

TSALKIN, V.I. 1971: *Cattle Breeding of the Northern Black Sea Littoral in Late Bronze and Early Iron Ages* (Moscow) (in Russian).

TSETSKHLADZE, G. R. 1994: Greek Penetration of the Black Sea. In G.R. Tsetskhladze and F. De Angelis (eds.), *The Archaeology of Greek Colonisation. Essays Dedicated to Sir John Boardman* (Oxford), 111–36.

TURAEV, B.A. 1911: Scarabs from Berezan Island. *IAK* 40, 118–20 (in Russian).

UVAROV, A.S. 1851: *Investigation of Antiquities of the Southern Russia and Black Sea Littoral* (St Petersburg) (in Russian).

VAKHTINA, M.Y. 1989: Greek Settlements on the Northern Black Sea Littoral and Nomads in the 7th-6th Centuries BC (the Problem of Initial Contacts). In Raev, B.A. (ed.), *Nomads of Europe-Asian Steppes and Ancient World* (Novocherkassk), 74–88 (in Russian).

VINOGRADOV, Y.A. 1991: Investigations on the West Edge of Myrmekion. *KSIA* 204, 71–7 (in Russian).

VINOGRADOV, Y.A. 1991a: Early Complexes of Myrmekion. In Molev, E.A. (ed.), *Questions of History and Archaeology of Bosporus* (Voronezh/ Belgorod), 12–19 (in Russian).

VINOGRADOV, Y.A. and MARCHENKO, K.K. 1985: Concerning the Beginning of the Second Stage of the Development of Lower Bug Area Rural Settlements in Ancient Times. In Kryzhitskii, S.D. (ed.), *Problems of Study of Olbia. Abstracts of Papers* (Parutinc), 14–5 (in Russian).

VINOGRADOV, Y.A. and MARCHENKO, K.K. 1989: Das Nordliche Schwarzmeergebiet in der skythischen Epoche. Periodisierung der Geschichte. *Klio* 71(2), 539–55C.

VINOGRADOV, Y.A. and MARCHENKO, K.K. 1991: Northern Black Sea Littoral in the Scythian Time. The Historical Periodization. *SA* 1, 145–55 (in Russian).

VINOGRADOV, Y.A., MARCHENKO, K.K. and ROGOV, E.Y. 1989: Concerning the Cultural and Historical Unity of the Rural Population in Lower Bug Area in Ancient Times. In Gudkova, A.V. (ed.), *Ancient Black Sea Littoral. Abstracts of Papers* (Odessa), 16–7 (in Russian).

VINOGRADOV, Y.A. and TOKHTASYEV, S.R. 1994: The Early Fortification Wall of Myrmekion. *VDI* 1, 54–63 (in Russian).

VINOGRADOV, Y.G. 1971: New Material on Ancient Greek Economy. *VDI* 1, 64–76 (in Russian).

VINOGRADOV, Y.G. 1971a: The Earliest Greek Letter from Berezan Island. *VDI* 4, 74–100 (in Russian).

VINOGRADOV, Y.G. 1976: Concerning the Political Unity of Berezan and Olbia. In Sokolskii, N.I. (ed.), *Artistic Culture and Archaeology of the Ancient World* (Moscow), 75–84 (in Russian).

VINOGRADOV, Y.G. 1979: Griechische Epigraphik und Geschichte des nördlichen Pontosgebietes. *Actes du VIIe Congrès International d'Épigraphie Grecque et Latine* (Bucuresti-Paris), 299–327.

VINOGRADOV, Y.G. 1981: *Olbia. Geschichte einer altgriechischen Stadt am Schwarzen Meer* (Konstanz) (XENIA,1).

VINOGRADOV, Y.G. 1983: *Polis* in the Northern Black Sea Littoral. In Golubtsova, E.S. (ed.), *Ancient Greece* 1 (Moscow), 366–420 (in Russian).

VINOGRADOV, Y.G. 1989: *Political History of Olbia Polis in the 7th-1st Centuries BC (Historical and Epigraphic Studies)* (Moscow) (in Russian).

VINOGRADOV, Y.G. 1994: A Maiden's Golden Burial from Berezan, the Island of Achilles. *Expedition* 36(2–3), 18–28.

VINOGRADOV, Y.G. 1994a: Greek Epigraphy of the North Black Sea Coast, the Caucasus and Central Asia (1985–1990). *ACSS* 1(1), 63–74.

VINOGRADOV, J. and DOMANSKIJ, J. 1996: Berezan' archaïque à la lumière des dernières déccouvertes, in O.D. Lordkipanidzé and P. Lévêque (eds.), *Sur les traces des Argonautes* (Besançon), 291–96.

VINOGRADOV, Y.G., DOMANSKI, Y.V. and MARCHENKO, K.K. 1988: The Development of Interrelations between Local Populations of the Northern Black Sea Littoral and Greek World in the 7th-4th Centuries BC. In Lordkipanidze, O. (ed.), *Local Ethnic and Political Units in the Black Sea Littoral* (Tbilisi), 28–34 (in Russian).

VINOGRADOV, I., DOMANSKI, I. and MARCHENKO, K. 1990: Sources écrites et archéologiques du Pontus Nord-Ouest. Analyse comparative. In O. Lordkipanidzé and P. Lévêque (eds.), *Le Pontus-Euxin vu par les Grecs* (Besançon), 121–39.

VINOGRADOV, J.G. and KRYZICSKIJ, S.D. 1995: *Olbia: Eine altgriechische Stadt im nordwestlichen Schwarzmeerraum* (Leiden).

VINOGRADOV, Y.G. and SHCHEGLOV, A.N. 1990: Creation of the Territorial State of Chersonesus. In Golubtsova, E.S. (ed.), *Hellenizm: Economy, Policy, Culture* (Moscow), 310–71 (in Russian).

VINOGRADOV, I. and ZOLOTAREV, M. 1990: : La Chersonèse de la fin de l'archaïsme. In O. Lordkipanidzé and P. Lévêque (eds.), *Le Pontus-Euxin vu par les Grecs* (Besançon), 85–119.

WARD-PERKINS, J.B. 1974: *Cities of Ancient Greece and Italy: Town Planning in Classical Antiquity* (New York).

WASOWICZ, A. 1975: *Olbia Pontique et son territoire* (Besançon).

WASOWICZ, A. 1982: *Zagospodarowanie przestrzenne antycznych miast greckich* (Warsaw).

XENOPHONTOVA, I.V. 1984: Pottery of the First Centuries AD from Excavations on Berezan Island (According to Materials of the State Hermitage). *TGE* 24, 138–47 (in Russian).

YAILENKO, V.P. 1974: Concerning the Dating and Reading of Achillodoros' Letter from Berezan. *VDI* 1, 133–54 (in Russian).

YAILENKO, V.P. 1975: Interpretation of Achillodoros' Letter from Berezan. *VDI* 3, 133–49 (in Russian).

YAILENKO, V.P. 1979: Berezan Graffito – Offering to a Friend. In Piotrovskii, B.B. (ed.), *Problems of Ancient History and Culture* (Erevan), 536–43 (in Russian).

YAILENKO, V.P. 1979a: Some Graffiti from Olbia and Berezan. *KSIA* 159, 53–60 (in Russian).

YAILENKO, V.P. 1980: Graffiti from Leuke, Berezan and Olbia. *VDI* 2, 89–99 (in Russian).

YAILENKO, V.P. 1980a: Graffiti from Leuke, Berezan and Olbia. *VDI* 3, 75–116 (in Russian).

YAILENKO, V.P. 1982: *Greek Colonization. The 7th-3rd Centuries BC* (Moscow) (in Russian).

ZEEST, I.B. 1960: *Amphorae of Bosporus* (Moscow, *MIA* 83) (in Russian).

ZENKOVITCH, V.P. 1960: *Morphology and Dynamics of the Soviet Shores of the Black Sea* 2 (Moscow) (in Russian).

ZHURAVLYOV, O.P. 1983: The Cattle-Breeding, Hunting and Landscape Peculiarities of the Ancient Olbian State (Bone Remains). *Peculiarities of Morphology of Vertebrate Animals in the Ukraine* (Kiev), 38–45 (in Russian).

ZHURAVLYOV, O.P. 1983a: Bone Remains of Mammals in Olbia and Berezan. *Arkheologiya* 42, 80–4 (in Russian).

ZHURAVLYOV, O.P. 1987: Palaeozoological Data and History of Cattle Breeding in Lower Bug Region in Ancient Times. In Stanukovitch, A.K. (ed.), *Methods of Physical Sciences in Archaeology* (Moscow), 35–41 (in Russian).

ZHURAVLYOV, O.P., MARKOVA, E.P. and SYTCHYOVA, L.V. 1990: Concerning History of Cattle Breeding in the Rural Area of Olbia *Polis*. In Kryzhitskii, S.D., Buiskikh, S.B. and Otreshko, V.M. *Ancient Settlements of Lower Bug Region (the Archaeological Map)* (Kiev), 98–113 (in Russian).

ZOLOTARYOV, M.I. 1986: New Material for Interrelations between Olbia and the Western Crimea in the 6th-5th Centuries BC. *VDI* 2, 88–94 (in Russian).

ZUBAR, V.M. 1993: *Tauric Chersonesus in Ancient Times* (Kiev) (in Russian).

Index

Uvarov, A.S.   13, 19

Vinogradov, Y.G.   1, 18, 111
Vorskla   28, 43

warriors, Scythian   129
Wasowicz, A.   79
wattle   62, 105
weapons   43, 47, 53, 84, 95
weights   102

wells   3
wine   30, 52, 54
wood   24, 34, 42, 76

Yagorlitskii industrial region   53
Yalenko, Y.P.   1

Zhuravlyov, O.P.   53
Zmeinyi   1, 116